PAKISTAN'S POLITICAL LABYRINTHS

This book explores Pakistan from different vantage points. It examines a variety of events in contemporary Pakistan through a comprehensive analysis of identity and power politics, media landscapes, military recruitment, role of madrasahs, terrorism and militancy, and civil war, as well as outlines future trajectories. It studies themes such as Pakistan's relationship with India, the legacy of Jinnah, gender and fundamentalism, and urbanization and unrest that have plagued the northern areas. It further looks at the nation after the capture of Osama bin Laden and the changing nature of its relationship with the US in its aftermath.

Including contributions from experts in the field and policymakers across the world, this volume will interest scholars and researchers on Pakistan studies, politics and international relations. It will also appeal to government think tanks.

Ravi Kalia is Professor of History at the City College of New York and specializes in South Asian studies. He is designated as Distinguished Role Model by the Asian Alumni Group and is recipient of the Distinguished Service Award by the City College of New York.

PAKISTAN'S POLITICAL LABYRINTHS

Military, society and terror

Edited by Ravi Kalia

NEW DELHI LONDON NEW YORK

First published 2016
by Routledge
2 Park Square, Milton Park, Abingdon, Oxon OX14 4RN

and by Routledge
711 Third Avenue, New York, NY 10017

Routledge is an imprint of the Taylor & Francis Group, an informa business

© 2016 Ravi Kalia

The right of Ravi Kalia to be identified as the author of the editorial material, and of the authors for their individual chapters, has been asserted in accordance with sections 77 and 78 of the Copyright, Designs and Patents Act 1988.

All rights reserved. No part of this book may be reprinted or reproduced or utilised in any form or by any electronic, mechanical, or other means, now known or hereafter invented, including photocopying and recording, or in any information storage or retrieval system, without permission in writing from the publishers.

Trademark notice: Product or corporate names may be trademarks or registered trademarks, and are used only for identification and explanation without intent to infringe.

British Library Cataloguing-in-Publication Data
A catalogue record for this book is available from the British Library

Library of Congress Cataloging-in-Publication Data
A catalog record has been requested for this book

ISBN: 978-1-138-92655-4 (hbk)
ISBN: 978-1-315-68319-5 (ebk)

Typeset in Goudy
by Apex CoVantage, LLC

Printed and bound by CPI Group (UK) Ltd, Croydon, CR0 4YY

CONTENTS

	List of contributors	vii
	Introduction	ix
1	Pakistan: issues of self-identity and parity with India APARNA PANDE	1
2	Riding the tiger: the threat to Pakistan from terrorism J. ANDREW GREIG	22
3	Pakistan's power game and the new media landscape GILLES BOQUÉRAT	40
4	Militant recruitment in Pakistan: a new look at the militancy–madrasah connection C. CHRISTINE FAIR	59
5	Destabilizing elements: the Punjabi militant threat to Pakistan STEPHEN TANKEL	86
6	The battle for Karachi: changing patterns of a permanent civil war LAURENT GAYER	106
7	Military rule: facilitating factors and future prospects STEVEN BARRACCA	125

CONTENTS

8 Women at risk: militancy in Pakistan   155
TAHMINA RASHID

9 At the margins of Pakistan: political relationships between Gilgit-Baltistan and Azad Jammu and Kashmir   174
MARTIN SÖKEFELD

Index   189

CONTRIBUTORS

Steve Barracca is Associate Professor of Government at Eastern Kentucky University, where he teaches courses on comparative politics and political theory. His research focuses on democratization and civil–military relations in Latin America and in Pakistan.

Gilles Boquérat holds a PhD in History from the University of Paris 1-Sorbonne and is specialized on South Asian affairs. He has spent a number of years in India (Jawaharlal Nehru University, French Centre for Human Sciences, New Delhi) and in Pakistan (Institute of Strategic Studies, Islamabad). He has also been in charge of the South Asia Program at the French Institute of International Relations and is now associated with the Foundation for Strategic Research in Paris.

C. Christine Fair is Assistant Professor at Georgetown University at the Center for Peace and Security Studies (CPASS) within the Edmund A. Walsh School of Foreign Service. She has authored, among other publications, *The Madrassah Challenge: Militancy and Religious Education in Pakistan* (2008), and has written numerous peer-reviewed articles covering a range of security issues in South Asia.

Laurent Gayer is Research Fellow at the Centre National de la Recherche Scientifique (CNRS, France), posted at the Centre d'Etudes et de Recherches Internationales (CERI), Paris. He is the author of the recently published *Karachi: Ordered Disorder and the Struggle for the City* (2014).

J. Andrew Greig retired from the US Foreign Service with the United States Information Agency and the Department of State. He served as senior country desk officer for Pakistan and as an analyst in the Bureau of Intelligence and Research. His overseas postings included France,

India, and Turkey. He has a PhD from the University of California, Los Angeles in South Asian History.

Aparna Pande is Research Fellow and Director of Hudson Institute's Initiative on the Future of India and South Asia. She is the author of *Explaining Pakistan's Foreign Policy: Escaping India* (2011). Her major field of interest is South Asia, with a special focus on India, Pakistan, foreign policy, security studies, religion in politics, and political Islam.

Tahmina Rashid is Associate Professor in International Studies, at the University of Canberra, Australia. She is the author of *Contested Representations: Punjabi Women in Feminist Debates in Pakistan* (2006).

Martin Sökefeld is Professor and Head of the Department of Social and Cultural Anthropology at Ludwig-Maximilians-University, Munich. His recent publications include *Struggling for Recognition: The Alevi Movement in Germany and in Transnational Space* (2008).

Stephen Tankel is Assistant Professor in the School of International Service at American University and a non-resident scholar in the South Asia Program at the Carnegie Endowment for International Peace. He is currently on leave, working as an Advisor for Asian and Pacific Security Affairs at the Department of Defense. He is the author of *Storming the World Stage: The Story of Lashkar-e-Taiba* (2011).

INTRODUCTION

This volume follows the earlier one, *Pakistan: From the Rhetoric of Democracy to the Rise of Militancy*, published in the spring of 2011.

Even as the earlier volume was in the production process, a series of events occurred that underscored the enormous structure of the Pakistani state and its Establishment. And equally, the growing distrust between the United States and Pakistan as its ally in the war on terror. On 27 January 2011, Raymond Davis, a CIA contractor, killed two reportedly armed men who tried to rob him in Lahore, the capital of Pakistani Punjab. Davis was arrested for the alleged crime – thus saved from a lynching mob – but the episode quickly gained byzantine proportions. On the one hand, it exposed America's expanding network of CIA operatives working clandestinely in Pakistan, and on the other, it revealed America's growing distrust of its non-NATO ally. For the Pakistani Establishment, the Davis affair was emblematic of American arrogance. Davis ultimately left Pakistan after the Obama administration paid blood money to the families of the victims.

On 2 May 2011, the US special forces raided Abbottabad, the cantonment town founded by the English General James Abbott in 1853 and that now is home to the Pakistan Military Academy, killing Osama bin Laden in his mansion. Instead of investigating how bin Laden came to live there for several years, the military took a nationalistic stance by focusing on the violation of Pakistani sovereignty by the US forces. The Obama administration, weary of its relations with Pakistan, elected not to press the point. There is thinking in certain academic and policy quarters that, given Pakistan's nuclear arsenal, it is safer to keep Pakistan in an embrace rather than letting it spin out on its own.

In retaliation, the ISI (Inter-Services Intelligence) disclosed the identity of the American CIA station chief in Pakistan one week after the Abbottabad raid. A few weeks later, the Pakistani journalist Saleem Shahjad was

INTRODUCTION

abducted and killed allegedly by the ISI. On 8 July 2011, the BBC reported that, according to Admiral Michael Mullen, Shahzad's killing had been 'sanctioned' by the top Pakistani military brass, including Generals Kayani and Pasha because he had been investigating al-Qaida and other militant groups infiltrating into the Pakistani navy and military. He reported that the militant group was behind 22 May deadly assault on the Mehran base in Karachi because talks had failed over the release of several naval personnel arrested on suspicion of links to al-Qaida affiliates.

Soon, human rights groups were calling Pakistan the most dangerous place in the world for journalists to operate, saying they were under threat from Islamist militants, on the one hand, and from Pakistan's military and intelligence agencies, on the other.

As the Americans and Pakistanis continued to argue about cutting ties with the Haqqani network and other insurgent groups, and Pakistan continued to mechanically and vociferously deny American allegations of protecting terrorist organizations, on 24 November, NATO airstrikes on two checkpoints killed 24 Pakistani military personnel, raising anti-American rhetoric in Pakistan, and forcing the military to close the supply route to Afghanistan for the NATO forces.

In the midst of all this erupted the so-called Memogate scandal involving Hussain Haqqani, Pakistani ambassador to the United States. This was a memorandum addressed to Admiral Mike Mullen, the Joint Chief of Staff, ostensibly seeking American help following the killing of bin Laden to avert a military takeover of the civilian government in Pakistan, as well as assisting in a Washington insider takeover of the Pakistani government and military apparatus. The timeline of events indicate that the memo was delivered in May (2011), but came to light when Mansoor Ijaz, a Pakistani American businessman and a friend of Ambassador Haqqani, on 10 October 2011, wrote a *Financial Times* opinion piece, bringing initial public attention to the affair. The memo, which at first was questioned to even exist, was allegedly drafted by Ambassador Haqqani on President Zardari's request, and delivered to General Mullen by former US national security advisor General James Jones, also a friend of Ijaz. The scandal led to Ambassador Haqqani's resignation, and he was charged with treason. In his *Magnificent Delusions* (2013), Haqqani claims that to save his life, he took refuge in Prime Minister Gilani's home, and ultimately, as a consequence of pressure brought by the Obama administration, as well as Republican senators such as John McCain, he was given a safe passage back to the United States and he resumed his academic work at Boston University.

INTRODUCTION

In addition to the surreal, if not incestuous, relationship between the United States and Pakistan, the Memogate reveals the multilayered labyrinths of the Pakistan Establishment. Yet another episode illustrating the Pakistan labyrinth occurred in 2013, when the *Times of India* on 30 June reported the tweet by Pakistani scholar Ayesha Sadiqqa, an indefatigable crusader for democracy, in which she claimed that the ISI had infiltrated the think tanks in Washington and lamented that the ISI was sending 'unqualified' people. A number of top US and British scholars, including two former US ambassadors to Pakistan, denounced what they called Siddiqa's 'unsubstantiated but extreme allegations'. The over-the-top reaction to Sadiqqa's tweet remains puzzling, given Ghulam Nabi Fai, a Kashmiri separatist in Washington, was convicted of lobbying after receiving slush funds from Pakistani intelligence agency.

As in the previous volume, so also in this one, effort has been made to diversify contributions by reaching out to young scholars from different regions of the world to explore Pakistan from their vantage point. Some are prominent and have established their presence in the field as well as on talk shows, others are emerging as sound scholars in their own right, and yet others who work in different countries, but deal with similar issues as in Pakistan: Aparna Pandey deals with Pakistan–India relations and addresses the issue of 'parity' with India that has been central in Pakistan since the time of Jinnah, Christine Fair examines the role of madrasahs as breeding grounds for militants, Gilles Boquérat looks at the media and its role in Pakistan, Laurent Gayer delves into Karachi and the violence that has come to define the city, Martin Sökefeld explores the Northern Areas of Pakistan, Steven Tankel takes a closer look at jihadist proxies in the Punjab, and Tahmina Rashid looks at the role of women in militancy.

I thank the contributors for their work and the patience they have shown in waiting for the publication of this volume that has been delayed by nearly a year for reasons beyond the control of this editor or Routledge, the publisher. Thanks also to the editorial staff at Routledge for piloting this volume to its completion.

1

PAKISTAN

Issues of self-identity and parity with India

Aparna Pande

Introduction

States have constructed identities and these identities often determine their behaviour in the international system. This chapter argues that what lies at the core of the tensions between India and Pakistan is the question of identity. Each state has crafted a view of itself, its origins, and creation and, in doing so, has also created a corresponding view of the 'other'. These images have totally different ideological bases and hence, the clashes that occur on every major issue are seen as existential.

Identity plays a key role in defining nationhood: as noted by political scientist Benedict Anderson, nations are 'imagined political communities'.[1] Indian leaders, conscious of a multireligious and multicultural state, have always portrayed India as a secular country, emphasizing links to the 5,000-year-old civilization. In the case of Pakistan, the founding fathers made a conscious decision to construct an ideology-based national identity that would be different from India's.

Over the decades, an ideology-driven Pakistani national identity was crafted to 'escape' a shared Indian heritage. This fostered the creation of an ideological state that, in turn, has bolstered the control of the military–intelligence establishment, not only in security and foreign policy but also in domestic politics.

This chapter will demonstrate how Pakistan's security establishment has benefitted from the legacy of Partition, the crafting of an ideology-driven identity, and the fear of perceived Indian hegemonic ambitions. All of these factors have influenced the military–intelligence establishment in pursuing its goals to achieve parity with India, both conventional and nuclear. Further, Pakistan's efforts to form ties with the United States, China, and countries in the Muslim world have also been shaped by the ambition to stand up to India, and these ties have principally benefited the security establishment.

Colonial and pre-Partition legacy

According to a 2009 report by the British Council (Pakistan), more than 75 per cent of Pakistanis consider themselves to be Muslims first, and Pakistanis second.[2] In a May 2011 poll by the Gilani Research Foundation, a Pakistan-based polling organization, 67 per cent of Pakistanis asserted that they are in favour of state-led Islamization of society.[3] How did this happen in a country that was founded by a Westernized elite as a homeland for South Asia's Muslims and not originally imagined as an Islamic state?

The increasing radicalization of Pakistani society and the move away from the more inclusive South Asian Islamic culture can be traced back to the construction of an ideology-driven Islamic Pakistani identity. The country's Islamist narrative has been crafted in such a fashion that even secularists have inadvertently contributed to both its rise and spread in Pakistan. The roots of this narrative can be traced back to the views of the well-off Indian Muslims in nineteenth-century India, when Muslim power was in decline.

As rulers in the Indian subcontinent since the tenth century, Muslims never considered themselves a numerical minority, even though India remained largely Hindu. With the advent of British rule and the gradual introduction of parliamentary democracy came a steady realization among the Indian Muslim elites of their numerical minority. In the age of parliamentary democracy, numbers mattered far more than in the earlier era of Muslim monarchy.

The reaction of the Indian Muslim elites to the establishment of British rule saw the development of two broad strands of nationalism. For some Muslim leaders, the answer was territorial nationalism: Indian Muslims were Muslim in religion and Indian in nationality. These leaders joined the Indian National Congress, a secular nationalist party, but Muslims formed only a small percentage of the Congress leadership.[4]

In contrast, other Muslim leaders saw religious nationalism as the defining characteristic of their Indian Muslim identity. The argument put forth was that Hindus and Muslims were not just followers of different religions but different communities or nations. This was the crux of the 'two-nation theory', which in later years was put forth as the justification for the creation of the independent state of Pakistan.

The majority of India's Muslim leaders during the Raj were modern Western-educated Muslims and not part of the traditional religious elite. Yet they looked towards religion as the defining aspect of their identity.[5] After independence too, Pakistan's secular leaders saw no conflict between acceptance of the religious narrative and their secular credentials.

In a Hindu-majority country such as India, elections under a joint electorate system would invariably have resulted in a situation where the majority of those elected would be Hindus. If the Muslim elite wanted a substantial say in any legislative set-up, they had to ensure that a certain minimum number of Muslims were elected. They could achieve this objective either by ensuring that all political parties had a certain number of Muslim candidates (in effect, using the minority's block voting clout) or they could ask for separate electorates (i.e. community-based electorates.) The system of separate electorates, whereby Muslim leaders would only get votes from Muslim voters (and Hindu leaders from Hindu voters), ultimately reinforced separation between the communities, even though the right to vote was very limited. Even if the feeling of separation had not been felt by the masses, this disconnect had been reinforced among the elite.

The establishment of the All India Muslim League in 1906 at Dhaka (formerly Dacca) was a seemingly logical manifestation of the belief that Muslims needed organizations – separate from Hindu-led organizations – that would represent them and help safeguard their interests. The need for separate electorates, reservation of seats for Muslims in the legislative assemblies of Muslim-minority provinces, and inclusion of the Muslim League in any discussion about the future of India were some of the early demands of the Muslim League. The leaders of the Muslim League believed that championing these causes would be adequate to help them win sufficient seats and ensure the party's position as the 'sole spokesman' of the Muslims, as historian Ayesha Jalal explains.[6]

In the aftermath of the 1936 electoral defeat, the Muslim League changed its overall policy. Since the 1946 elections would decide who would rule India after the British, it became incumbent on the Muslim League to secure its position as the sole Muslim voice and party in the Raj. Instead of safeguards for the Indian Muslim minority, the party's new demand was centred around the two-nation theory, meaning that Hindus and Muslims – as the two religions present in India – had equal right to decide the future of India. Further, realizing the vast cultural, ethnic, and linguistic differences among Muslims living in the various provinces of British India, the Muslim League emphasized their religious commonality in order to gain support.

The Muslim League did exceptionally well in the 1946 elections, precisely because of the support of Muslim clerics and the use of religious slogans. Receiving 75 per cent of the total Muslim vote in the provincial assemblies and a majority of the Muslim vote in the national assembly as well, the League could now claim its status as the spokesperson for Muslims.[7] Despite various attempts, the Muslim League and the Indian National Congress were too far apart for reconciliation at this stage. And thus, two independent countries, India and Pakistan, came into existence on 15 August 1947. The violence-ridden partition of the British Raj, the mass migrations, and the massive refugee crisis did nothing to improve the trust on either side of the border. Around 14 million people migrated and crossed borders. Another million were killed in the large-scale riots that took place. The refugee crisis and riots were not just an emotional issue; they had practical consequences as well. The entry of over 8 million people,[8] mainly homeless and moneyless, into the newly created and still weak country of Pakistan, only accentuated the feelings of insecurity and being under siege. India was seen as deliberately causing riots or problems and sending more refugees into Pakistan so as to break it up from within. The refugee problem was part of a larger crisis: the large number of minorities in both countries – Hindus in Pakistan and Muslims in India.

After 1947, this mistrust has been visible in the belief held by a majority of Pakistanis that India and Indian leaders have never accepted Partition or the rationale for the creation of Pakistan. Pakistan's leaders have always imagined their Indian counterparts to be questioning of the logic of Partition, both in 1947 and in subsequent years, thereby challenging Pakistan's very identity and existence.[9]

Identity

At the core of India–Pakistan relations is the question of identity. Pakistani leaders and strategists fear not simply a military defeat by India, but the reabsorption of the separate Islamic Pakistani identity within a larger Indian national identity. In effect, India is seen as a threat to Pakistan's very existence as an independent nation.

The 'idea' of Pakistan has a very short history: the word originated in the 1930s; the 'Lahore Resolution' (later referred to as the Pakistan Resolution) of 1940 discussed the two-nation theory; and, in 1947, Pakistan was created. Constructing a Pakistani identity was thus considered a matter of national survival.

Over the years, the idea that Pakistan was founded on the basis of an ideology, which the Pakistani state had to implement and safeguard, was put forth by both civilian and military leaders. Pakistan's first Prime Minister, Liaquat Ali Khan, often talked about the Pakistani ideology and the primary role Islam played in this ideology. For Pakistan's first military ruler, General Ayub Khan, who ruled from 1958 to 1969 and played a crucial role in the country's formative years, man's 'greatest yearning is for an ideology for which he should be able to lay down his life . . . Such an ideology with us is obviously that of Islam. It was on that basis that we fought for and got Pakistan, but having got it, we failed to order our lives in accordance with it'.[10] Pakistan was officially declared the Islamic Republic of Pakistan in 1956 and its evolution in an Islamic direction has been consistently enforced by state policy. For Pakistan's leaders, a national ideology based on and derived from Islam has always been the answer to nagging questions of national identity; thus it is through Islam that they chose to define Pakistani nationalism.

The Indian Muslim elite, which founded Pakistan, saw it as the homeland of Indian Muslims. However, they faced many challenges on this front, not the least of which was shared history with India. Pakistan had little history of its own to appeal to except that of the Indian civilization (including India's Muslim history), which it had broken away from. It could have taken one of two roads: acknowledge its Indian history and lay itself open to constant critique over its raison d'être or try and craft a narrative of history that matched its current ambitions. Pakistan's leaders opted for the latter and in doing so, searched for episodic evidence in the relatively recent history of Indian Muslims.

The creation of a national identity that would be separate, viable, and sustainable meant that Pakistan wove a very intricate pattern of ideological differentiation with India. The crafting of history in Pakistan's textbooks, the creation of a Pakistan Studies curriculum, and the depiction of any gesture from the Indian side as an offer from the Hindu *bania* (moneylender) show the extent to which a certain ideology was created in Pakistan.[11] The elite constructed Pakistan's history in such a manner that, in the words of a leading Pakistani thinker, Khaled Ahmed, 'it appears natural to people that to be Pakistani you have to be anti-Hindu: it is part of the definition, like the core of the being. You have to define yourself in opposition to the other. India has become the definite other for the Pakistanis'.[12]

Pakistan's official narrative of its history reinforces the belief that Pakistan was created not in 1947 but rather twelve centuries earlier, when Islam was introduced to India as a result of the annexation of Sindh (in AD 712) by the Arab–Muslim Umayyad Empire. The shared history of the peoples of South Asia has been rewritten in school curricula to stress the divergence and difference between the two principal religious communities of South Asia – Hindus and Muslims.[13]

Each one of Pakistan's Constitutions – 1956, 1962, 1973, and even the Legal Framework orders under military rule – has reiterated the important role of Islam and asserted that no law in the country should contravene any of the tenets of Islam. The harshest policies of Islamization took place under General Zia ul Haq (1977–89), President and Army Chief, who not only believed that Pakistan was founded in the name of Islam but also declared that the Pakistani military were the 'guardians of ideological as well as geographical frontiers' of Pakistan.[14]

Under General Zia, there was state-led Islamization of Pakistani society, legal system, educational system, and even the military. There was a gradual Islamization of the lower ranks of the civil service and bureaucracy in Pakistan.

Those with an ideological and religious orientation were favoured in recruitment for the military. This created a combustible cocktail in which there was an increasingly religious and ideological military, whose foreign policy goals included keeping Pakistan safe from India and continuing involvement in the anti-Soviet jihad in Afghanistan.

That General Zia's views are still prevalent in the military was self-evident when, on the eve of Pakistan's sixty-second Independence in August 2009, Chief of Army Staff, General Ashfaq Pervez Kayani, reiterated, 'Islam is the soul and spirit of Pakistan. It is our strength and we will always be an Islamic republic'. Further, General Kayani emphasized that the Pakistani army would continue to defend the country 'against all internal and external threats'.[15]

Fear of Indian hegemony

> 'What India wants is a subservient Pakistan, which should remain constantly under Indian influence, like some of the smaller states, unfortunately, in the region at the present moment who are nevertheless trying to assert their independence. Pakistan cannot accept that position. India should know that very well.'
>
> —General Zia ul Haq, 1981[16]

Pakistan's leaders have always perceived India as being hegemonic and imperialist. Even after the creation of Pakistan, there was a firmly held belief that its territorial integrity was still under threat and there was a need for self-preservation.[17] As late as the 1970s, a leading Pakistani political scientist wrote that, for Pakistan, its borders with India had not only physical but ideological significance 'as they represented a monument to the Muslim's successful defiance of Hindu majority rule, as well as the territorial projection of the ideology of Islam – the basis for the creation of Pakistan'.[18]

Not only do Pakistanis fear that India plans to undo Partition, but that the end goal of all Indians is to create *Akhand Bharat*, an Undivided India. This was a term used by Hindu revivalist organizations as well as right-wing

Hindu nationalist parties. *Akhand Bharat* territorially refers to the entire Indian subcontinent as being one entity. Pakistanis often refer back to the statement made by Hindu right-wing nationalist organizations at Partition about the indivisibility and territorial unity of the Indian subcontinent as proof of Indian imperial designs.[19] Though never a mainstream belief in India, these views are nevertheless widely promoted in Pakistan.

In the initial decades after Independence, Pakistan's primary fear vis-à-vis India was that of India breaking up Pakistan through military or other means. Not only did the various provinces have to be kept intact, but also Pakistan could only be complete once Kashmir joined the country.

Jammu and Kashmir was one of the 562 princely states that were part of the British Raj. They were all bound to the British Raj via treaties under the 'Doctrine of Paramountcy'.[20] At Independence in 1947, these states were asked to accede to either Pakistan or India, based on two conditions: geographical contiguity of the state and the wishes of its people. Kashmir was contiguous to both India and Pakistan; it was a Muslim-majority region and was ruled by a Hindu Dogra ruler. Maharaja Hari Singh refused to join either country, and like some of the other princely states would have preferred independence.

Fear that India might try to annex the Muslim-majority province of Kashmir and refusal by the British commander-in-chief of the Pakistani Army to allow the army to enter Kashmir-led Pakistan to adopt a different strategy.[21] The Pakistani establishment became impatient and mobilized a tribal *lashkar* (irregular army), which was convinced that it was fighting a jihad to free Kashmir. The *lashkar* entered Kashmir, defeated the Maharaja's forces, and almost reached Srinagar. In the meantime, Maharaja Hari Singh asked for Indian assistance and signed the Instrument of Accession to India. This led to a war between the two countries in 1947–48, resulting in an UN-declared ceasefire. As of now, Kashmir is divided along the ceasefire line or Line of Control (LoC).

For India, the existence of a Muslim-majority state within the Indian Union attests to the secular nature of India's polity, notwithstanding India's overwhelming Hindu majority. There is a fear that allowing secession of one part of India could open the gates for possible balkanization of modern India. Thus India's position has been that Jammu and Kashmir lawfully acceded to India in 1947, when the Maharajah signed the Instrument of Accession. Over the years, successive Indian governments have been willing to consider acceptance of the Line of Control as the international boundary between Pakistan and India to resolve the dispute. However, there is also a demand for Pakistan to end all support to Kashmiri terrorist groups and to give up the option of use of force to gain control of Kashmir.

Pakistan's nationhood is based on the 'two nation theory', and thus if a Muslim-majority province stays part of India, then the ideological basis for a separate homeland for Muslims in the subcontinent comes into question.[22] Pakistan has demanded that a plebiscite should be held in Indian-controlled Kashmir in accordance with the United Nations resolutions, to ascertain the will of the people about joining India or Pakistan. Pakistan also believes that India has been violating the human rights of Kashmiri Muslims, which has resulted in a popular and indigenous uprising against Indian occupation since 1989.

According to historians such as Charles Tilly, territorial conflicts are very important in the formation of nascent states. These conflicts provide both internal and international legitimacy to the state, nurture feelings of nationalism, and accelerate the process of centralization of the state.[23]

The Kashmir issue plays such a crucial role in Pakistan's foreign policy. The rise in power of Pakistan's military and its deepening role in foreign and defence policies can be traced to the Kashmir conflict of 1947–48, which was the first time that the military portrayed itself as the defender of the new nation.

Tied in with the issue of Kashmir is the water dispute between India and Pakistan. Pakistan and India share the Indus river system, which comprises the Indus River and its five tributaries. In 1960, the two countries signed the Indus Water Treaty, under which the three eastern rivers fall under India's share and the three western rivers, under Pakistan's. Indian policymakers assert that India has always abided by the Indus Water Treaty, and even during times of war and conflict (1965, 1971, 1999), has never cut off the supply of water to Pakistan. However, as the lower riparian state, Pakistan has always feared that India might 'cut off the jugular', i.e. cut off the supply of water.

In 1971, Pakistan suffered a second partition and loss of its Eastern wing, East Pakistan, resulting in the creation of Bangladesh. Till 1971, East Pakistan was the most populous province of Pakistan. However, among the East Pakistani elite and populace, there was a feeling of second-class citizenship, of being deprived of its due share in the economic growth of the country, a feeling of low representation in the civil and military services, and of inadequate representation in the political system. By the late 1960s, these issues had boiled down to a demand for more autonomy that, in the end, led to a military crackdown, civil war, and a war with India. The 1971 break up and separation of East Pakistan as Bangladesh, instead of diluting the two-nation theory, only reinforced this belief of Pakistan's policymakers and elite. Speeches by Indian leaders, either expressing solidarity with East Pakistanis or threatening Pakistan, only increased the paranoia.

The desire for parity and the fear of Indian hegemony are reflected not just on the military plane, but also the economic one. Since 1947, India and Pakistan have traded with each other and the only time trade came to a complete halt was between 1965 and 1974. Yet, the extent of trade remained negligible and limited until recently. The amount of legal trade has ranged from $100 million in the late 1990s, to $300 million in 2003, to around $2 billion in 2008.[24]

Until recently, there was no India–Pakistan trade agreement and Pakistan only allowed a limited list of commodities to be imported from India. This was in spite of the various studies by Pakistan's Ministry of Commerce and the Karachi Chamber of Commerce, which revealed how beneficial trade with India would be, due to low transportation costs, low prices, and cultural similarities leading to similar tastes and preferences.[25] In accordance with the World Trade Organization (WTO), India granted Pakistan Most Favoured Nation (MFN) status as early as 1996; however, Pakistan agreed to award the same to India only in 2011. The reason why there is such little trade is political, not economic. There is a desire for parity in this sphere too.

When, in 1971, East Pakistan broke off and Bangladesh was created, the fear of India trying to undo Partition and wipe out Pakistan's existence became a distinct possibility in the Pakistani view. India did not attack West Pakistan, however, and also allowed the creation of a separate country, Bangladesh. If *Akhand Bharat* had been the real aim of Indira Gandhi, then India would have merged East Bengal with West Bengal and not just walked away. Similarly, a weakened West Pakistan would have been easy prey for India's army. The calculated decision not to undo Pakistan was reflected in a letter from Prime Minister Indira Gandhi to President Nixon in December 1971, in which Gandhi stated that India does 'not want any territory of what was East Pakistan and now constitutes Bangladesh. We do not want any territory of West Pakistan'.[26]

The theory of *Akhand Bharat* as India's ultimate strategic goal has been disproved by the history of events. Yet, this did not keep it from maintaining its salience in Pakistani strategic thinking. The paradigm was adjusted and adapted. Even after Pakistan has obtained nuclear weapons, and thus, nuclear deterrence, the fear of India trying to break up Pakistan has not dissipated. This is because it is not a fear rooted in realistic analysis but is rather psycho-political in nature.

Ties with Afghanistan

Pakistan's ties with Afghanistan need to be examined in the context of Pakistan's fear of Indian hegemonic ambitions and seen as a way to prevent a perceived strategic encirclement of Pakistan by India and its allies.

Having a hostile neighbour along one border (India), Pakistan has always sought a friendly country along its other border (Afghanistan). A pro-Pakistan regime in Afghanistan that was opposed to India was hence deemed crucial to the foreign and security policies of Pakistan. Any close ties between India and Afghanistan were anathema to Pakistan's leaders and strategists.

Pakistani defence and security planners believed that 'in spite of the great length of territory in West Pakistan, there is no depth in the area'.[27] This refers to the concept of 'strategic depth': a military term that refers to the distance between the front lines and the combatants' key centres of population or military production. In the view of Pakistan's military planners, the key question facing the country has been the fear that Pakistan's territorial structure is such that it is vulnerable to an Indian attack. Pakistan thus does not have the capability to withdraw into its own territory, absorb an initial thrust, and still save its key cities. Fearing India, a country with which it shares borders that are not easily defensible, and also fearing that Pakistan lacked 'strategic depth' vis-à-vis India, Pakistan sought strategic depth in its western neighbour, Afghanistan.

Seeking military parity: Pakistan's defence policy

The issue of strategic depth and the need for at least one of Pakistan's borders to be safe feed into the Pakistani security establishment's fear of an imminent attack from India. The key reason is that the terrain along the India–Pakistan border is level and plain. With people on both sides of the border sharing ethnic and linguistic similarities and no mountains or other geographical barriers separating the two countries, this fear has been all-consuming. In the initial decades after Partition, the main communication links built by the British to tie their empire together, railway tracks and roads, between Pakistan's initial capital, Karachi, and its key city, Lahore, lay very close to the Indian border. Thus, in 1947, from the position of Pakistan's leaders, the fear of 'Hindu India' marching across Punjab and Rajasthan into the heart of Pakistan was a reality they had to guard against. This fear has been self-sustaining over the years.

The source of this fear stems from the disparity between the armed forces of the two countries. The British Indian army was divided between India and Pakistan so that Pakistan got one-third. The existential fear had manifested itself early in Pakistan's life as an independent country, during the 1947–48 war over Kashmir. It reinforced the constructed belief that India had not accepted Partition and prevented Pakistan from receiving its due share of the British Indian assets.

This perceived reality and fear led to the singular goal of Pakistan's defence policy: military parity with India at any cost – a quest bearing similarity to Jinnah's quest for political parity between the Hindus and Muslims. The result has been Pakistan's high military expenditure, the search for allies such as the United States, Saudi Arabia, and China, who would supply military aid, and the defence establishment's obsessive focus on its eastern frontier, with most of its army being trained for war with India. It also resulted in a security policy that sanctioned the use of asymmetrical warfare and non-state actors to pursue foreign and security policy interests in South Asia, particularly against India.

To compensate for its weaker position in material and manpower, the Pakistani military establishment invoked the old Raj myth of martial races, arguing that numerically weaker Pakistan could stand up to India because Pakistan had most of the martial races. The 'martial races' concept was a designation created by the British Indian officials in eighteenth-nineteenth-century India. At its core lay the assumption that certain ethnic groups are inherently more warlike than others. Pakistan's military leaders persisted in this misconception after Partition. Confident that since the 'martial races', such as the Punjabis, Balochis, and Pathans, were now part of Pakistan, leaving non-martial races in India, Pakistan's victory in any conflict with India would be ensured, even if India had a larger army. This misconception was summarized in the claim that 'one Muslim Pakistani was equal to five Hindu Indians'. Pakistanis tend to ignore the fact that the Indian Army comprises people from all parts of India, especially Gurkhas, Rajputs, Muslims, and Sikhs – all of them being martial races.

After the ignominious defeat in the 1971 war and the fear that Indian conventional military strength was growing very quickly, Pakistani military and intelligence planners turned seriously to asymmetrical or irregular warfare. Many Pakistani strategic planners had looked on irregular warfare favourably, even in the early decades after Partition, and this strategy was deployed in the first war with India in 1947–48. Strategic thinkers such as Aslam Siddiqui argued that though Pakistan needed external aid to build up its military strength, Pakistan should still be ready for the day the 'marriage with the West' dissolves.[28] It was argued that Pakistan had an ideology and manpower and that in parts of Pakistan (like Baluchistan and the Frontier areas), there was a tradition of irregular warfare that could be harnessed by the state. Unlike a regular army, irregular forces (read 'jihadis') were not a burden on the treasury and since they were independent entities, the state could disclaim responsibility from any action they undertook.

The success of the anti-Soviet Afghan jihad of the 1980s demonstrated to the security establishment of Pakistan the advantages of using irregular warfare. With the end of that jihad in the early 1990s, there was not only an ideology but also a large pool of radical Islamists who were encouraged to include not just Afghanistan but also central Asia and, especially, India in their ambit and scope.

Tied to this was the idea that, unlike Pakistan, which was based on an ideology and had religious unity, India was an unnatural state and would easily fall apart. A study in the 1990s conducted by the Command and Staff College at Quetta claimed that a 'misguided belief in Indian unity in the past' has led Indians 'into believing that a vast country like India can exist as a single political entity'.[29] Militarily, the argument put forth is that India could easily be 'cut down to size' if the right policies are followed.

The Pakistani security establishment's support for radical Islamist groups who are focused on Afghanistan (Afghan Taliban, Haqqani network, and allied groups) and India (Lashkar e Taiba, Jaish e Muhammad) is based on the belief that these groups are ideal proxies. The Afghan groups would help Pakistan achieve a pro-Pakistan, anti-India Afghan government, and the India-focused groups would keep the Indian state tied down.

Nuclear policy: deterrent and parity

Until the 1971 break up of Pakistan, Pakistani leaders believed that their large population gave them some sense of parity with India. The loss of East Pakistan – hence, the majority of Pakistan's population – coupled with the disastrous military defeat at the hands of India, did not result in a realization that maybe it would be impossible for Pakistan to have a military balance with its much larger neighbour. Instead, the desire for military parity with India became more important so as to prevent any further break up of Pakistan. In January 1972, the head of Pakistan's Army, Lieutenant General Gul Hasan, stated in an interview with his American interlocutors the need for American aid in order to maintain the army 'at pre-war size'. When asked by the Americans if this would be possible keeping in mind both the reduction in size of the Pakistani territory and the elimination of the need to now maintain a force in East Pakistan, Gul Hasan answered that 'a credible force would still be needed to serve as deterrent against any hostile intentions by India'.[30] Thus, the desire for balancing India remained paramount even after the creation of Bangladesh.

Concluding by the early 1970s that conventional military parity with India was difficult, if not impossible, Pakistan's civilian and military policymakers looked to nuclear weapons. Nuclear weapons were seen as the magic wand that would make Pakistan India's equal, guarantee territorial integrity even without the support of allies, and gain respectability in the Muslim world as the first Muslim country with nuclear weapons. The primary goal of Pakistan's nuclear weapons programme was, and continues to be, military parity with India.

Starting in 1972, Pakistan was able to build a nuclear weapons programme mainly through international help, both overt and covert. The groundwork, however, was done by Dr Abdul Qadeer Khan, who used information and material obtained from his former place of work, a Uranium enrichment facility in the Netherlands, along with assistance from an illicit international network of suppliers to support Pakistan. The 'Islamic' bomb of Zulfikar Ali Bhutto's dreams was built with aid from Pakistan's allies in the Middle East, such as Libya, Saudi Arabia, and the other Gulf countries.[31] By the late 1980s, Pakistan had built a bomb, though under American pressure, the Pakistani leadership did not 'turn the final screw'.[32]

In May 1998, the Hindu-right wing BJP government of India conducted nuclear tests and this increased pressure on Pakistan to follow suit. The United States tried to dissuade Pakistan from testing its nuclear weapons. However, statements by the Indian Home Minister, L.K. Advani, directed at Pakistan, asking Pakistan to accept the new reality simply increased Pakistan's fears of an existential threat from India and reinforced the desire for parity. Exploding five devices on 28 May 1998, the Pakistani rationale for the blasts was reflected in the centrality of India in their strategic outlook and the desire for parity: 'We have done it. We are India's equal'.[33] Content not to test the nuclear weapons as long as India did not do so, Pakistan felt justified in testing if only to ensure the balance. The only way Pakistan could contain and prevent India's hostile intentions was to have a balance in weapons.

Ties with the US

Faced by what they viewed as an existential fight for Pakistan's very survival, Pakistan's military and civilian policymakers have always tried to maintain a balance with India in the field of military, and later, nuclear, technology. However, India being the bigger power in area, population, economy, and conventional forces, other ways to address this imbalance often needed to be discovered. In many ways, this was a continuation of the attempts in the 1930s and 1940s by the Muslim League to balance the relationship between itself and the Congress.

In total size, India is around four times Pakistan, and in population, India has almost as many Muslims as Pakistan does, with a total population of over a billion. India's economy is much larger, with the GDP of India around ten times that of Pakistan. India spends only 2.4 per cent of its GDP on its military, as compared to 3.4 per cent by Pakistan, and yet, outspends Pakistan around six to one. The Indian Army is around double that of Pakistan's.[34] Thus, in order to achieve a measure of parity with India, Pakistan has both invested a large part of its budget on military expenditures as well as entered into military alliances with the West, especially with the United States, as well as with China.

During the early 1950s, Pakistan entered into a number of Cold War security arrangements with the United States and obtained economic and military assistance in return for giving access to the Americans to Pakistan. American aid, both in the military sphere and in the economic sphere, played a significant role in framing Pakistan's pro-US foreign policy. The role of the top brass of the military, who benefited from the defence and military deals with the US, should not be overlooked either. Pakistan signed a number of alliances in this period: agreements with Turkey, and later, with the US in 1954. It also joined the South East Asia Treaty Organization (SEATO) in 1954 and the CENTO (Central Treaty Organization) in 1955. In 1959, Pakistan and the US signed an agreement that ensured that Pakistan would get economic and military assistance from the US to preserve the 'independence and integrity of Pakistan', and in return, Pakistan promised to provide the US with an air base in Peshawar.[35]

During the Cold War, Pakistan was the eastern-most anchor of America's 'northern tier of containment' but with the end of the Cold War, there was a reduction in Pakistan's importance as an American ally. Post-September 2001, Pakistan was once again roped in as a strategic ally in the War on Terror. From the point of view of the United States, Pakistan has always been more of a key tactical ally for specific American geopolitical interests in the region rather than a strategic partner in larger American foreign policy interests.

Though Pakistan gained militarily from all these agreements and was also able to build ties with pro-West Muslim nations, in some ways, these alliances did not solve the primary concerns of Pakistani foreign policy. In all these pacts, Pakistan was forbidden from using the assistance provided for any aggression outside of these agreements that, given the Cold War situation, were basically directed against Communism. However, Pakistan's main concern was India and on that front, these alliances did not directly aid Pakistan. Therefore, ties with other Muslim countries and China, India's bête noire, were seen as critical.

Ties with China

Pakistanis and Chinese usually describe their friendship as 'loftier than the Himalayas and deeper than the Indian Ocean'.[36] Chinese support, both economic and military, over the years, has been a great asset to Pakistan. In some respects, it is *realpolitik*: both countries have their worries about India, and so, find the other useful.

Pakistan's relations with China started in 1954 at the Bandung Conference. After the Indo–China war of 1962, Pakistan–China relations developed deep roots during the Ayub Khan regime. Foreign Minister Zulfikar Bhutto argued, 'China is Pakistan's neighbor and it is essential for us to maintain good relations with all our neighbors on the basis of friendship and equality'.[37] Clearly, India was excluded in this calculation.

During the 1965 Indo–Pakistan War, China took an openly pro-Pakistan and an anti-India stance. Chinese government spokesmen described India's extension of the war beyond Kashmir into Pakistani Punjab as 'naked aggression'.[38] The Chinese government also accused India of provocative actions on the Indo–Chinese border and threatened to retaliate – a move designed to offset India against Pakistan.

Pakistan seeks in China what it has always wanted from an ally – a country that will build Pakistan's economic and military resources to help it achieve parity with India, and who has an antagonistic relationship with India, and hence, will support Pakistan in any conflict with India.

While China has supplied Pakistan with aid over the years, it is limited to the military (including nuclear) arena and to investment in areas of the economy that would benefit China, especially infrastructure (e.g. Karakoram highway, Gwadar port). Further, Sino–Indian ties have improved since the 1990s and in the last decade, China has urged Pakistan to resolve conflicts with India peacefully.

Pan-Islamism

For Pakistan's founding elite, domestic politics and foreign policy were to complement each other. Pakistan's foreign policy was cast in the same terms as its domestic policy: because India is dominated by Hindus, with whom Muslims have little in common, Pakistan must draw closer to the Muslim states to its west. Pakistan's first Prime Minister, Liaquat Ali Khan, claimed, 'Even when we were subject people we regarded the distress of Muslim countries as our own . . . today we are bound by those natural postulates of Islamic Fraternity which were formulated for our guidance thirteen centuries ago'.[39] To fortify the ideology of the state, the national identity within and without, there were constant attempts at emphasizing the universal nature of Islam; hence, the pan-Islamist nature of Pakistan's foreign policy.

However, due to the deeper belief in nationalism and the strength of anti-colonialism in other recently decolonized Muslim countries, Pakistan's attempts at pan-Islamism failed during the 1950s. The 1970s, however, provided fertile ground for reviving the deal. The 1971 civil war and the creation of Bangladesh led to an intensifying of various beliefs. India was trusted even less and the need for allies was seen as even more important – especially, allies from the Muslim world. The unwillingness of the United States to militarily safeguard Pakistan's unity was seen as proof of American perfidy. Pakistan had to build its own deterrent to India and there was a tendency to rely even more on the Ummah.

Events in 1979, including the Iranian Revolution, the Soviet invasion of Afghanistan, and the anti-Soviet Afghan jihad led to increasing aid and growing ties between Pakistan and the Gulf States in the Middle East.

Between 1972 and 1977, Pakistan concluded a series of military protocols with Saudi Arabia, Libya, Jordan, Iraq, Oman, the U.A.E., and Kuwait. Under these agreements, training facilities were provided in Pakistani defence institutions for members of the armed forces of these countries. By the late 1970s, there were 893 Pakistani advisors and 914 Middle East military trainers.[40] By the 1980s, Pakistan had military missions in 22 countries, making it the largest exporter of military manpower in the Third World.

Pakistan built not only close military ties, but also very close economic ties, with the Middle Eastern states. In return for Pakistani technical labour working in the Gulf, the Gulf sheikhdoms invested in both agriculture and industry in Pakistan.[41] During 1974–75, the oil-producing countries of the Middle East, including Iran, provided Pakistan with enormous aid. They gave balance-of-payments support of $770 million in addition to pledging another $391 million in support for specific projects.[42] By the late 1970s, the single largest source of Pakistan's foreign exchange was the over-$2 billion in remittances sent by the one million Pakistanis labouring in the Gulf region.[43]

Though Pakistan was able to build relations with many Muslim countries over the years, none of them were willing to totally break off ties with India, even if they disagreed with Indian actions at certain times. Even Pakistan's closest Muslim allies, such as Turkey, Saudi Arabia, and Iran, have very close ties with India. Pakistan was unable to achieve its objective of isolating India in the Muslim world, despite tremendous efforts on the parts of its diplomats and policymakers.

Jihadism

The educational curricula and government policies, which championed Islam at home and pan-Islamism abroad, created an atmosphere over the years in which it became difficult for the government to act against groups who justified violence against perceived enemies of Islam. Domestically, these perceived enemies range from Muslim minority sects to non-Muslim minorities. Internationally, in addition to India, any countries that ally with India, whether the US, Israel or any others, have been labelled enemies of Islam, and hence, of Pakistan.

The Pakistani state has often condoned the actions of Islamist groups and even provided covert support. The state, especially the military–intelligence establishment, saw potential in ties with these Islamist groups for both its domestic and foreign policy agendas.

In the foreign policy arena, Islamist groups and their militant offshoots have helped the Pakistani state fight asymmetrical covert wars with both of Pakistan's immediate neighbours, India and Afghanistan. A majority of the Islamist militant groups operating in Indian-administered Kashmir have ties with some Pakistani Islamist group or the other, and Pakistan's military–intelligence establishment sees these groups as proxies, helping tie down a larger adversarial neighbour. Similarly, state support for Islamist groups and militias operating in Afghanistan serve both domestic and foreign policy goals: subdue the rise of Pashtun irredentism and work towards setting up a pro-Pakistan, Pashtun-led Afghan government. The blowback from radical madrasas has been the flourishing of radical literature and ideology. Khaled Ahmed, a leading Pakistani scholar, states, 'Intolerance is embedded in the evolution of the Islamic state', and that is what lies at the roots of Pakistani intolerance.[44]

In the domestic arena, Islamist groups have helped curtail the influence of the secular liberal forces and political parties as well as groups championing ethno-linguistic nationalism (e.g. Bengalis, Sindhis, Baluchis, Pashtuns). During the 1971 conflict in East Pakistan, militias belonging to the Jamaat e Islami fought alongside the regular army and helped suppress Bengali Muslims.

Way out

'. . . all nations bear some marks of their origin. The circumstances that accompanied their birth and contributed to their development affect the whole term of their being. . .'
—De Tocqueville, *Democracy in America*, Vol. 1, Ch. 2

What has happened in Pakistan is that over the years, the ideology-driven identity and nationalism have resulted in the emergence of an ideological state. What this has meant is that any criticism of this identity or any aspect of it is perceived as being anti-Pakistan. The fear of internal break up is so strong that any talk of ethnolinguistic nationalism is seen as threatening to Pakistan's existence.

Over time, the more tolerant Sufi strain of Islam of the subcontinent has been replaced by an intolerant radical version that has helped in the emergence of radical jihadi groups. This has aided some sections of the security apparatus in using the ideological identity and non-state actors for both domestic politics and foreign policy.

Instead of welding the nation together, this over-emphasis on an Islamist ideology has ended up dividing the Pakistani nation. In order to survive as a state, Pakistan will have to tame ideology. It is one thing to talk about ideology; it is quite another to use it to run a state.

A Pakistani nationalism and identity that is defined territorially and is accepting of ethno-linguistic differences within, and of similarities with neighbours, would help Pakistan move forward.[45] This would, however, require a drastic rewriting of the national narrative (including school curricula) so that it is consistent with history. Further, space needs to be created within Pakistani society for tolerance and acceptance of dissent. This would require a state where the civilians are able and willing to wrest the framing of the national narrative and identity. This may prove elusive, given that many of the country's civilian and military leaders have already embraced a partially radical or Islamist view of Pakistan's origins and purpose.

Notes

1 Benedict Anderson, *Imagined Communities: Reflections on the Origins and Spread of Nationalism* (London: Verso Books, 1983), pp. 5–7.
2 British Council Pakistan, *The Next Generation*. Full report available at http://www.britishcouncil.pk/pakistan-Next-Generation-Report.pdf.
3 Gilani Research Foundation, *Religion and Governance: Islamization of Society*. Full report available at http://www.gallup.com.pk/Polls/31–05–11.pdf.
4 Judith Brown, *Modern India: the Origins of an Asian Democracy* (New Delhi: Oxford University Press, 1985), p. 178.
5 Sir Sayyid Ahmed Khan, leading Muslim reformer, intellectual, and founder of the Muslim Anglo-Oriental College at Aligarh (later Aligarh Muslim University) was among those who believed that the way out for Muslims lay in support for the British and not in allying with the Hindus – or the Hindu-led Congress – for Indian nationalism. The paradox lies in that Sir Sayyid Ahmed Khan had many Hindu friends and often described Hindus and Muslims as 'the

two beautiful eyes' of India. The pattern was repeated later. Indian Muslim leaders, such as Pakistan's founding father, Mr. Muhammad Ali Jinnah, who had many Hindu and Parsee (Zoroastrian) friends, was a modern Muslim, and yet, espoused the two-nation theory for political reasons.

6 Ayesha Jalal, *The Sole Spokesman: Jinnah, the Muslim League and the Demand for Pakistan* (Cambridge: Cambridge University Press, 1994).
7 The figures and details related to the 1946 elections have been taken from Jalal, *The Sole Spokesman*, p. 172.
8 Around 6 million refugees entered India.
9 Statements made by many Congress leaders at the time of Partition only fed into these beliefs. As Acharya Kripalani, then President of Congress Party, said, 'Neither the Congress nor the nation has given up its claim of a united India' (Ibid, p. 9). The wording of the resolution passed by the Indian National Congress committee on the eve of Partition read: 'The picture of India we have learnt to cherish will remain in our minds and hearts. The All India Congress Committee earnestly trusts that, when present passions have subsided, India's problems will be viewed in their proper perspective and the false doctrine of two nations will be discredited and discarded by all'. Cited in K Sarwar Hasan (ed.), *Documents on the Foreign Relations of Pakistan*, Pakistan Institute of International Affairs, 1961, p. 261. Statements such as the following, written in a book by the first President of India, Rajendra Prasad, were also read in a certain way: 'It cannot be denied that, irrespective of who rules, and what were the administrative or political divisions of the country, the Hindus have never conceived of India as comprising anything less than what we regard as India today'. Rajendra Prasad's book reissued in 1946, cited in Ian Stephens, *Pakistan* (New York: Frederick Praeger, 1963), p. 83.
10 Muhammad Ayub Khan, *Friends Not Masters: A Political Autobiography* (Karachi: Oxford University Press, 1967), pp.196–197.
11 Interview with Pakistani scholars and foreign service officials and journalists, July 2008.
12 Interview with Khaled Ahmed, Lahore, July 2008.
13 For detailed analysis of textbooks in various subjects, please see the following report titled *Subtle Subversion*, accessible at http://www.uvm.edu/~envprog/madrassah/TextbooksinPakistan.pdf.
14 Speech given to the graduates at the Officers Training Academy at Kakul, *Pakistan Times*, 14 April 1978.
15 'We are against terrorism, not religion, says Kayani,' *Dawn*, 14 August 2009.
16 Interview to Joseph Kraft, 11 March 1981. Cited in Islamabad Directorate of Film and Publications: Ministry of Information and Broadcasting, Government of Pakistan, *President of Pakistan General Zia ul Haq: Interviews to Foreign Media*, Vol IV, p. 79.
17 Speech by Liaquat Ali Khan on his trip to the United States in 1950, Liaquat Ali Khan, *Pakistan: The Heart of Asia* (Cambridge: Harvard University Press, 1950), pp. 11, 15, 121.
18 Mujtaba Razvi, *The Frontiers of Pakistan: A Study of Frontier Problems in Pakistan's Foreign Policy* (Karachi: National Publishing House, 1971), p. 13.
19 Statements such as the following made by the Hindu Maha Sabha at the time of Partition were oft-repeated: 'India is one and indivisible and there will never

be peace unless and until the separated parts are brought back into the Indian Union and made integral parts thereof'" *The Statesman*, Delhi, 9 June 1947.
20 Doctrine of Paramountcy basically meant it is your state, but you recognize the British as paramount power and through treaties, you are bound to the British Empire in India.
21 For the first few months after Independence, especially while Auchincleck was overall Commander-in-Chief and Mountbatten was the Governor General, they refused to allow the armies to fight each other.
22 As stated by Zulfikar Ali Bhutto, former prime minister of Pakistan, 'If a Muslim majority can remain a part of India, then the raison d'être of Pakistan collapses. . . . Pakistan is incomplete without Jammu and Kashmir both territorially and ideologically'. Zulfikar Ali Bhutto, *Myth of Independence* (London: Oxford University Press, 1969), p. 180. (Although the creation of Bangladesh out of East Pakistan in 1971 has also undermined the two-nation theory.)
23 Charles Tilly, 'War Making and State Making as Organized Crime' in Peter Evans, Dietrich Rueschemeyer, and Theda Skocpol, *Bringing the State Back In* (Cambridge: Cambridge University Press, 1985), pp. 169–191.
24 S. Akbar Zaidi, 'India – Pakistan Trade', *South Asian Journal*, 2004, Vol 4. http://www.southasianmedia.net/Magazine/Journal/indiapakistan_trade.htm; Figures for 2000 onwards taken from Ministry of Commerce & Industry, Government of India, http://www.fibre2fashion.com/news/images/newspdf/Indo_pak_trade_69945_50777.pdf?PDFPTOKEN=1b984f1fa99a4f789d1142f496a0d1337 7282b8a|1327439970#PDFP.
25 Karachi Chamber of Commerce and Industry (KCCI), Research and Development Cell, Karachi. *Freer Trade With India: Its Raison d'être and Impact*, March 1996, p. 1. Cited in 'S. Akbar Zaidi, 'India – Pakistan Trade', *South Asian Journal*, 2004, Vol 4.
26 Department of State, Confidential, 17 December 1971, Letter from Indira Gandhi to President Nixon, Dated 15 December 1971. Taken from Roedad Khan, *The American Papers: Secret and Confidential India, Pakistan, Bangladesh Documents, 1965–1973* (Karachi: Oxford University Press, 2000), p. 744.
27 *Dawn*, 18 January 1956.
28 Aslam Siddiqui, *Pakistan Seeks Security* (Lahore: Longman & Greens, 1960), p. 64–65.
29 For details, please see Col. Javed Hassan, *India: A Study in Profile* 1990, Services Book Club, A Study conducted for the Faculty of Research and Doctrinal Studies, Command & Staff College, Quetta.
30 Department of State, Telegram, Secret, From American Embassy Islamabad, 22 January 1972, Subject: Conversation with Pak Army Commander-in-Chief Lt Gen Gul Hasan. Taken from Roedad Khan, *The American Papers: Secret and Confidential India, Pakistan, Bangladesh Documents, 1965–1973* (Karachi: Oxford University Press, 2000), p. 787.
31 'We know that Israel and South Africa have full nuclear capability. The Christian, Jewish and Hindu civilizations have this capability. The communist powers also possess it. Only the Islamic civilization was without it, but that position was about to change'. Taken from Zulfikar Ali Bhutto, *If I am Assassinated* (New Delhi: Vikas Publishing House, 1979), p. 138.
32 Quotation taken from Dennis Kux, *The United States and Pakistan 1947–2000: Disenchanted Allies* (Baltimore, MD: The Johns Hopkins University Press, 2001), pp. 257–260, 272–273.

33 John Ward Anderson, 'Pakistan Sets off Nuclear Blasts: Today we have settled a score, Premier Says', *Washington Post*, 29 May 1998.
34 For figures, please see World Bank, World Development Indicators. 2013. http://data.worldbank.org/data-catalog/world-development-indicators/wdi-2013; International Institute for Strategic Studies, The Military Balance 2014.
35 *Bilateral Agreement between the U.S. and Pakistan.* 5 March 1959: 'The Government of the USA regards as vital to its national interest and to world peace the preservation of the independence and integrity of Pakistan . . . and . . . in case of aggression against Pakistan the Government of the USA will take such appropriate action including the use of armed forces as may be mutually agreed upon'.
36 'Hu Jintao meets with Pakistani Senate Speaker and National Assembly Speaker', 25 November 2006. http://www.chinaconsulatesf.org/eng/xw/t281994.htm.
37 Bhutto, *Myth of Independence*, p. 131.
38 *Survey of China Mainland Press*, Hong Kong, No. 5075, 14–18 February 1972, p 46. Cited in Latif A. Sherwani, *Pakistan China America* (Karachi: Council for Pakistan Studies, 1980), p. 213.
39 M. Rafique Afzal (ed), *Speeches and Statements of Quaid-I-Millat Liaqat Ali Khan, 1941–51*, Research Society of Pakistan, 1967, p. 216.
40 The above-mentioned statistics and numbers have been taken from Roedad Khan (ed), *The American Papers: Secret and Confidential, India, Pakistan, Bangladesh Documents, 1965–1973* (Karachi: Oxford University Press, 1999), pp. 937–943.
41 Richard Wheeler, 'Pakistan in 1975', *Asian Survey*, 16(2), 1976, p.118.
42 W. Eric Gustafson, 'Economic Problems of Pakistan Under Bhutto', *Asian Survey*, 16(4), 1976, p. 373.
43 W. Howard Wriggins, 'The Balancing Process in Pakistan's Foreign Policy', in Lawrence Ziring et al. (eds), *Pakistan: The Long View* (Durham, NC: Duke University Press, 1977), pp. 301–40.
44 Khaled Ahmed, 'Roots of our Intolerance', *Express Tribune*, May 22, 2011.
45 Not all Pakistani leaders were in favour of a religious-based identity. A leading Indian Muslim and one of Pakistan's prime ministers during the 1950s, Huseyn Shaheed Suhrawardy advocated a territorial-based national identity. However, his views never gained sufficient favour or support.

2

RIDING THE TIGER

The threat to Pakistan from terrorism[1]

J. Andrew Greig

Riding on a tiger must be exhilarating; the strength of a tiger is a trope for power, prowess, and stealth, and, so long as one stays on its back, one would be safe from its claws and teeth. The problem comes after dismounting.

So it is with Pakistan's decades-long flirtation with militant jihad and the use of terrorism as an instrument of state policy. In the 1980s, Pakistan, working through its Inter-Services Intelligence Directorate (ISI), the secret service branch of the all-powerful army, engineered attacks on the forces of the Soviet Union in Afghanistan, using Afghans as proxies, motivating them with calls to jihad, or 'holy war', and providing them with supplies and money secured from the United States and Saudi Arabia. This war, in which the roles of Pakistan, the US, and Saudi Arabia were ostensibly covert, is now popularly known as Charlie Wilson's War.[2] Pakistan was seeking a means of neutralizing a perceived existential threat from possible Indian inroads in Afghanistan and India's strategic partner, the USSR. When the Soviet invasion ended, the US withdrew from the region. Pakistan, unable and unwilling to follow suit, became involved in the civil war that followed, siding with the Taliban, hoping to gain advantages cheaply in order to keep the main focus of its army against archenemy, India. It also began increasingly to foster terrorist groups to conduct a covert war against India. Those groups enjoyed the covert sponsorship of the ISI even while the military and political leadership denied any links and avoided the censure of the international community. The result has been the growth of an extremist militancy that is alien to Pakistan's majority Barelvi Sunni population, but which is increasingly infecting the political discourse there. Retaliation from these groups include persecutions and pogroms of minority groups and mortal threats against public figures, including several attempts made on the life of former president, Pervez Musharraf, during his long military rule and the assassination of Benazir Bhutto, Musharraf's most likely successor, shortly after returning to Pakistan in December 2007. No longer is any politician safe, as political violence has escalated to epidemic proportions in a nation that has always tolerated a high level of political violence. Those in Pakistan, who are riding the tiger, may soon find it hard to avoid being mauled.

Pakistan is also host to many international terrorist groups espousing a radical ideology of violent militant jihad, using terror as a marker. Pakistan's territory is used for safe havens, staging areas, and training camps by a variety of terrorist groups. Too many examples give the deep impression that virtually every terrorist incident since 11 September 2001 worldwide has had some connection to Pakistan. Even after the death of Osama bin Laden on 2 May 2011 in Abbottabad, much of the remaining al-Qaida leadership still hides in Pakistan. Umar Patek of the Jemaah Islamiyya, the South East Asian affiliate of al-Qaida, was the bomb-maker for the Bali bombings of 2002, until his arrest in January 2011 in Abbottabad (coincidentally, and somewhat ironically, Abbottabad is the 'West Point' of Pakistan's army) and sentencing to 20 years in Indonesia[3]. Arabs, Chechens, Uzbeks, and Uighurs have all been captured or killed by US-led drone strikes in Pakistan. Most of the London transport bombers of 7 July 2005 and their supporters and contacts were of Pakistani origin and trained in Pakistan. The terrorists who besieged the Indian financial capital, killing hundreds, including in hotels, train stations, and Jews at a synagogue, were of Pakistani origin trained by the ISI. So was the perpetrator of the failed attempt to bomb Times Square on 1 May 2010, Faisal Shahzad. The Kashmiri militants who have so poisoned India and Pakistan's bilateral relations were recruited and trained under the auspices of the ISI for decades.

The high costs of terrorism

Not only does terrorism threaten the national leadership, it now poses serious challenges to the people of Pakistan. Terrorism is part of daily life in Pakistan and an important negative element in its economic, civic, and legal, security, and foreign affairs. Its continuing threats to life and its economic costs are unsustainable. Pakistan will continue a downward spiral towards economic and political failure until its society and leadership summon the will to seriously attack terrorism and militancy. Figures compiled by the South Asia Terrorism Portal, relying on press and official reports, state that more than 54,550 Pakistanis, including over 19,500 non-combatants, have died since 2003.[4] Barely over 2,650 of those can be attributed to US drone strikes, according to the same source, so the overwhelming majority of deaths have been caused either by terrorists or Pakistan's security forces.[5] In addition, hundreds of thousands of Pakistani civilians have been displaced and their lives and livelihoods destroyed because of terrorist-related violence and disruption. The economic costs of this violence are also substantial and unsustainable; the direct and indirect costs of terrorism in the decade since 9/11 are estimated at $68 billion by the government of Pakistan.[6] This number includes an estimate of losses to the country's exports and lost foreign investments and business due to the heightened risks, as well as a slowed economic activity in general. It does not include downsizing of programmes run by international and non-governmental development agencies, lost business, decreased foreign investment, and missed educational opportunities due to denials of technology transfers, heightened risk assessments, and more stringent visa restrictions. Although unquantifiable, those costs are real and serious and will have long-term consequences for an already impoverished nation.

In addition, terrorism has so deeply infected the body politic in Pakistan that it is unclear that Pakistan's institutions are able any longer to contain it. Extremist violence has closed broad areas of Pakistan to its citizens and the authorities. At the current time, no part of Pakistan is completely free from the threat of terrorist violence, be it a market in Peshawar, a military base in Karachi, a government office in Islamabad, or a mosque or village virtually anywhere. These uncontrollable and unrelenting challenges to law and order strike at the heart of the state and government of Pakistan, which can no longer reliably promise to protect its citizens from their compatriots. For instance, in early 2007, militants ensconced in the Lal Masjid (Red Mosque) in Islamabad were terrorizing citizens and taking police personnel hostage in Islamabad, the nation's capital. After months of negotiations and procrastination, army commandos took control of the mosque in July that year, resulting in the deaths of several hundred of the militant occupiers (numbers vary widely), and arrested the surviving leadership of the mosque. Subsequently, the Lal Masjid was rebuilt and returned to the same leadership and the courts released the surviving leader, Abdullah Aziz, and recently awarded damages to rebuild the rest of the complex.[7] In another embarrassing incident in May 2011, terrorists successfully occupied a naval base in Karachi and held it for hours. They destroyed some military hardware, including aircraft, and, more worrisome, raised serious questions about Pakistan's security apparatus to protect itself and its nuclear arsenal even in Pakistan's most populous city.[8] In rural Pakistan, warlords, militants, and criminals using terrorist tactics now virtually control swathes of the country, intimidating local authorities and populations in ways that appear unstoppable. Since 2005, fighting between various militant groups and Pakistani security forces have escalated in the Federally Administered Tribal Areas (FATA), Bajaur, Swat, North Waziristan, and South Waziristan. All attempts at ceasefires and treaties have failed to date. Instead, traditional tribal elders are being targeted for assassination and are being replaced by anti-government militants.[9] For instance, North Waziristan is still largely under the control of the Haqqani network along the Pak–Afghan border and their ally, the warlord Hafiz Gul Bahadur, even after a much-vaunted Pakistani army offensive in 2009.[10] By October 2012, no one was safe. A 14-year-old Pakistani girl, Malala Yousafzai, was shot point blank by the Pakistani Taliban because she dared to stand up for female education. Malala recovered fully from her wounds, and has gone on to be a worldwide celebrity, espousing the cause for which she was targeted. Recently, she co-won the 2014 Nobel Peace Prize for her work. Nonetheless, many Pakistanis suspect her motives and Malala continues to live outside of Pakistan.[11]

Extremist views also continue to wreak havoc on political discourse in Pakistan. The increasingly virulent rhetoric of 'Islam and threats to Pakistan' no longer allows for any serious dissent or discussion. Instead, public figures that stand up for positions that, only a few years ago, seemed reasonable find themselves targets of assassins or denounced as blasphemers or traitors. In a famous example, Salman Taseer, the governor of Punjab, was assassinated early in 2011 for publicly speaking out against Pakistan's blasphemy laws. His murderer was applauded as he was led into the court of justice, unrepentant.[12] Seven months later, armed men in Lahore abducted Mr. Taseer's son;[13] subsequently, these armed gang demanded the release of Salman Taseer's convicted murderer. The government of Pakistan apparently does not have the means to provide for the safety of its members or their families. Instead, Pakistani authorities use counter-terrorism laws to perversely punish citizens who participate in the fight against terrorism. For instance, Dr. Shakeel Afridi, who cooperated with the CIA effort to locate and kill Osama bin Laden, has been sentenced to 33 years' imprisonment because he allegedly 'supported' an anti-government warlord when he paid a ransom after he had been kidnapped.[14] Militant jihadis use terrorist tactics to skew the debate, altering perceptions by Pakistanis about what is happening to them, and narrowing the options for positive solutions to Pakistan's increasingly threatening social and economic problems.

Public opinion in Pakistan has become increasingly volatile and xenophobic in a climate of fear. Thus far, Pakistanis largely see the problem as coming from outside forces, most notably, the United States and its drone strikes. Instead of realizing that most of the violence and hardship endured is the product of Pakistan's own tolerance of and support for terrorism, they choose to blame forces over which they have no control. Shortly after Osama bin Laden was killed by US forces in May 2011, only 12 per cent of Pakistanis had a positive view of the US, and nearly the same number (14%) saw his death as a good thing.[15] While this may be construed as a reaction to the US's recent, more aggressive response to terrorists seeking a safe haven in Pakistan, the public's low opinion of the US has been substantially the same for years, antedating drone strikes. Nonetheless, it appears that the steadily declining popular support for an aggressive counter-terrorism response to militancy indicates that too many Pakistanis believe their problems derive from foreign interference, especially from the West in general and the US specifically, perhaps in league with India and Israel, and not with their own government's inaction or incapacity. They are apparently willing to forego insisting on needed reforms in governance and development, in favour of a national narrative of Islam under attack from hostile outside forces. Implicit in this narrative is an acceptance that their government is unable or unwilling to protect them from violence committed by Pakistanis in Pakistan. Unfortunately for Pakistani authorities, such resignation carries with it the seeds of delegitimization. If the government cannot ensure basic security, is unable to protect them from general lawlessness and economic exploitation, and cannot provide for the common good, then the imperative to follow its laws and pay taxes falls by the wayside. With such existential issues on their minds, it is understandable that most Pakistanis see no positive hope in a battle against extremist militancy. However, Pakistan is at a tipping point and could easily slip into a deep economic depression, militant theocracy, and aggressive and dangerous military isolation. What few reminders of democracy that are left behind by the British will be ultimately lost, even as they are being turned on their head now. The resulting chaos augurs ill for the region, which has several nuclear states, although none more volatile than Pakistan.

Pakistan's security tripod

To understand how terrorism became such a danger to the Pakistani state, it is first necessary to examine briefly terrorism's role in Pakistan's security apparatus. Pakistan's security tripod rests on its large land force (approximately 1,000,000 regular and paramilitary soldiers), a substantial nuclear capability, and terrorism. Pakistan's military is one of the largest in the world, but it is directed almost exclusively against India. The national neuralgia allows the army to commandeer inordinate amounts of scarce national resources and to interfere in politics with near impunity. In fact, this large army has been far more successful in the political arena than on the battlefield; it has never actually won a war against India, the only foreign entity it has fought.

Nor has it distinguished itself in suppressing revolts. In 1971, its incompetence resulted in creating the political conditions for the secession of Bangladesh (East Pakistan). After a monsoon-driven flood, the slowness of the army in distributing relief to East Pakistan led to a humanitarian crisis and popular disaffection that grew into a political crisis that the army tried to suppress through violence. Instead, they found themselves in a humiliating war with India and independence for Bangladesh. The army's response was slightly better after the earthquake of 2005 centred in Muzaffarabad, but it was slower than both the international community, and, very embarrassingly, a charity linked to a major terrorist organization, the Jamaat-ud Dawa (JuD), a branch of the Lashkar-e-Tayyiba (LeT).

In fighting internal unrest from Pashtun and Balochi separatist militants, its counter-terrorist tactics have been largely counter-productive. Pashtuns in the Swat Valley in northern Pakistan raised the flag of revolt in 2007, insisting on the imposition of a strict version of Sharia or Islamic law. The army's heavy-handed military bombardments in Swat, involving attacking civilian locations with aerial bombing and artillery barrages, dislodged the Taliban militants who had taken over the local governments, but not before many homes were incinerated and efforts to achieve peace deals were abrogated. The leader, Sufi Muhammad, was arrested and released. A peace settlement granting the primacy of Sharia law fell apart over the issue of the final verdict resting with Pakistan's Supreme Court. Nonetheless, Pashtuns who had been forced to flee have been able to return, but Sufi Muhammad's son-in-law, Maulana Fazlullah, continues attacks against Pakistan from safe havens in Afghanistan. As in the Lal Masjid operation, defeat was snatched from the jaws of victory.

As for Pakistan's nuclear arsenal, estimated at between 100 and 200 nuclear warheads and the means to deliver them in the region (namely, to India), it is a threat and a deterrent to other nations, but it is not a viable military option. Its use would certainly occasion a nuclear response, the deaths of tens of millions of Pakistanis, the destruction of its major cities and infrastructure, and the complete breakdown of all semblance of the state of Pakistan. In short, it would be suicide masquerading as national honour. Pakistan has, of course, been deeply implicated in the proliferation of nuclear technology; Abdul Qadeer Khan sold, very possibly as state policy, the means to enrich uranium to Iran, Libya, and North Korea before he was caught, and, for a time, placed under house arrest.[16] Nonetheless, nuclear capability has given Pakistan considerable leverage in the world community, and it is highly improbable Pakistan will surrender its nuclear capability. It holds before it the examples of a tolerance of North Korean bluster, international acceptance of India's civilian nuclear programme underscored by a bilateral agreement with the US, and the limited options available to the world in the face of Iran's nuclear enrichment programme. Pakistan undoubtedly contrasts those ginger-footed accommodations to the invasion of Iraq because Saddam Hussain was erroneously believed to be seeking nuclear capability and NATO actions against Muammar Qaddafi, who had surrendered Libya's nuclear materials purchased from A.Q. Khan.

The remaining leg of the tripod – terrorism – has proven to be marginally effective in meeting Pakistan's short-term regional goals. By and large, Pakistan has outsourced terrorism in support of its national goals to militant jihadi groups, which were able and willing to undertake recruitment, training, and operations against entities and powers perceived as threats, even while offering Pakistan a fig leaf of deniability. For example Pakistan's past support for the Taliban in Afghanistan served to further their policy of 'strategic depth', i.e. to maintain a non-hostile and weakened Afghanistan, ensuring that neither India nor the USSR (now Russia), nor any other power, such as the US, Iran, or the Central Asian republics, could gain traction on their western border. To do this, Pakistan backed certain Taliban clients, such as Mullah Omar, and allied factions, such as the Haqqani network, and has often seemed to undermine the establishment of a stable central government in Kabul. This covert policy has put it at odds with the interests of the US and its NATO/ISAF partners, which have sought, for over a decade, to establish a central government that will be able to prevent Afghanistan from returning to failed state status and once again harbouring international jihad groups such as al-Qaida. Unless Pakistan re-examines its relationship with the Afghan insurgency, it might find itself isolated and unable to play any role but a destructive one – one that will be very expensive in reputation and influence. One US observer, Ashley Tellis, for example has put forth the opinion that Pakistan stands on the brink of strategic defeat because its clumsy meddling in Afghan affairs is alienating Afghanis and the government in Kabul, as well as NATO, the US, Iran, India, the Central Asian republics, and Russia.[17] Time, of course, will tell if he is correct.

Terrorism as a tool of state: Afghanistan

In September 2011, Admiral Michael Mullen, Chairman of the Joint Chiefs of Staff, made news when he publicly stated on record that the Haqqani network was responsible for the 13 September 2011 attack against the US Embassy in Kabul as well as other terrorist incidents, resulting in harm to American forces in Afghanistan and that they enjoy sanctuary as well as active support from Pakistan through the ISI.[18] While Admiral Mullen's testimony is certainly not proof of ISI connivance with the Haqqani network, the fact that he was stating it as part of his testimony to the US Congress indicates that such is the official view of the Department of Defense, and, we may infer, of the US government. No serious attempts were made to 'walk back' those comments afterward. In all likelihood, the accusation is one that had been made privately to the government of Pakistan earlier, along with repeated pleas, both public and private, for Pakistan to rein in the Haqqani network's attacks on NATO forces in Afghanistan by denying them safe haven in Pakistan.

The Haqqani network is a cross-border Afghani/Pakistani insurgent group organized along basically semi-autonomous familial and tribal units, although these units have shown considerable willingness to accept orders from the leadership, which has passed from Jalaluddin Haqqani, once CIA's blue-eyed boy in the fight against the Soviets in Afghanistan and killed in May 2012 by a US drone, to a son, Sirajuddin. Its main headquarters is in Miran Shah, North Waziristan, Pakistan. Its ties with the ISI and with al-Qaida date from the days it was a proxy in the fight against the Soviet Union in Afghanistan. Since then, the Haqqani network has become central to the jihadi movement on the global, regional, and local levels, working as an enabler for allied groups that share its local concerns and its militant aims. On a global level, the Haqqani network's links to al-Qaida stretch back three decades. It has enabled al-Qaida and Osama bin Laden with support for global jihad, as well as provided an opportunity for international militant jihadis, from the Sudan to Bosnia, to gain battle experience. The captures of Khost and Gardez in 1991 showed both al-Qaida and the ISI that the Haqqani network was a valuable partner in militant jihad, both globally and regionally.[19] In the regional arena, the Haqqani network continues to attack US and NATO's ISAF forces with regularity and ferocity, as the recent attack on the US Embassy in Kabul demonstrated.[20] According to the US, they do so with the covert support of the ISI.

The Haqqani network also poses a clear and present danger to the current governments in both Afghanistan and Pakistan. While the Haqqani threat to the Karzai government is, perhaps, in Pakistan's perceived interest in denying any rivals a foothold in Afghanistan, and therefore, the ISI might feel justified in supporting them, ISI support for the Haqqani network is a major irritant in the bilateral relations between the Karzai administration and the government of Pakistan. Presumably, the government of Pakistan is willing to risk this friction with Afghanistan, as it has apparently calculated that the Karzai government will fall shortly after NATO/ISAF forces leave in 2014, and its relations with the Haqqani network and the Quetta Shura of the Taliban will serve it in good stead. Unfortunately for the government of Pakistan, the Haqqani network also supports the Tehrik-e Taliban Pakistan (TTP), a virulently anti-government group that targets Pakistani authorities, especially the military. The Haqqani network's links to al-Qaida and the TTP have freed it from a complete dependence on the ISI. It is one of the paradoxes of Pakistan's support for terrorism that the Haqqani network has been able to maintain its close ties with al-Qaida and the TTP, even while continuing as Pakistan's proxy in Afghanistan. The Haqqani network has been able to serve so many masters by adding value to each of its interactions, and by acting as a mediator between these three actors.[21] It has, apparently, become so ensconced in its safe havens in North Waziristan, especially around Miran Shah, that Pakistan security forces will not directly confront Sirajuddin Haqqani's estimated 10,000 to 15,000 seasoned fighters.

Admiral Mullen went on to state in his testimony to the Senate Armed Services Committee that the remnants of Taliban regime, deposed immediately after 9/11, are ensconced in Pakistan, and are still led by Mullah Omar. They are known as the Quetta Shura, taking their name from Quetta, capital of the Balochistan province of Pakistan. From there, they direct what they can of the Taliban insurgency across the border and raise money. Their resources come from wealthy Arab supporters in the Gulf and Saudi Arabia, from opium trafficking, and from contributions from Pakistani supporters, including the ISI. In addition, local branches of the Taliban hold sway, as a sort of shadow government, in provinces. They raise money through collecting taxes from the local population and through providing security and transport services to opium and drug traffickers. The movement of truckloads of drugs and raw materials, as well as large caches of cash, requires protection that can only be supplied by these local Taliban groups, which are really little more than organized crime networks. They owe little allegiance to the Quetta Shura, which does not provide them with sufficient resources or fighters to maintain control over them.

Links between al-Qaida, the Taliban, and Kashmiri militant groups date back to at least December 1999, as evidenced by the hijacking of Air India flight 814.[22] In the view of US policymakers and intelligence analysts, they seem to have endured. Kashmiri militants and their Pakistani supporters, with the connivance of the ISI, were being trained in camps in Afghanistan as early as the late 1980s. The contacts and connections formed in those camps with al-Qaida members have endured. For the past 10 years, raids on al-Qaida safe houses in Pakistan turned up militant Pakistanis, primarily from LeT or the Jaish-I Muhammad.[23] In 2010, journalist Steve Coll reported: 'American officials believe that ISI has considerably more leverage with the Afghan Taliban than it is willing to admit', and this had led to some friction between the US and Pakistan.[24] Awareness of Pakistan's perfidy among the American public and political establishment could jeopardize American financial support. Increasingly, non-humanitarian assistance is conditioned on Pakistan's cooperation on Afghanistan.[25] The Kerry-Lugar Bill of 2009 requires Pakistan's 'ceasing support, including by any elements within the Pakistan military or its intelligence agency, to extremist and terrorist groups, particularly to any group that has conducted attacks against United States or coalition forces in Afghanistan, or against the territory or people of neighboring countries'.[26] Moreover, it could trigger punitive counter-measures by the US and its allies or direct military action against the Afghan Taliban in Pakistani territory.

ISI support for the Haqqani network and the Afghan Taliban, both designated as terrorist organizations by the United States and the United Nations, is presumably intended to drive up the cost of resistance to Pakistan's designs on Afghanistan and to keep Pakistan's interests integral to any Afghan settlement. While Admiral Mullen did not recommend disengaging from Pakistan, which he still saw as key to the resupply of NATO/ISAF forces, subsequent events have shown that Pakistan's usefulness as a conduit was undermined by its closing of the supply route from late November 2011 until July 2012. Regardless of public outrage from all sides in Pakistan, the US administration of President Barack Obama stepped up its use of unmanned drones against terrorists sheltered in Pakistan's tribal regions along the Afghan border and developed an alternate supply route through Russia and Uzbekistan to Afghanistan. As Pakistan has slid into irrelevancy, the US has sought allies in Uzbekistan, and the other members of the Shanghai Cooperation Organization and institutionalized its strategic ties with Afghanistan.[27] Whereas Pakistan, early in its history, had strategic relationships with the US – the CENTO and SEATO Alliances, channelling aid to those battling the Soviets in Afghanistan, and supporting the NATO/ISAF efforts against al-Qaida and the Taliban – the relationship has since deteriorated into one of mutual suspicion and wary transactions. Pakistan now risks souring even its transactional relationship with the US.

The origins of extremist Islamic militancy in Pakistan date primarily from the time of the rule of General Zia ul-Haq, although they started in the ill-starred administration of Zulfikar Ali Bhutto. To be sure, Deobandi and Ahl-e Hadith Islamic thinkers were present at the foundation of Pakistan, but their beliefs were a minority among generally more liberal South Asian Muslims. Zia ul-Haq instituted measures to enforce Sunni beliefs in Pakistan, which had the effect of alienating the substantial but minority Shia community. A power struggle ensued, with the Shias encouraged by the Iranian revolution in 1979. Hardline Sunni groups soon rose, and, against the backdrop of the anti-Soviet jihad in neighbouring Afghanistan, Zia ul-Haq's government provided official, unofficial, and covert support to some of the more extremist Deobandi and Ahl-e Hadith groups, such as the Harakat-ul Jihad-al-Islami (HuJI), which splintered into the Harakat-ul Mujahideen (HuM), of which a further splintering was the Jaish-e Muhammad (JeM). They all operated and oftentimes trained together in Afghanistan alongside the Taliban. For them, Zia ul-Haq found partners in the US and Saudi Arabia. The Sipah-e Sahaba Pakistan (SSP) and Lashkar-e Jhangvi (LeJ) saw their missions as primarily to beat back the influence of Shi'ism, and regularly attacked their sectarian opponents. The SSP and LeJ benefited in terms of personnel training and resources from the ideological links with HuJI, HuM, and JeM, even after the Soviets were driven from Afghanistan.[28]

Terrorism as a tool of state: India

Resentment simmered in Islamabad for almost two decades after Pakistan's humiliating loss to India in the civil war that tore Pakistan asunder and formed Bangladesh in 1971. Pakistan had learned that overt hostilities with India would fail, and so, its best bet of revenge was through proxies. The opportunity finally presented itself in 1989, when Pakistan moved to exploit an indigenous uprising in Kashmir. A conflict dating back to the days of Partition in 1947, India and Pakistan both claimed the princely state of Jammu and Kashmir and had fought two wars over it already. Diplomacy had also failed, and Kashmir remained divided along a ceasefire line that was demarcated as the Line of Control (LoC) in 1972. The status of Kashmir is at the very heart of Pakistan's enduring neuralgia about India. Pakistan's goals in Kashmir have devolved into undermining the ability of India to govern its portion of Jammu and Kashmir by covertly fomenting civil unrest and encouraging terrorism against India and its allies. To this end, although the government of Pakistan vehemently denies it, the ISI has covertly supported militant groups, of which the most prominent and dangerous examples are the aforementioned HuM and JeM, and LeT.[29] Spectacular terrorist attacks on India by militants from these groups serve the interests of the Pakistani state by raising the price of India's hold on Kashmir and by deflecting attacks within Pakistan. In the 1992–93 time frame, LeT was by no means the ISI's first choice of proxies, according to the statement of the then Director-General, Javed Nasir, who described the LeT as 'a very small one that was only just coming up'. That relationship soon grew, perhaps because its relative weakness made LeT more malleable than its rivals in the eyes of the ISI.[30] The LeT was certainly more attuned to the wishes of the government of Pakistan than the indigenous rebels, the Jammu–Kashmir Liberation Front, which preferred Kashmir's independence over accession to Pakistan.

Ironically, the LeT has, since that time, apparently grown beyond the absolute control of the ISI. The LeT is led by Hafiz Muhammad Saeed, who lives openly at the LeT's headquarters in Muridke, outside of Lahore. Its public wing, the Jamaat-ud Dawa (JuD), raises funds throughout Pakistan and the Middle East, especially Saudi Arabia, in the name of Islamic charity, one of the duties of the pious. They were especially successful in fundraising, for instance, in the wake of the 2005 earthquake in Muzaffarabad. Once dependent for funds on the ISI, and generally amenable to some degree of command and control from the ISI, its ability to raise funds independently has released it from a client–patron relationship with the ISI. Although Pakistan's authorities have occasionally placed Saeed under house arrest, they have never taken serious steps to inhibit his public activities. Even after the US recently placed a $10 million price on his head for his alleged role in the November 2008 Mumbai attack, no action has been taken against him.[31] The position of the government of Pakistan is that the JuD, and the LeT, are not culpable, and that they are not, in any case, acting for the state of Pakistan. Nonetheless, David Headley Coleman (born Daood Sayed Gilani), a Pakistani American arrested for his role in the planning of the Mumbai attack, states that the ISI was involved in his management.[32] The head of the ISI admitted that some 'rogue' ISI elements might have been involved in the Mumbai attack, but that was different than the ISI providing 'authority, direction, and control'.[33] The LeT is a major and dangerous irritant in the Indo–Pak relationship, but it does not really seem to affect policy, largely due to exceptional restraint on the part of Indian authorities. For instance, the LeT (in league with the JeM) is credited with spearheading the 13 December 2001 assault on the Indian Parliament. They are also implicated in the 11 July 2006 Mumbai train bombings that killed over 200 people, the bombing of the Indian Embassy in Kabul on 7 July 2008, and the 26 November 2008 attack on Mumbai, which included the Taj Mahal Hotel and killed 172 people.[34]

While it appears on the surface that militant groups operating in Kashmir seem to be working in Pakistan's interest, their impact on Pakistan's security is not benign. There is the danger that attacks by LeT, as with other militant extremist groups linked to Pakistan's ISI, will alienate the world community and lead to Pakistan's isolation from the international community and access to desperately needed world economic resources. In the case of the US, since FY2002 (the first year after the 9/11 attack), the US has obligated a total of around $22 billion, two-thirds of it in military aid and reimbursements. This money was explicitly intended to underwrite Pakistan's fight against militant terrorism in the region. Instead, Pakistan has supported the very groups opposed to the US, NATO, the Afghan government, and India. As Pakistan-watcher C. Christine Fair stated in Congressional testimony, 'Pakistan is the firefighter, the arsonist, and the vendor of a variety of propellants'.[35]

It is not inconceivable that Pakistani militant groups will, in the future, conduct an attack that will so enrage the Indian government that military reaction will ensue. Such was nearly the case in 2002. In the aftermath of the attack on the Indian Parliament on 13 December 2001, tensions between India and Pakistan rose to a dangerously high level. Javed Ashraf Qazi, a former head of the ISI, has admitted that JeM was responsible for mounting this attack, but Maulana Masud Azhar, a Pakistani jihadist, had engineered the attack.[36] Masud Azhar owed al-Qaida, and the ISI, a great deal for his release from an Indian jail on New Year's Eve, 1999, in return for a hijacked Indian airliner.[37] The escalation of Indo–Pak tensions was extremely advantageous for al-Qaida, for at the time, the US counter-strike against al-Qaida for the 11 September 2001 attacks on the World Trade Center and the Pentagon was underway. When Pakistan re-deployed troops away from its western border, al-Qaida and Taliban elements were able to escape into the tribal regions of Pakistan. Ahmed Rashid and Bruce Reidel, two authors whose insights cannot be easily dismissed, seem to imply that the timing of the attack on the Indian Parliament may have been more than a coincidence, since it served so well the interests of both al-Qaida and the ISI.[38] The temperature rose again dramatically in May 2002, when three LeT terrorists dressed in Indian military uniforms first attacked a tourist bus in Kaluchak in the Indian state of Jammu and Kashmir and, when fired upon by Indian troops, took refuge in Indian military family quarters, where they killed several family members of the Indian Army personnel. The aftermath of that event has left Pakistan with an entrenched militant insurgency in its tribal regions. It is far from certain that any future attack against Indian or American interests will be benignly overlooked.

Terrorism against the state: Pakistan

A third strain of militancy has arisen within Pakistan that poses a direct threat to its body politic. In fact, it might pose the gravest threat not only to Pakistan but also to the peace and stability of a region which has so many nuclear-armed actors and intransigent conflicts. The early militants were largely anti-Shia, conservative Sunnis such as Ahl-e Hadith, Deobandi, and heavily influenced by hardline Salafist and Wahhabi ideologies. They opposed modernizing trends in Pakistani society, on the one hand; and on the other, they were incensed by the veneration of Sufi saints, a widespread characteristic of Islam in South and Central Asia, and the generally more liberal, less-rigid brand of South Asian Islam known as Barelvi. The first was a departure from the original Islam espoused by Salafist ideas, and the second was a deviation from the strict monotheism of Wahhabism. The US involvement in Afghanistan gave these groups a sense of grievance against their own government for cooperating with Western non-Muslims, an immediate motive. The long US involvement also provided the jihadists the means to receive training, hone their military skills, and gain battle experience in Afghanistan, even as they were fighting against the US and what they see as a collaborationist government in Islamabad. Furthermore, tribal and communal links to the Afghan Taliban led in the late 2000s to the formation of militant groups that are collectively called the Tariq-e Taliban Pakistan (TTP). They are ideologically committed to the imposition of a conservative, rigid interpretation of Sharia religious law in Pakistan. Various TTP leaders, acting as warlords, have already challenged the government of Pakistan in Bajaur, Swat, North and South Waziristan, and elsewhere in the FATA (Federally Administered Tribal Areas), as already mentioned above. One leader, Baitullah Masood, is held culpable in the death of candidate for president, Benazir Bhutto. The occupation of the Lal Masjid in downtown Islamabad, cited earlier, has added to the sense of insecurity in Pakistan. It has taken considerable energy on the part of Pakistan's security forces to dislodge these groups. In the process, the army has often felt compelled to resort to heavy-handed artillery barrages that destroyed homes and livelihoods, killed civilians, and created hundreds of thousands of internally displaced refugees – all actions guaranteed to produce an alienated population.

The high tide of terrorism in Pakistan leads to the inescapable conclusion that the state has produced a situation that the government and security apparatus in Pakistan will have to confront at some time in the near future. Its economy is a shambles. Energy and water supplies are woefully insufficient. The fiscal situation is dire. Pakistan's population is overwhelmingly poor and illiterate and the trends are worsening. The situation is deteriorating. Pakistan's relations with all its neighbours and near neighbours are difficult, and could unravel at any time. Its relationships with its allies, especially the US, are in tatters, and it is unlikely that Pakistan will find a relationship to replace it. China seems to be the only potential candidate. It has backed Pakistan in the past but its investment in a new port at Gwadar on the coast of Balochistan seems intended to move goods in and out of Central Asia. That will require less mischief-making on the part of Pakistan in the interior of Asia. Nonetheless, China has stuck with North Korea, the Sudan, and Burma for years, refusing to use its influence to open up those closed societies. If Pakistan is content to join that club, they may yet muddle through. Pakistan will still have to find the resources to protect itself from its internal enemies – the terrorists it has fostered – and it is not clear that there is either the political will or the ability to do so. It is predictable that those terrorist organizations and their vested supporters will resist. They have shown time and again their willingness to shed blood – theirs and of others – to accomplish political goals. Pakistan will still have to tame the tiger before it can safely dismount from it.

Notes

1 The opinions and characterizations in this chapter are those of the author, and do not necessarily represent official positions of the United States Government. This article was written and approved for publication by the Department of State over two years ago. Upon receiving the galley proofs, I could only update some numbers and check online references, but I could not substantially rewrite it to reflect developments in Pakistan, Afghanistan, and India over the past two years, and they have been substantial. All three nations have held successful elections and seen peaceful transfers of power, for instance. Nonetheless, the essential premise of the article is as true today as when I wrote it. Terrorism still poses an existential threat to Pakistan's society and stability and is still used as a means of achieving state ends.
2 The term is taken from the title of an account by George Crile. *Charlie Wilson's War* (New York: Atlantic Monthly Press, 2003). In 2007, the book was made into a film with the same name, starring Tom Hanks and Julia Roberts.
3 Sarah Schonhardt. 'Militant Gets 20 Years in Prison for Bali Bombing'. *The New York Times*, 21 June 2012. http://www.nytimes.com/2012/06/22/world/asia/indonesian-militant-gets-20-years-in-prison-for-bali-bombing.html?_r=1 (accessed on 29 October 2014); Eko Listiyorini. 'Indonesia Sentences Umar Patek to 20 Years for Bali Bombing Role'. *Bloomberg Business News*, 22 June 2012. http://www.businessweek.com/news/2012-06-21/indonesia-sentences-umar-patek-to-20-years-for-bali-bombing-role (accessed on 29 October 2014).
4 SATP Datasheet. 'Fatalities in Terrorist Violence in Pakistan, 2003–2012'. Updated on 19 October 2014. http://www.satp.org/satporgtp/countries/pakistan/database/casualties.htm (accessed on 29 October 2014). The methodology of counting casualties has some obvious faults; for one thing, journalists are usually unable to independently verify the numbers as sites are closed off immediately either by the militants or by the military authorities.

RIDING THE TIGER

5 SATP Datasheet. 'Drone attack in Pakistan, 2005–2014'. Updated 12 October 2014. http://www.satp.org/satporgtp/countries/pakistan/database/Droneattack.htm (accessed on 29 October 2014).
6 Government of Pakistan. Ministry of Finance. *Economic Survey, 2010–2011*. Special Section 1: 'Cost of War on Terror for Pakistan Economy', pp. 219–220.
7 Obaid Abbassi. 'Lal Masjid cleric acquitted in four cases'. http://tribune.com.pk/story/285881/lal-masjid-cleric-acquitted-in-four-cases/; Pervez Hoodbhoy. 'Lal Masjid: Rewarding an insurrection'. *Express Tribune*, 21 May 2012. http://tribune.com.pk/story/381761/lal-masjid-rewarding-an-insurrection/ (both accessed on 29 October 2014).
8 Salmon Masood and David Sanger. 'Militants attack naval base in Karachi'. *The New York Times*, 22 May 2011. http://www.nytimes.com/2011/05/23/world/asia/23pakistan.html (accessed on 29 October 2014).
9 SATP. 'Attack on Tribal Elders in Pakistan'. Updated 12 October 2014. http://www.satp.org/satporgtp/countries/pakistan/database/Tribalelders.htm (accessed on 29 October 2014).
10 Sadia Sulaiman and Syed Adnan Ali Shah Bukhari. 'Hafiz Gul Bahadur: A Profile of the Leader of the North Waziristan Taliban'. *Terrorism Monitor*. VII: 9. 10 April 2009. http://www.jamestown.org/uploads/media/TM_007_9_03.pdf (accessed on 29 October 2014).
11 'Malala Yousafzai's Nobel peace prize receives mixed response in Pakistan'. *The Guardian*, 10 October 2014. http://www.theguardian.com/world/2014/oct/10/malala-yousafzai-nobel-peace-prize-pakistan-reaction (accessed on 29 October 2014).
12 Karen Brulliard. 'Salman Taseer Assassination Points to Pakistani Extremists Mounting Power'. *Washington Post*, 5 January 2011. http://www.washingtonpost.com/wp-dyn/content/article/2011/01/04/AR2011010400955.html (accessed on 29 October 2014).
13 Salman Masood. 'Gunmen Seize Son of Slain Pakistani Official'. *The New York Times*, 26 August 2011. http://www.nytimes.com/2011/08/27/world/asia/27pakistan.html (accessed on 29 October 2014). For over two years, negotiations with the Taliban and two Pakistani governments have been unable to secure Mr. Shahbaz Ali Taseer's release, and he remains a prisoner of the Taliban as of this writing.
14 AFP. 'Dr. Shakil Afridi jailed for "militant links"'. *The Express Tribune*, 30 May 2012. http://tribune.com.pk/story/386265/dr-shakil-afridi-jailed-for-militant-links/ (accessed on 29 October 2014).
15 Pew Global Attitudes Project. 'U.S. Image in Pakistan Falls No Further Following bin Laden Killing'. Released 21 June 2011. http://www.pewglobal.org/2011/06/21/u-s-image-in-pakistan-falls-no-further-following-bin-laden-killing (accessed on 29 October 2014).
16 Seymour Hersh. 'The Deal: Why is Washington going easy on Pakistan's nuclear black marketers?' *The New Yorker*, 8 March 2004. http://www.newyorker.com/archive/2004/03/08/040308fa_fact (accessed on 29 October 2014).
17 Ashley Tellis. 'Pakistan's Impending Defeat in Afghanistan'. *Carnegie Endowment for International Peace*, 22 June 2012. http://carnegieendowment.org/2012/06/22/pakistan-s-impending-defeat-in-afghanistan/c6sn (accessed on 29 October 2014).

18 Statement of Admiral Michael Mullen. U.S. Navy. Chairman of the Joint Chiefs of Staff, on Afghanistan and Iraq. U.S. Senate Armed Services Committee. 22 September 2011. http://armed-services.senate.gov/statemnt/2011/09%20September/Mullen%2009-22-11.pdf (accessed on 20 October 2012).
19 Don Rassler and Vahid Brown. *The Haqqani Nexus and the Evolution of al-Qa'ida*. Harmony Program. Combating Terrorism Center at West Point, July 2011, pp. 18–33. http://www.ctc.usma.edu/wp-content/uploads/2011/07/CTC-Haqqani-Report_Rassler-Brown-Final_Web.pdf (accessed on 29 October 2014).
20 Jack Healy and Alyssa Rubin. 'U.S. Blames Pakistan-based Group for Attack on Embassy in Kabul'. *The New York Times*, 14 September 2011. http://www.nytimes.com/2011/09/15/world/asia/us-blames-kabul-assault-on-pakistan-based-group.html?pagewanted=all (accessed on 29 October 2014).
21 Don Rassler and Vahid Brown. *The Haqqani Nexus and the Evolution of al-Qa'ida*. Harmony Program. Combating Terrorism Center at West Point, July 2011, p. 10. http://www.ctc.usma.edu/wp-content/uploads/2011/07/CTC-Haqqani-Report_Rassler-Brown-Final_Web.pdf (accessed on 29 October 2014).
22 Bruce Reidel. *The Search for Al Qaeda: Its Leadership, Ideology, and Future* (Washington, DC: Brookings Institution Press, 2008), p. 83.
23 Gary Schroen. *First In: An Insider's Account of How the CIA Spearheaded the War on Terror in Afghanistan* (New York: Presidio Press, 2005), p. 383.
24 Steve Coll. 'Letter from Afghanistan: War by Other Means'. *The New Yorker*, 24 May 2010. http://www.newyorker.com/reporting/2010/05/24/100524fa_fact_coll (accessed on 29 October 2014).
25 Matthew Waldman. 'The Sun in the Sky: The Relationship Between Pakistan's ISI and Afghan Insurgents'. London School of Economics, Development Studies Institute, Discussion Paper 18. http://image.guardian.co.uk/sys-files/Guardian/documents/2010/06/13/SISFINAL.pdf (accessed on 29 October 2014).
26 Enhanced Partnership with Pakistan Act 2009, Title II, Section 203(c)(2)(A). (The Kerry-Lugar Act). http://www.gpo.gov/fdsys/pkg/PLAW-111publ73/html/PLAW-111publ73.htm (accessed on 29 October 2014).
27 'Nato strikes alternate supply route deals through Central Asia'. *Dawn*, 4 June 2012. http://dawn.com/2012/06/04/nato-strikes-alternate-supply-route-deals-through-central-asia/. Also see, 'Central Asia group seeks bigger Afghanistan role'. *Dawn*, 6 June 2012. http://dawn.com/2012/06/06/central-asia-group-seeks-bigger-afghanistan-role/ (both accessed on 20 October 2012); Matthew Rosenberg and Graham Bowley. 'U.S. Grants Special Ally Status to Afghans, Easing Fears of Abandonment'. *The New York Times*, 7 July 2012. http://www.nytimes.com/2012/07/08/world/asia/us-grants-special-ally-status-to-afghanistan.html (accessed on 29 October 2014). Nonetheless, shipping supplies through Central Asia is considerably more expensive, perhaps as much as 10 times as much.
28 Stephen Tankel. *Storming the World Stage: The Story of Lashkar-e-Taiba* (New York: Columbia University Press, 2011), pp. 23–31.
29 Jamal Afridi. 'Kashmir Militant Extremists'. *Backgrounder, Council on Foreign Relations*, 9 July 2009. http://www.cfr.org/kashmir/kashmir-militant-extremists/p9135 (accessed on 20 October 2012).
30 Stephen Tankel. *Storming the World Stage: The Story of Lashkar-e-Taiba* (New York: Columbia University Press, 2011), p. 40.

RIDING THE TIGER

31 Declan Walsh. 'U.S. Offers $10 Million Reward for Pakistani Militant Tied to Mumbai Attacks'. *The New York Times*, 3 April 2012. http://www.nytimes. com/2012/04/04/world/asia/us-offers-10-million-reward-for-pakistani-militant. html?pagewanted=all (accessed on 29 October 2014).
32 Sebastian Rotella. 'U.S. Prosecutors Indict 4 Pakistanis in Mumbai Attacks'. *Washington Post*, 26 April 2011. http://www.washingtonpost.com/politics/us_ prosecutors_indict_4_pakistanis_in_mumbai_attacks/2011/04/26/AFaDLhsE_ story.html?wprss=rss_homepage (accessed on 20 October 2012).
33 Bob Woodward. *Obama's Wars* (New York: Simon & Schuster, 2010), pp. 46–47.
34 'Accused in India massacre claims ties to Pakistani secret service'. *The Globe and Mail*, 11 April 2011. http://www.theglobeandmail.com/news/world/accused-in-india-massacre-claims-ties-to-pakistani-secret-service/article581121/ (accessed on 29 October 2014); 'Rana, Headley implicate Pak, ISI in Mumbai attack during ISI chief's visit to US'. *The Times of India*, 12 Apr 2011. http://arti cles.timesofindia.indiatimes.com/2011–04–12/us/29409412_1_rana-and-headley-isi-tahawwur-hussain-rana (accessed on 29 October 2014).
35 Fair C. Christine. '2014 and Beyond: U.S. Policy Towards Afghanistan and Pakistan, Part I' *Testimony to the House Committee on Foreign Affairs, Subcommittee on the Middle East and South Asia*, 3 November 2011, p. 4. http://foreignaf fairs.house.gov/112/fai110311.pdf (accessed on 20 October 2012).
36 Bruce Riedel. *Deadly Embrace: Pakistan, America, and the Future of the Global Jihad* (Washington DC: Brooking Institution, 2011), p. 69.
37 According to Bruce Reidel, who worked at the US National Security Council at the time, the hijacking had been one part of a multipronged Millennium Plot by al-Qaida operatives. The other parts included bombing a hotel and Christian sites in Amman, Jordan, a car bomb at Los Angeles International Airport, and an attack on US Navy ship docked in Aden, Yemen. All were to take place on 1 January 2000. The others were all frustrated. *Deadly Embrace: Pakistan, America, and the Future of the Global Jihad* (Washington DC: Brooking Institution, 2011), p. 57–59.
38 Ahmed Rashid. *Descent into Chaos: The United States and the Failure of Nation Building in Pakistan, Afghanistan, and Central Asia* (New York: Viking, 2008), p. 113; Bruce Riedel. *Deadly Embrace: Pakistan, America, and the Future of the Global Jihad* (Washington DC: Brooking Institution, 2011), p. 69–70.

3

PAKISTAN'S POWER GAME AND THE NEW MEDIA LANDSCAPE

Gilles Boquérat

Despite spells of military rule and censorship, the media in Pakistan has shown a fair degree of resilience and witnessed, over the last decade, a notable expansion in the electronic segment. Apart from several hundred periodicals and dozens of newspapers, one can now access information and entertainment from around a hundred TV channels and countless licensed or illegal radio stations. The choice has been made here to focus on a limited number of publications and television channels that appear more pertinent for analysis due to their influence. The fourth estate has always been seen in ruling circles as a potentially destabilizing institution and occasionally became the victim of repressive force. In its 2014 press freedom index, Reporters Sans Frontières rank Pakistan 158 out of 180 countries. Covering sensitive issues can be dangerous. As of November 2014, the Committee to Protect Journalists has listed 51 Pakistani journalists killed since 2002 while conducting their professional activities, and for 16 others, the motive remains unclear.[1] This figure does not include those who were injured, arrested, or kidnapped. The offence and crime against journalists usually go unpunished and are not even properly investigated. However, in spite of these restraining factors on the exercise of free expression, the media plays a significant role in shaping public opinion. It has even taken a new dimension during the last decade with the proliferation of private television channels likely to influence a larger number of persons in a nation where the adult literacy rate (15 years and above) was officially 57 per cent of the total population in 2012–13.[2]

'People should only know what the establishment wants them to know'[3]

The evolution of the media in Pakistan is directly linked to political upheavals that the country has been going through. Its history goes back to pre-Partition days, when two newspapers took upon themselves the struggle against 'anti-Muslim propaganda' and the struggle for the creation of Pakistan. The Urdu *Nawa-e-Waqt* came into being in 1940 (it became a daily newspaper in 1944). The following year, Mohammad Ali Jinnah launched *Dawn*, which became the mouthpiece of the Muslim League, and an organ for advocating the demand for Pakistan. Attempts by the authorities to exercise supervision on the press have existed from the outset. It was reported that the address made by Jinnah on 11 August 1947 before the first Constituent Assembly, in which he asserted that a citizen's religion has nothing to do with the business of the state, displeased some leading members of the emerging Pakistani establishment, starting with Chaudhry Muhammad Ali, the Secretary General of the new nation. They unsuccessfully tried to convince *Dawn* to black out the secularist passages of the speech in the press.[4]

The authorities have never stopped looking for critical appreciation from the media. Benefits accrue to media house owners and editors willing – and, sometimes, forced – to express their loyalty to the powers-that-be at the local and national levels. They include advertisement revenue from public notices, a generous quota for imported newsprint (partly profitably resold in the black market), travels abroad, under-evaluated land deals, as well as the purchase of numerous copies of their publications by government agencies. Another pressure tactic used is the threat of a tax audit, or, alternatively, the promise of a lenient attitude towards undeclared revenues. A secret fund is available for compliant journalists. A budget line-item, 'other expenditures', of the Ministry of Information and Broadcasting was ostensibly used to 'manage' public opinion or to 'neutralize' criticisms by a strongly biased media.[5] Following a constitutional petition filed by two private television channel anchors who had requested the Supreme Court to probe the matters of media accountability, details of money paid from the secret fund to journalists were made public for the first time in April 2013. It is a game of influence peddling in which the military establishment also participates.[6] Zealously independent editors run the risk of damaging their operations. In recent years, the rise in revenues drawn from private sector advertisements has somewhat reduced the level of dependence on state funding.

Zuhair Siddiqi, who had worked for the *Civil & Military Gazette* (a daily newspaper founded in 1872, which closed in 1963), observed that 'government could, almost always, find support for its arbitrary action against a newspaper in one section or another. The support was generally extended in the name of "national interest, the glory of Islam, the ideology of Pakistan" or some other mundane consideration'.[7] Even before the coup by General Ayub Khan in 1958, the practice of suspending dissident publications had already developed. In fact, within the first seven years after independence (1947–1953), in the Punjab province alone, 31 newspapers were banned for varying periods of time. With the introduction of military rule under Ayub Khan, journalists and newspapers suspected to be sympathetic towards communism were targeted. The first victim was the Progressive Papers Limited (PPL), a left-wing publishing house that controlled *Imroze* and the *Pakistan Times*.[8] Under the Pakistan Security Act of 1952, PPL was taken over by the military leadership and renamed National Press Trust in 1964.[9] In an effort to legally regulate the functioning of the media, the Press and Publication Ordinance (PPO) was promulgated in 1960, then amended in 1963, with the intention to strengthen penalties against wayward publications, in addition to the sanctions already considered by the penal code. The ordinance gave the authorities the means to intimidate all those associated with the publishing process – from the media owner to the printer. To cap the supervisory powers of the state, the government in 1961 took control of the news agency, Associated Press of Pakistan (APP), at a time when only a few newspapers could afford to have correspondents throughout Pakistan, and even fewer of them abroad.

The long arm of the state was particularly felt during the presidential elections of 1965, when Ayub Khan was challenged by Fatima Jinnah (Jinnah's younger sister).[10] The 'press advice' was also amply used during the conflict with India in 1965. Likewise, the national media was gagged during the secessionist Bengali movement (1971). The army headquarters fed the editors with triumphant communiqués and concealed military excesses and setbacks.

The practice did not disappear with the return of a civilian government. Zulfikar Ali Bhutto hardly showed any tolerance for a critical press. Under Zia-ul-Haq, even more harsh legal measures were imposed to ensure that the influence of the military and radical Sunni clerics was not challenged. Predictably, journalists close to the rightist Jamaat-i-Islami made an impact in newsrooms, enforcing an Islamic narrative of Pakistan, while those critical of Zia would face imprisonment and even public flogging. It became very difficult for a liberal and progressive publication to survive. Similarly, religious programmes were widely broadcasted on state-controlled Pakistan Television (PTV). In 1983, the Urdu press made much of Zia's announcement of the discovery of Jinnah's personal diary, in which Quaid-e-Azam's convictions seemed to echo the General's Islamization project. Even PTV and Radio Pakistan invited 'experts' to discuss the discovery until two close associates of Jinnah uncovered the fraud.[11] For the press not to report demonstrations against the regime was commonplace. Zia, nevertheless, allowed two English dailies to appear, The Frontier Post from Peshwar and Lahore and The Muslim from Islamabad, the latter managed by Agha Murtaza Pooya, a leading Shia figure who later became director of the Institute of Strategic Studies of Islamabad in the mid-1990s.

The return to a democratic process after the untimely death of Zia in August 1988 brought some relief to the press. The caretaker government of Ghulam Ishaq Khan proposed a less harsh version of the Press and Publication Ordinance. It was, nevertheless, still considered insufficient by journalists to ensure press freedom. After becoming prime minister, Benazir Bhutto made promises to restore the credibility of the media, ambitiously announcing that her government 'will abolish all the laws and rules which go against the liberty of the press. We will suppress the National Press Trust. We will give to the television and radio their autonomy so that they serve the people. . . . The practice/custom of the press advice will be suspended'.[12] Allocation of newsprint by the state was discontinued by Benazir Bhutto's government in April 1989 in favour of free access at market prices. This was later re-established by Nawaz Sharif in 1991. It was for the Audit Bureau of Circulation (ABC) to evaluate the circulation of newspapers, according to which the allocation of imported newsprint and attribution of advertisement campaigns by public organizations and enterprises was decided. ABC continues to remain a source of favouritism and corruption.

Those years saw the launch of a weekly Friday Times (1989), monthly Newsline (1989), and daily The News International (1991). In 1990, there was a short-lived experience with a private TV channel, NTM (Network Television Marketing). In 1995, the first FM radio station was launched. Enjoying a large majority after the general elections of February 1997, Nawaz Sharif found himself in a strong position to face the media. A conflict arose with the Jang group, which had refused to give him unconditional support. Mir Shakil-ur-Rahman complained of politically motivated harassment through freezing of the bank accounts of the group, retention of newsprint imports, and tax controls. Instrumentalizing frequent change of governments during the 1990s, it became easy for the military establishment to get the media to discredit an immature political class and pave the way for its return to power with the coup managed by General Pervez Musharraf in October 1999.

In the autumn of 2002, the PPO of 1962 was finally legally buried and replaced by a series of ordinances in charge of regulating media activities (Press, Newspapers, News Agencies and Book Ordinance; Freedom of Information Ordinance; Defamation Ordinance; Press Council Ordinance). The authorities were then feeling confident enough to abrogate the monopoly of PTV, which had indeed become an anachronism, especially with the competition coming from India, where the first private television channel (Zee TV) had been launched ten years earlier and which offered, via dish antennas, a diversity – breaking the monotony of PTV. The coverage of the 1999 Kargil conflict in which Indian private TV channels successfully reported to the world New Delhi's viewpoint was also an eye-opener.[13]

As a first step, private channels were only allowed to broadcast in Pakistan from foreign soil. The new television channels were supervised by the Pakistan Electronic Media Regulatory Authority (PEMRA), coming under the Ministry of Information. Its role was to impose a code of conduct to ensure the quality of the telecasted programmes.

Destabilized by the TV coverage of the protest of lawyers, following the flagrant dismissal of Chief Justice Iftikhar Muhammad Chaudhry in March 2007, Musharraf decided in early June to amend PEMRA to facilitate the suspension of broadcasting rights of private TV channels and to render possible the confiscation of their equipment. The suspension was applied on Geo TV and Aaj TV. In the wake of protests, the government, however, had to step back a few days later. The following month, TV images of the bloody assault on the Red Mosque in Islamabad reflected badly on Musharraf among a large segment of the population that viewed the dynamics of the War on Terror as imposition on Pakistan by the United States.

When Musharraf declared the state of emergency in November 2007, it was accompanied by new amendments reinforcing penalties on media broadcasting 'anything which defames or brings into ridicule the head of State, or members of the armed forces, or executive, legislative or judicial organs of the State'.[14] Musharraf, who has taken great pride in opening the doors to private TV channels, did not then measure how difficult it would be to rein in these new political actors. His successor, Asif Ali Zardari, had also to accept that no channel can be shut down without negative repercussion.

The media houses and the rising power of the electronic media

The print media covers eleven languages; the most read is in Urdu, followed by Sindhi. The readership is difficult to assess since there is, on one side, the tendency to exaggerate sales figures to attract advertisers, and, on the other side, a newspaper might be passed from hand to hand or be read to many others in a society with a low literacy rate. The Jang group claim to have the highest sales of newspaper in Urdu, *Daily Jang*, as well as the highest sales for the English daily, *The News International*. The English press has a readership essentially among the urban élite, yet exercises an influence on the decision makers in the political and economic spheres far exceeding that of the vernacular press. Besides, it often brings the headlines and the main themes, which are then taken up by the Urdu press, the latter giving conservative perspectives and terminologies to respond to the expectations of their readers. The English language press is also more open to op-ed articles written by members of the Pakistani diaspora.

Over the years, the print media has been dominated by three large groups. The first is the Urdu language *Jang* (War) (1940). It was established during the course of the World War II in Delhi by Mir Khalil-ur-Rahman (1927–92), who transferred his office to Karachi after Partition. It remains a family enterprise run by his sons, Mir Shakil-ur-Rahman and Mir Javed-ur-Rahman. The political leaning of this group is centre-right, even though one can find a wide range of opinions in articles discussing the religious identity of the country or issues of national security. The second media group is Dawn, publisher of the eponymous newspaper. After the creation of Pakistan, *Dawn* competed with the *Pakistan Times* for influence among the élite. Today, it stands as a reference daily with a liberal editorial line. Since 1969, the group has been also publishing the monthly named *Herald*.

The third media group is Waqt (Time). Its Urdu daily, *Nawa-i-Waqt*, was, for a long time, the most read, before being replaced by *Daily Jang*. With a display of fierce Islamic nationalism, the group also publishes the daily, *The Nation*, with views close to those of the establishment.[15]

These three groups did not take long in investing in the audio-visual field when private TV channels were permitted. Jang was the first, with Geo TV, which started telecasting in 2003 from Dubai programmes recorded in Pakistan, before being allowed to transmit directly from Pakistani soil in 2008. When the state of emergency was imposed in November 2007, Geo TV received orders from the Dubai authorities to stop the transmission of live programmes. In March 2009, Zardari's government suspended for some time the broadcasting of Geo TV when it actively supported the lawyers' 'long march' demanding the reinstatement of the Chief Justice. Geo TV has been a critical voice of the previous PPP-dominated government; it was all the more damaging since it is the most watched TV channel in Pakistan, accounting for over 50 per cent of all viewers. Geo has made a speciality of facing the wrath of parties feeling unjustly treated, be it political parties, the military establishment, religious or militant groups. Pakistan Tehreek-i-Pakistan supporters attacked the Geo office in Islamabad during the sit-in protest in the summer of 2014. Earlier in 2014, the military establishment initiated an onslaught on Geo for overstepping the red line by airing Hamid Mir's allegation against the ISI and its chief after he survived an assassination attempt. While the Ministry of Defence petitioned the media regulator, PEMRA to cancel its TV licence, the cable operators succumbed to pressure to blackout Geo News and were foot-dragging when the Supreme Court ordered its restoration in May 2014.

Dawn News started to broadcast in English in 2007. Since it was not able to establish an English-speaking audience, it gradually shifted to the Urdu medium in 2009. The Waqt group has also a TV network. For these media houses, the decision to venture into the electronic media was a way to increase their outreach. The number of people having access to a TV set is estimated at about 100 million whereas circulation of newspapers is around 4 million. In Pakistan, 50–60 percent of households have a cable TV connection. If the print media content still benefits from a more enduring value resulting from its capacity to discuss at length about serious matters and to conduct deeper investigation, the electronic media, bound by the immediacy of news and subject to a more superficial exposition of issues, has a capacity to cause political damage second to none.

Similarly, other print publications were attracted by the electronic media. *Business Recorder*, the first daily financial newspaper in the Muslim world, founded in 1965 by M.A. Zuberi (1920–2010) launched Aaj TV, the first channel to be allowed to telecast from Pakistan itself. Business Recorder/Aaj TV is another family group controlled by the three sons of the founder, ideologically close to conservative circles. The late Salman Taseer, PPP politician-businessman who became Governor of Punjab had launched in 2002 *Daily Times*, and a few years later, a business news channel called Business Plus TV. A media activity is rarely profitable, but it may serve other business interests of the owners as a promotional tool or as a channel of influence vis-à-vis the power centres that could bring financial returns.

Another case of political-commercial collusion is Dunya TV, launched in 2008 by Mian Amer Mahmood, ex-PML-Quaid-e-Azam Mayor of Lahore, who runs the Punjab Group of Colleges, the largest private higher education group in Pakistan. Dunya TV is the second most watched channel in Punjab. It is also worth mentioning the Century Publications Group, belonging to the Lakson group, a conglomerate run by the Lakhani brothers. They, for instance, look after the interests of Colgate-Palmolive and McDonald's in Pakistan.[16] The group launched the *Daily Express* in 1998, which became the third largest daily newspaper in Urdu. Ten years later, it launched an Urdu TV channel, Express News.[17] Urdu channels are more traditional and conservative in form and substance. The Lakson group launched in April 2010 a daily newspaper in English, *The Express Tribune*, in partnership with *The International Herald Tribune*. In the same year,

Pakistan Today was launched under the leadership of Arif Nizami (son of the founder of Nawa-e-Waqt, Hamid Nizami) after his eviction from the post of editor of *The Nation* by his uncle, Majeed Nizami. The rapid shift towards the electronic media could not have taken place without the support of the private sector, especially telecom companies capable of investing heavy budgets in advertising campaigns. Though radio remains the most easily accessible media (with no problem of power outages), it is not seen as a means of influence that can arouse the attention of large media conglomerates. Unlike television, the state-owned Pakistan Broadcasting Corporation continues, through Radio Pakistan and its multiple local channels accessible by more than 95 per cent of the population, to dominate the radio landscape.[18]

The equivocal links between journalism and the power centres

The separation between the media circles and the political world has always been tenuous. Journalism has, in some instances, been a springboard for a political/diplomatic career. In 1982, Mushahid Hussain Syed, at the age of 29, became the youngest editor of a daily newspaper (*The Muslim*). He currently occupies the post of secretary general of the Pakistan Muslim League (Quaid) and Chairman of the Senate Defence Committee. He was also the first Pakistani journalist to write for the Indian press.[19] During Nawaz Sharif's second stint as prime minister, he served as Federal Minister of Information (1997–99) and was subsequently arrested and imprisoned for one year after General Musharraf's coup d'état. Maleeha Lodhi is another person to have been once in charge of *The Muslim* (1987–90), before being the founding editor of *The News International*. She held important diplomatic positions as Ambassador to the United States (1994–97, 1999–2002) and High Commissioner to the United Kingdom (2003–08). Currently, she is an advisor to the Jang/Geo group.

Hussain Haqqani, who was at the centre of the 'Memogate' scandal,[20] had been a full-time journalist from 1980 to 1988, working for the Voice of America and for the Far Eastern Economic Review, before entering politics in support of Nawaz Sharif, who nominated him as Ambassador to Sri Lanka (1993–95). After defecting to the PPP, he was nominated in April 2008 for the ambassadorship to the United States (until his resignation in November 2011). Sherry Rehman, a prominent member of Pakistan People's Party, who succeeded him in Washington, had been, early in her professional life, editor of the monthly *The Herald*. She was nominated in March 2008 as Minister for Information and Broadcasting of Gilani's government. A year later, she quit her position, following differences with Zardari when the president imposed restrictions on the media at the time of a new crisis around the reinstatement of the Chief Justice.

Another glaring example of political rewards to 'agreeable' journalists is the selection of senior journalist Najam Sethi in March 2013 as the caretaker chief minister of Punjab to ensure incident-free national and provincial elections in that state. Sethi, the founder-editor of *Friday Times*, and editor of *Daily Times* from 2002 to 2009 (both liberal publications), was also hosting a talk show on Geo TV at the time of his appointment by the PPP government. Incidentally, Najam Sethi had been appointed a federal minister for accountability in 1996 in the caretaker government set-up under Malik Meraj Khalid, following the dismissal of Benazir Bhutto's second government by President Farooq Leghari.[21]

Although there is no more state monopoly, there is still one public network, PTV, which, apart from the existence of seven transmission channels (PTV News, PTV National with programmes in different regional languages, PTV Sports, PTV Bolan in Baluchistan, Azad & Jammu Kashmir TV, PTV Global, PTV World), is the only channel to be widely accessible with a reach of about 80 per cent that give it unparalleled access to the rural world in comparison to private channels accessible only through cable or satellite connections. The rapid increase in the number of TV channels compelled the enticement of journalists from the print media who were attracted by the elevated salaries. If the majority of them have remained confined to the editorial work, others have succeeded in making their mark on the electronic landscape by anchoring talk shows (Talat Hussain, Hamid Mir, Shahid Mahsood, Kamran Khan, etc.): all of them are partisan markers of the political debate. These popular talk shows (on prime time), four to five days per week, are a distinct element of the media scene, and thus, an appealing product to attract an audience. They are regularly criticized for their drama and sensationalism, arousing the attention of the viewers by verbal outbursts or giving currency to all the conspiracy theories. Trivializing the political debate by showing verbal jousting between politicians devalues the democratic rules of the political process. Targeting the civilian rulers and mocking politicians for their venality is considered fair game. The military establishment and the judiciary are, in comparison, largely spared from criticism, a disparate treatment ultimately reinforcing the imbalance between elected and unelected representatives at the top of the power structure.[22] It also plays into the hands of extremist groups prone to denounce greedy and immoral rulers and calling for Islamic rule. In March 2013, the National Assembly passed a resolution that demanded that TV channels remove anchor persons telecasting programmes against parliamentarians without verification of the facts for some personal agenda or for some unlawful gains.

TV channels have become political tools of prime importance because they offer to a population, the majority of which does not have access to print media, a certain proximity to the political class. For the political initiation of educated youth, the print media today has been replaced by the television, the Internet and the social media. Proscribed outfits are also adept at using social media to communicate and recruit. The government has played into the hands of conservative elements in blocking on and off social websites such as Facebook, Twitter, or YouTube in the name of protecting the sanctity of the faith.[23] YouTube has been banned since September 2012 to prevent access to blasphemous content while there is complacency vis-à-vis hate speeches or literature. According to the Pakistan Telecommunication Authority, the number of people using social media is under 30 million. There are around 8.6 million Pakistanis on Facebook while Twitter has over a million. Several newspapers and magazines have opened their websites to blogs, some of them are maintained by well-informed expatriate Pakistanis.

The media and the imprint of a religious narrative

In April 2014, the National Assembly unanimously adopted a resolution moved by a Jamaat-i-Islami MNA, urging the government to impose an immediate ban on telecasting 'immoral' programmes on private and public TV channels.[24] Vigilante TV shows had already taken the responsibility of moral policing.[25] It is not so much different from the 'moral cleansing' of the Lal Masjid cohort in 2007 taking the law into their hands and raiding Chinese massage parlours and telling owners of music centres to shut down their business. Besides seven religious channels (Ary QTV, Azaan TV, Hadi TV, Haq TV, Labbaik TV, Madani Channel, and a Christian channel, Isaac TV), religious programming is a common feature on most channels. Many of country's top channels have cultivated their own clerics for prime time television. For Khalid Zaheer, Dean of the Faculty of Arts and Social Sciences in the Central University of Punjab, their content is dogmatic, a repetition of what is already accepted by society without addressing the intellectual and practical challenges posed by the modern world.[26] The use of religious images (prayer scenes, mosques) by the advertisers is frequent.

Another media observer commented that '[The Pakistani] media is playing a dangerous game by whipping up emotions of an already confused and conservative populace (. . .) airing provocative programmes where warmongers are invited to speak or are taken on the phone as experts in is strengthening a particular mindset. This mindset is suicidal, bigoted and jingoistic'.[27] As a matter of fact, the media, above all the TV channels, is often seeking to exacerbate the religio-nationalist fabric of the nation through a vindictive discourse against foreign nations supposedly wishing the fall of Pakistan.

Traditionally, India – or 'Bharat' since some prefer the Sanskritized name to underline unchanging antagonism and the validity of the two-nation theory – attracts resentment essentially because of the past wars, the perceived repression in Kashmir, alleged discrimination against the Muslims in India, and for its ties to the former Karzai government in Afghanistan. One of the exponents is the red-capped Zaid Hamid, known for his televised sermons raising high the flag of a conquering Islam (and, if possible, on top of the Red Fort in New Delhi).[28] He targeted the Jang/Geo group for supporting an initiative aiming at rapprochement called 'Aman ki Asha (hope of peace)', in collaboration with *The Times of India*. Immediately after the Mumbai attacks in November 2008, the Pakistan government sympathized with India by claiming terrorism as a common enemy. But it soon turned into a media war when the Indian side underlined the Pakistani roots of the perpetrators of the terrorist attacks on Mumbai. On the Pakistani side, the military establishment estimated that the offer of cooperation by civilian authorities for the investigation of the Mumbai attacks could lead to the compromise of classified information. In some cases, the media ran conspiracy theories linking the Mumbai attacks to Indian intelligence activities with an aim to tarnish Pakistan's image and divert attention from Kashmir. It was also explained in the media as a ploy of the India–Israel–America axis to incriminate Pakistani authorities for not controlling terrorist activities originating from the Pakistani territory and as a consequence, putting a question mark over the safety of Pakistan's nuclear arsenal.

The representation of India among the Pakistanis is not without contradictions. Indian films and TV programming are as popular as ever on Pakistani TV screens, even if conservatives accuse it of spreading vulgarity and challenging Pakistan family values – a criticism also addressed to well-liked Turkish soap operas. The code of conduct allows the TV channel programmes to have only up to 10 per cent of foreign content (6 per cent Indian).[29] While Turkey, Saudi Arabia, and China get a favourable treatment in the Pakistani media (e.g. the deafening silence of the media regarding the crackdown on Uigurs in Xinjiang), the United States has replaced India as the primary source of animosity, though some commentators see it only as a reflection of offensive American actions. Even before the US–Pakistan relations were strained by a series of contentious incidents in 2011, the American Ambassador in Pakistan had once expressed his deep anguish towards the Jang group by stating that the group 'consciously publishing and broadcasting false and inflammatory stories, without regard to the fact that they could encourage violence against Americans or against US interests. It is purposefully using the reach of its television network to amplify unchecked hate speech and promote violence in a brazen attempt to uphold or even increase its market share in a down economy'. In this case, he wished that the programmes of Voice of America broadcasted on the Geo TV network should be transferred to a more responsible and less partial partner.[30]

The denunciation of the War on Terror in most media goes along with an ambiguous treatment of the Pakistani Taliban. The logic of PEMRA's decision to not show shocking images of attacks committed by the Tehrik-i-Taliban Pakistan (TTP), fearing that it may favour their cause, is double-edged as it also conceals their atrocities. Crimes committed by the TTP against the Pakistani security forces are seen as a consequence of the destabilizing effect of the presence of foreign forces in the region and the support that the Pakistani authorities provide to the latter. As for the Afghan Taliban, they are often represented as a nationalist movement fighting legitimately to defend the Pashtun community in Afghanistan. The recurrent use of a religious idiom to denounce the presumed antipathy of the West towards the Islamic world has done little to improve relations between Pakistan and the Western nations.

This defensive mindset of Pakistan is also reflected in actions against those Pakistanis who are suspected to be deviating from religious orthodoxy. Religious persecution in Pakistan has a long history: as early as 1953, some newspapers were accused of fanning the flames of hatred at the time of agitation against the Ahmadiya community that had been branded heretical by Sunni orthodox clerics. Similarly, in September 2008, Aamir Liaquat Hussain, former minister of Religious Affairs during Musharraf's regime, was at the centre of a controversy when he gave a hate speech against the Ahmadiyas during a programme (Aalime Online) on Geo TV. Some days later, two leaders of the Ahmadiya community were assassinated in Nawabshah (Sindh). Following this, Aamir Liaquat Hussain was expelled from Muttahida Qaumi Movement, the party from which he had successfully contested the general elections in 2002.[31] In August 2010, he became Managing Director of QTV, the most popular Islamic channel, part of the ARY Digital network, a subsidiary of ARY business holdings, founded in 1970 by a Pakistani businessman, Abdul Razzak Yaqoob, and based in Dubai. Aamir Liaquat Hussain rejoined the Geo TV Network in June 2012.

TV professionals emphasize the difficulty of addressing religious issues without offending sensibilities, to the extent of running the risk of being physically threatened. This environment shields the clergy from criticism and leaves the field open to individuals adopting extremist positions. By inviting hotheads to write commentary or spill vitriol in TV studios against Salman Taseer, who dared to defend Aasia Bibi, a Christian woman imprisoned for blasphemy and facing capital punishment, the media carries some responsibility in his assassination in January 2011. After the killing, politicians invited to television shows displayed less readiness to condemn the murder than to warn those who dare to question the blasphemy law. The Urdu press was no different for two reasons: first, in the opinion of the editors, the blasphemy law was just; and second, they feared reprisal because the extremists read no other newspaper but Urdu ones. The TTP have warned repeatedly that media outlets and journalists will be targeted if their coverage fails to reflect its positions favourably. The group even issued a fatwa accusing the media of siding with the 'disbelievers' and propagating promiscuity and secularism.[32]

In militant-infested zones, the marginalized reporters can always be mistaken for informers and have to be especially careful in their writings. Talking about the killing of terrorists or miscreants, and not martyrs, is a sure way to fuel the wrath of militant groups and to be on their hit-list. A media outlet also has a specific responsibility. The pruning of an article at the editorial level could have dramatic consequences: such as, for instance, the association of a journalist's report with a dispatch from a Western news agency. In January 2012, Mukarram Khan Aatif was assassinated near Peshawar by the Taliban, who accused him of working for the Voice of America, and thereby, opposing them.

The grip of the security establishment over the media

If civilian rulers jockey to gain the support of journalists and editors – reference is often made to 'lifafa' (envelop) journalism – the military establishment is not to be outdone in patronizing journalists, particularly when it is about discrediting civilian authorities or fighting those who could undermine the military establishment's image before the nation. After a terrorist attack against the Pakistan Naval Station Mehran on 22 May 2011, the ethical code of the PEMRA was invoked for denouncing news channels putting down the institutions in charge of the security of the country, and as a result, inciting 'anti-national sentiments'. For the army, the electronic media's penetration into households poses an additional challenge, especially when the security forces are the victims of videos uploaded by terrorist outfits on hosting websites. Such images relayed over the Internet can also represent an opportunity for the military. The images of a young woman flogged by Taliban in the Swat valley created a favourable atmosphere for the military operation in the spring of 2009.

Questions about the presence of Osama bin Laden in Abbotabad rapidly gave way on TV shows to the issue of the violation of airspace by American troops, thereby shielding the military from answering some thorny questions. One week after Abbotabad, the ISI leaked the name of the CIA operative in Islamabad to the media. Similarly, the media's denunciation of the Kerry-Lugar Bill was symbolic of protecting the military: the media denounced the American aid package on the grounds that the bill provided conditions that amounted to interference in domestic matters of Pakistan by reconfigurating the civilian–military relationship. Likewise, the 'Memogate'affair, which casted shame on Ambassador Hussain Haqqani and President Asif Ali Zardari for having 'sold the honour of the nation', diverted the whole focus away from the presence of bin Laden near the Kakul military academy.

In the 1960s, the military establishment suppressed the leftist ideas promoted by some publications. During the years of jihad in Afghanistan and Kashmir in the 1980s and 1990s, the military aim was to convince the journalist community that the strategic decisions of the general headquarters were correct and inextricably connected with the interests of the nation. Paradoxically, the demonization of the United States – or India – by the media can also be instrumentalized to consolidate Pakistan's bargaining position vis-à-vis Washington in order to appease an adverse public opinion. In the case of India, it justifies the large financial resources allocated to the armed forces.

The management of the communication between the military and the media is primarily the responsibility of the Inter Services Public Relations (ISPR).[33] ISPR is known to provide TV channels with a list of officers who could be invited to participate in debates and sending emails to media houses, passing off as war reporting. The military establishment also has its favourites among civilian analysts capable of defending army positions during talk shows and in the press.[34] The ISI has also an Information Management Wing. One wonders if the decision of private cable operators, after the NATO bloody attack in November 2011 against a border post manned by the Pakistani Army, to stop the broadcasting of BBC World News programmes was taken in an independent manner. The BBC had produced a documentary questioning the army's commitment to fight against the Taliban militancy.

The journalistic treatment of the privileges and abuses of the army is particularly problematic due to lack of transparency and the insecurity of media owners. The intelligence agencies (ISI, Intelligence Bureau) are not known for showing great tolerance towards those who question their power. In September 2010, Umar Cheema, a journalist working for *The News*, was kidnapped and tortured by ISI agents after denouncing corruption within the army. Saleem Shahzad, correspondent of *Asia Times Online* (which is based in Hong Kong), was killed after he raised the question of the infiltration of the army by al-Qaeda members following the attack against the PNS Mehran in Karachi. The commission charged with the inquiry on the murder of this investigative journalist, who specialized in the murky links between the intelligence agencies and extremist organizations, submitted its report in January 2012. Without holding anyone guilty, it only wished that the interaction between the intelligence agencies and the media be 'institutionally rationalized and regularly documented'. The ISI expressed its discontent for having been dragged into this affair by the local representative of the Human Rights Watch. The argument used against such kind of criticism is often to cast doubt on the patriotic feelings of journalists fuelling the alienation of the Western media vis-à-vis Pakistan and its armed forces.

The journalists are not exempt from intimidations. They are routinely asked, for instance, to disclose their sources of information – and have to put up with the overreaching powers of the security forces. This situation is even more acute for journalists operating in conflict zones, where exercising their profession with complete independence and without relying exclusively on information provided by the ISPR is an arduous task. During a survey carried out in the Swat valley in 2009, all the journalists interviewed admitted that between the threatening attitude of the security forces and that of the local Taliban, sometimes, it becomes incumbent to sacrifice the truth and to cover only apolitical issues or else to secretly inform NGOs working on human rights violations.[35]

Because of the constraints imposed by the security forces and extremists, the information on militancy-hit tribal areas is incomplete and often contradictory. The difficulty of retrieving first-hand information is illustrated by the often varying estimates of the number of victims of the War on Terror and the difficulty in verifying assessments made by the army, as in the case of the Zarb-i-Azb operation launched in June 2014. What is true of the situation in the FATA applies also to Baluchistan.[36] Because of weak media imprint due to low ratings (national newspapers do not have local editions from Quetta) and the absence of significant stake for private advertisers in a poor province, bullied journalists are left to themselves and caught, both literally and metaphorically, in the crossfire between conflicting demands and threats coming from the military, security agencies, sectarian groups, and Baluch insurgents. The journalists are targeted for not toeing the line of the sectarian militants, for being seen as representatives of the Punjabi establishment by the separatists, and for being 'too nosy' if investigating on the army's law and order operations and the phenomenon of missing persons.

In conclusion, talking about the print media in Pakistan requires, first of all to make a distinction between an English-language minority press, yet influential, comparatively liberal; and a majority Urdu press voicing 'the ideology of Pakistan', a reflection of a society for which reference to the religious identity pushes it towards conservatism and which inclines to think of Pakistan as a nation besieged by hostile forces. The main constraints that journalists are confronted with result from the protection of the financial/political interests of the media moguls and from the inability of their employers and the civilian authorities to protect them in face of threats coming from both state and non-state actors.

The sustainability of a print media with standards of excellence is becoming more delicate as the consumption of information is increasingly through television screens, the Internet, and the social media – all vectors of communication more reactive, and consequently, more difficult to manipulate. The implications are mixed. While the wide appeal of the electronic media could foster political awareness, notably among the urban middle class, which usually do not turn out to vote in large numbers, it is also more difficult for the military establishment to control their content, and, as a result of their sheer number and their democratic oversight, a freedom of expression to which the military establishment has not been accustomed. Nonetheless, as long as it will be easier to raise the alarm for the shortcomings of the civilian power than to report the wrongdoings of the military establishment, the media will not significantly contribute to correct the balance of power at the top of the state structure. Moreover, if television can offer to a reclusive section of the population a semblance of proximity to a political world and a social reality to which they are unaccustomed, without having even to master traditional learning tools, the commercial dynamics and sociopolitical acceptability brings to the fore a discourse reflecting a mindset imbued with conformist views.

Notes

1 Six media workers were also killed. https://cpj.org/killed/asia/pakistan/ (accessed on 15 November 2014).
2 The figures for women are even worse. According to the findings of Pakistan Social and Living Standards Measurement Survey 2012–13 done by the Pakistan Bureau of Statistics, the female adult literacy rate is 50 per cent in Punjab, the highest in the country, and the lowest is recorded in Baluchistan at 18 per cent.

3 Zamir Niazi, *The Press in Chains*, Karachi: OUP [2nd rev. & updated ed.], 2010, p. 188.
4 Ibid., p. 59.
5 *Dawn*, 2 June 2012.
6 When not in power, the military establishment has often used the media to cut the civilian government down to size. In the summer of 2014, it instigated the current affairs TV channels to give favourable coverage of Imran Khan and Tariq Qadri anti-government agitation demanding the resignation of Nawaz Sharif.
7 Niazi, *The Press in Chains*, op. cit., pp. 74, 110–11.
8 Faiz Ahmed Faiz (1911–1984), the influential intellectual and poet, had been the editor of *Pakistan Times* from 1947 to 1951. A later-day significant leftist publication has been the weekly *Viewpoint*, set up in 1975 by Mazhar Ali Khan (1917–1993), editor of the *Pakistan Times* from 1951 till it was taken over by the Ayub regime in April 1959 and the father of Tariq Ali – the British essayist of the *New Left Review*. *Viewpoint* was, from 1975 to 1993, one of the few publications of the Left in Pakistan before disappearing in turn. It actually saw a resurgence on the Internet. See, http://www.viewpointonline.net.
9 The National Press Trust was finally privatized in 1996, the year which also saw the end of the *Pakistan Times*, five years after the closure of Imroze.
10 Mir Khalil-ur-Rahman, founder of the Jang group, gave in to the pressure of the authorities for the publication of all the speeches of Ayub Khan on the first page in six columns whereas Fatima Jinnah had to be satisfied at best with three columns. Inam Aziz, *Stop Press* (Karachi: Oxford University Press, 2008), p. 80.
11 Nadeem F. Paracha, 'Pinning Jinnah', *Dawn*, 16 October 2011.
12 Speech of Benazir Bhutto, 2 December 1988. Quoted in Aziz, *Stop Press*, op. cit., p. 167.
13 A recommendation has been made in the Green Book published by the General Headquarters of the Pakistan Army to acquire a TV channel as well as a radio station to counter 'Indian propaganda'. *The Express Tribune*, 21 December 2013.
14 *Dawn*, 4 November 2007.
15 This overview would not be complete without mentioning the Islamist press, an umbrella term for publications focussing on the centrality of the Islamic identity and appealing to the unity of the community of believers in the face of physical and moral threats coming from the West and its local allies. It ranges from the Jamaat-e-Islami publications (including the daily *Jasarat* and its online edition) to the firebrand papers of militant groups, such as *Ghazwa* (the Battle), a weekly of the Jamaat-ud-Dawa, wanting to install a Khilafat and baying for martyrdom. They are more than hundred, circumventing any ban through circulation in the madrasa network or in the mosques on the occasions of the Friday prayers. Those publications have benefitted from the laxity of the authorities in the name of superior strategic interests or under the pressure coming from the clergy. If a decision is taken to close down some publications, as it happened in March 2002, when the federal and provincial governments banned 22 magazines, they resurface in the market under different names.
16 One of the 20 richest families, the Lakhani are Ismaelis based in Karachi. Two of the four Lakhani brothers were accused by Musharraf, shortly after his accession to power, to have paid bribes to the preceding government (Nawaz Sharif). Arrested in 2000, Sultan Ali Lakhani spent 9 months in jail. He is today the

CEO of Express Media Group, Pakistan's second largest media group, and in 2011, received the Hilal-i-Imtiaz, the second highest civilian award,
17 Express 24/7, a 24-hour news channel, was started in 2009, but had to close down at the end of 2011 due to lack of sufficient revenues; it was then the only English-language channel surviving after the decision of *Dawn News* to switch to Urdu.
18 Many illegal FM channels are being operated in tribal areas by religious groups and individuals. It was this laxity that had permitted Maulana Fazlullah (Maulana Radio) to take charge of the airwaves in the Swat Valley for a long time till transmissions were scrambled before his eviction in a military operation in the spring of 2009.
19 He escorted the Indian journalist Kuldip Nayar at the time of his meeting in 1987 with A.Q. Khan. The ISI-managed interview gave place to an article in *India Today* (11 March 1987), which removed all doubts on the reality of Pakistan's nuclear capacity.
20 A memorandum prepared by Hussain Haqqani, supposedly at the instigation of President Zardari, and conveyed to Admiral Mullen, sollicited, in the aftermath of the operation against Osama Bin Laden in May 2011, American support against a potential military coup.
21 Once a committed Marxist associated with the Baloch insurgency of the 1970s, Najam Sethie faced, during Zulfikar Ali Bhutto's time, imprisonment in the Hyderabad conspiracy case directed against the National Awami Party. In May 1999, he was held for a month under the custody of the ISI for allegedly making derogatory remarks about Pakistan while in India, inducing accusations of being a RAW agent.
22 Politics also interferes in the evaluation of the audience level. Based only on some 700 electronic boxes – for 15 million television sets – and half of which are located in Karachi and Hyderabad, cities largely controlled by the Muttahida Qaumi Movement (MQM), a party not known to enjoy the contradiction. Nusrat Javed, a talk show host on Aaj TV, was fired in the summer of 2011 by his employer after having mocked the leader of MQM, Altaf Hussain.
23 An Islamic social network site, 'Millat Facebook', was launched in May 2010 after the Lahore High Court temporarily banned Facebook on charge of blasphemy but has since been facing financial bankruptcy.
24 In one instance, PEMRA asked the Pakistan Broadcasters Association to stop airing a controversial ad on a contraceptive.
25 A programme on Samaa TV in January 2012 created quite a stir when the host engaged in moral policing in a Karachi park. For a change, the indignation of the liberal press and the social media forced the channel (or was it pressure from advertisers?) to dismiss the host. Maya Khan soon joined ARY channel, and on one show in July 2012, helped an Islamic cleric convert a Hindu Dalit boy to Islam.
26 http://www.newslinemagazine.com/2011/10/interview-dr-khalid-zaheer-religious-scholar-2/ (accessed on 26 January 2013).
27 Harris Khalique, 'War euphoria', *The News*, 30 September 2011.
28 In this view, the Tehrik-e-Taliban Pakistan is a creation of the Research and Analysis Wing (RAW, the main external intelligence agency of India) with the objective of destabilizing the country whereas the Jamaat ud-Dawa and the Lashkar-e-Toiba play a positive role in waging war in Kashmir.

29 It was announced in December 2013 that PEMRA has banned the relay in Baluchistan of popular Afghan television channels by cable operators.
30 http://wikileaks.org/cable/2008/11/08ISLAMABAD3712.html# (accessed on 31 October 2013). In the case of controversial anti-Islamic movie trailer, 'Innocence of Muslims', the American government had to finance advertisements on Pakistani TV to broadcast that it had nothing to do with the video of the Egyptian-born American producer.
31 Inflammatory statements are banned by the code of conduct edicted by PEMRA in 2009. It stipulates that no programme will be broadcast if it contains derogatory remarks against any religion, sect, or community or if it uses images or contemptuous words against any religious, sectarian, or ethnic group. The practice, however, shows that this rule continues to be disregarded.
32 The fatwa defines three major categories for journalists: 'murjif', 'muqatil', and 'Sa'ee bil fasad'. 'Murjif' is someone who engages in propaganda against Muslims during a war between Islam and disbelief, 'Muqatil' is someone who incites disbelievers and their allies to act against Muslims while the third category includes those who corrupt Muslim society through different means, such as replacing the Islamic ideology with secular ideologies. Hasan Abdullah, 'Media now in TTP crosshairs', *Dawn*, 23 January 2014.
33 From 2008 to 2012, the head of ISPR was Major-General Athar Abbas, whose elder brother, Zafar Abbas, is the editor of Dawn; one of the two younger brothers, Azhar Abbas was the managing director of Geo TV. He resigned in August 2013, invoking editorial differences, to become president of the Bol media group. The other brother, Mazhar Abbas, is Director, Current Affairs for *Express News*, after having been deputy director of ARY News TV, and former secretary-general of the Pakistan Federal Union of Journalists.
34 A regular participant to talk shows is Sheikh Rasheed Ahmed, a minister under Pervez Musharraf. Of Kashmiri origin, he formed its own political party in 2008, the Awami Muslim League Pakistan, and participated in the public meetings of the Difah-i-Pakistan Council, along with people such as Samiul Haq, Hamid Gul, Hafiz Mohammed Saeed, and others. He is now close to Imran Khan, the Pakistan Tehreek-i-Insaf leader.
35 Syed Irfan Ashraf, 'Media's biased image', *Dawn*, 11 January 2010.
36 Journalists in Baluchistan have paid a particularly heavy tribute. The latest instance is the killing in Quetta on 28 August 2014 of Irshad Mastoi, secretary general of the Baluchistan Union of Journalists, and Ghulam Rasool, both working for Online International News Network.

4
MILITANT RECRUITMENT IN PAKISTAN
A new look at the militancy–madrasah connection

C. Christine Fair[1]

Ever since the terrorist attacks of September 11, 2001, Pakistan's *madaris* (pl. of *madrasah* or seminary) have attracted the attention of policymakers in the United States and elsewhere. Pakistan's *madaris* are posited both to be incubators of militants in Pakistan and to be responsible for creating communities of support for militancy in Pakistan, South Asia, and beyond. Consequently, the United States and other countries have strongly encouraged Pakistan's various civilian and military leaders alike, to reform these institutions and close down those *madaris* for which there is evidence of links to militant groups, or *tanzeems*, as they are known in Pakistan.

Consonant with the perceived threat posed by these religious schools, the popular, academic, and policy literatures on Pakistan's *madaris* continue to expand. These analyses have produced contradictory findings. While several prominent authors have argued that *madaris* are critical to militant production in the region and beyond,[2] others have cast doubt upon these claims, noting that few known militants have had madrasah backgrounds.[3] This chapter argues that the extant literature likely has overestimated some risks associated with Pakistan's seminaries while underestimating or even failing to identify more empirically supportable threats associated with Pakistan's educational landscape. This disparity has arisen in part because analysts have tended to ask the wrong questions, focusing narrowly upon the disputed connections between *madaris* and militancy and failing to discriminate adequately across different militant organizations, which have their own distinct personnel requirements.

This essay seeks to reframe the policy debate surrounding the role of *madaris* in the production of militants in Pakistan and elsewhere. The main argument is that analysts must examine the human capital requirements of specific *tanzeems*, taking into consideration the objectives, tactics, theatres, and 'quality of terror' produced, as well as the preferred 'target recruitment market' of each particular group in question. Necessarily, this implies that some groups pose more risks than others, based on the scope of their operations, ties with other organizations (e.g. al Qaeda, Taliban), reach (local v. global), and lethality of operations pursued (suicide terrorism v. bazaar attacks). Such an analytical approach is more agile and affords more nuanced conclusions about the connections between education and militancy and about concomitant policy implications. Such an approach does not seek static answers to the madrasah question; rather, this approach permits analysis to evolve as groups develop their objectives, targets, theatres, and indeed, the quality of terror that they can perpetrate.

This approach permits the following conclusions. First, groups that operate in more challenging terrains, assail hard targets or attack targets that are either high-value or for which opportunity costs of failure are high are *less* likely to use militants that are exclusively madrasah trained than are groups that operate in easier areas of operation and engage either soft targets or targets with low opportunity costs of failure. Second, considering the prospect that madrasah education could confer some operational benefits – as in sectarian groups – madrasah graduates may be preferred in some operations. In other words, madrasah graduates may be suitable for some kinds of attacks but not for others. Third, even if madrasah students are more inclined towards jihad, madrasah students may not be selected by a given militant group if the group has other more desirable candidates to recruit. Militant groups could become more dependent upon madrasah students over time *if* militant recruitment standards change or if the militant recruitment market changes. Fourth, *madaris* produce religious entrepreneurs who justify violence and contribute to communities of support. Madrasah graduates also may build families that support some kinds of violence and may be the schools of choice for such families. In sum, this analytical framework suggests that *madaris* merit continual observation as they may contribute both to the demand for terrorism and to the limited supply of militants. For the same reasons, Pakistan's public school sector deserves much more attention, however, than that sector currently enjoys.

The remainder of this chapter is organized as follows. The first section reviews the literature, laying out the various claims about madrasah enrolments, numbers of *madaris*, madrasah students' socio-economic backgrounds, and – finally, and perhaps, most importantly – reviews the literature arguing for and against the connections between militancy and *madaris*. The second section looks very carefully at the various analyses of the presence (or lack thereof) of *madaris* products in militant groups. Drawing from this complex and multidisciplinary literature, the third section lays out a new analytical framework. The fourth section revisits the connections between *madaris* and militancy through this new analytical optic. The fifth and concluding section draws out the policy implications of this approach.

The maddening madrasah debates

As noted above, despite the proliferation of studies of Pakistan's *madaris*, many important questions persist. First, scholars have vigorously disagreed about the number of *madaris* and the penetration of *madaris* in the educational market. In the popular press, an array of reports suggested that anywhere from 500,000 to two million children are enrolled in Pakistan's *madaris*, without any clarity about the level, intensity, or duration of madrasah attendance.[4] The most influential – yet, still incorrect – account of the penetration of *madaris* in the educational market was offered by the International Crisis Group (ICG) in 2002. Relying upon interview data to obtain estimates of madrasah students, the ICG claimed that some one-third of all students in Pakistan attend *madaris*; however, those estimates were derived from an erroneous calculation that, when corrected, yields estimates that vary from 4 per cent to 7 per cent.[5] This miscalculation is regrettable because the report is otherwise very illuminating.

In 2005, Tahir Andrabi, Jishnu Das, Asim Khwaja, and Tristan Zajonc published a study (hereafter referred to as the 'Andrabi study') that employed data both from household-based economic surveys (Pakistani Integrated Household Surveys, or PIHS, from 2001, 1997, and 1991) and from the 1998 Pakistani census[6] as well as from household data collected in 2003 in three districts in the province of Punjab. The Andrabi study, without adjusting for bias in the data, calculated that *madaris* enjoyed a market share of less than 1 per cent. That is among all students enrolled in school full time, less than 1 per cent attend *madaris*. In contrast, the study found that public schools account for nearly 70 per cent of full-time enrolment and private schools account for nearly 30 per cent.[7] It should be noted that the Andrabi study asked only about the kind of school attended not about the kind of education obtained. The Andrabi study did not adequately consider the fact that religious education is not the exclusive purview of *madaris*. Indeed, religious education takes place in public schools, under private tutors, in part-time mosque schools, and even in various kinds of private schools.

Since household-based surveys exclude some potential madrasah students (e.g. orphans and homeless children) and are somewhat dated, Andrabi, Das, Khwaja, and Zajonc adjusted their estimates accordingly for excluded groups and population growth. Accounting for these biases, they estimated generously that 475,000 children might attend *madaris* full time, less than 3 per cent of all full-time enrolments.[8] The Andrabi study's upper estimates are on the same order of magnitude as the ICG's corrected figures, suggesting that *madaris* do not enjoy the market penetration that is widely believed of them.

Another serious caveat to the Andrabi study is that the data the study employed excluded various important areas of the Federally Administered Tribal Areas (FATA) and protected areas of the Northwest Frontier Province (NWFP), where madrasah enrolment could be much higher.[9] The Andrabi study presented evidence that this may be the case: intensity of madrasah enrolment was highest along the Pakistan–Afghanistan border, reaching 7.5 per cent of enrolments in the district of Pishin. This raises the possibility that intensity of madrasah utilization could be just as high, if not higher, in all or parts of the FATA. For these reasons, the study could have underestimated madrasah enrolments, particularly in areas such as the FATA and restricted areas of the NWFP. The Andrabi study did not make any attempt to correct estimates for this exclusion, likely because there is little empirical base upon which such correction could be attempted.

A second area of empirical discord surrounds the number of *madaris* in Pakistan. In 2000, Jessica Stern claimed that there were 40,000–50,000 *madaris* in Pakistan; in 2001, Peter Singer estimated a number of 45,000, albeit with dubiety about this figure. The *9/11 Commission Report*, citing Karachi's police commander, claims that there are 859 *madaris* educating more than 200,000 youth in Karachi alone.[10] In contrast, official Pakistani sources estimate that there were fewer than 7,000 *madaris* in Pakistan's four provinces in 2000.[11] Unfortunately, there are no definitive data sources in place to reconcile these different claims until Pakistan's Ministry of Education completes its planned census of all educational institutions in Pakistan.

Yet a third area of empirical concern is the socio-economic backgrounds of madrasah students. Conventional wisdom holds that *madaris* are the resort of the poor students; yet, this claim rests uneasily upon the various robust studies of student socio-economic background that utilize 2001 PIHS data. Table 4.1 shows the income breakdown of student families for public schools and *madaris*. Perusing the data in Table 4.1 underscores the simple fact that madrasah students are not generally poorer than those students in public schools. It is true that 43 per cent of madrasah students come from the poorest households (defined as those with annual incomes less than 50,000 Pakistani rupees [Rs], or U.S. $865 in 2001 dollars)[12], compared to only 40.4 per cent for those in public schools; however, more madrasah students (11.7%) than public school students (3.4%) come from Pakistan's wealthiest families (those with incomes of Rs 250,000

Table 4.1 Distribution of school enrolment by education system and income (%): Pakistan overall

Annual income (Rs)	Public schools	Madaris
<50,000	40.4	43.0
50,000–100,000	38.1	29.7
100,000–250,000	18.1	15.6
>250,000	3.4	11.7

Source: This table is derived from analysis of PIHS 2001, compiled and published by the Social Policy and Development Center, *Social Development in Pakistan Annual Review 2002–03. The State of Education* (Islamabad: SPDC, 2003, p. 160. Available at http://www.spdc-pak.com/publications/sdip2003.asp)

[$4,325] or greater). In fact, more than one-quarter of madrasah students come from Pakistan's wealthier families (those with incomes of at least Rs 100,000 [$1,730]) compared to only 21 per cent of students in public schools.[13]

Further discounting the theory that *madaris* are schools of last resort, the Andrabi study found that of all the households that use *madaris* (full time) for at least one child, fewer than one-quarter use *madaris* for all of their children. Instead, the vast majority of madrasah households adopt a mixed strategy to educate their children, using public and even private schools for some children in addition to a madrasah for at least one child.[14] This strategy suggests that parents choose *madaris* for reasons other than poverty or the paucity of other options.

Differences in estimates of the inventory of *madaris*, the numbers of madrasah students, and claims about madrasah student backgrounds stem from a variety of factors, such as differing sampling units used by different researchers (household-based surveys versus interviews with Pakistani officials), varying and inadequate definitions of *madaris* and how they differ from the ubiquitous informal 'mosque' schools (which impart only primary Islamic education),[15] over-reliance on one kind of data with little or no effort to check against other data sources,[16] and, finally, deficiencies in the way in which *madaris* are registered by the state and how the state stores such registration data.[17]

Finally, and perhaps, more importantly, debates persist over the connections between *madaris* and militancy. With great certainty, some scholars and government agencies alike have posited the linkages between *madaris* and militancy in Pakistan and beyond.[18] Other analysts have written exculpatory articles suggesting that *madaris* do not significantly contribute to militancy or have not been observed to do so beyond a handful of well-known and notorious *madaris* with historical connections to jihad.[19] How does one resolve the various claims and counter-claims about the linkage between *madaris* and militancy in Pakistan and beyond? Indeed, much of the ancillary inquiries about the number of *madaris*, their market share, and the characteristics of their students are rendered moot if indeed the *madaris* pose no real security threat. If *madaris* are not 'instruments of mass terrorist instruction', then interest in these institutions and debates about their numbers and penetration would arguably be arcane. The next section of this paper seeks to reconcile these claims and counter-claims in an effort to identify the most important contemporary security challenges posed by *madaris*.

Evidence from 'supply-side' studies: exculpating *madaris*?

Against the vocal assertions that *madaris* are 'instruments of mass instruction' and comprise an essential element of militant production in Pakistan and elsewhere, several scholarly articles as well as editorial pieces have sought to add a corrective view to the madrasah policy fixation. At first blush, many of these studies can be called 'supply side' because of their purported focus on the characteristics of militants who supply labour to militant groups. One recent example is afforded by Peter Bergen and Swati Pandey, who examined the backgrounds of 79 terrorists involved in five of the worst anti-Western terrorist attacks (e.g. the 1993 World Trade Center bombing, the 1998 bombing of two US embassies in Africa, the September 11 attacks, the 2002 Bali nightclub bombings, and the London bombings in July 2005). Bergen and Pandey found madrasah involvement to be rare and further noted that the masterminds of the attacks all had university degrees.[20]

Bergen and Pandey's findings comport with the earlier conclusions of Alan Krueger and Jitka Maleckova as well as those of Claude Berrebi, who studied the attributes of suicide terrorists and found that suicide terrorists generally tend to have educational levels that exceed the societal mean and are less likely to live in poverty relative to the average person.[21] Bergen and Pandey's findings also comport with those of forensic psychiatrist Marc Sageman, who compiled profiles of 172 Salafist jihadists that have targeted foreign governments or their people. Upon analyzing these collected profiles, Sageman's study found that terrorists are less likely to be poor and undereducated than are other individuals in the societies from which they are drawn.[22]

These conclusions – that actual militants do not tend to be undereducated or to come from *madaris* – at first blush conflict with the findings of other prominent researchers, such as Paul Collier and Anke Hoeffler, who do find evidence (albeit not necessarily in Pakistan) that higher income and educational attainment should reduce the risk of political violence, principally by increasing the economic opportunity costs of participation in rebellion and other forms of violence.[23] These findings also conflict with those of Jessica Stern, whose interviews with madrasah students led to the conclusion that those students do indeed contribute to *tanzeem* manpower in Pakistan.[24] These ostensible differences between the work of Collier and Hoeffler as well as Stern, on the one hand, and the various supply-side studies, on the other hand, can be explained to a great extent by the recent work of Ethan Bueno de Mesquita.[25]

Bueno de Mesquita's theoretical models suggest that terrorist groups, like other employers, impose standards of quality in their recruitment efforts and pick the most qualified person for the intended mission, subject to whatever resource constraints the organization faces. Here, quality refers to human capital endowment or aptitude. Thus, 'high quality' means a person who is above average in human capital endowment or aptitude. This does not suggest that *tanzeems* require sophisticated human resources tools to make these determinations. Rather, *tanzeem* recruiters, like other conventional employers, may rely upon proxies for quality to evaluate a candidate. These proxies include the recruit's educational background, previous employment, the recruit's reputation or standing in a community. Recruiters may also assess the recruit during periods of personal interaction.[26] *Tanzeems* can pick higher quality candidates as long as there are more persons willing to join a group than there is actual need for additional personnel. In other words, as long as supply exceeds demand, groups can select based on quality. Pakistani *tanzeems* are likely to be able to impose quality standards because most of them require cadres that number in the hundreds or at most in the thousands. Under prevailing conditions in Pakistan, willing supply of militant labour likely exceeds the demand *tanzeems* have for labour.

Assuming that *tanzeems* utilize their human and other resources rationally, they will match personnel to specific operations in accordance with both the skills of the operative and the requirements of the mission. One would expect higher-quality persons to be assigned to targets that are high value or for which the opportunity costs of failure are high. Given the availability of more qualified candidates, a madrasah student likely would not be the target market for many *tanzeems* unless the student also attended a public school or is otherwise numerate and literate. Notably, some *madaris* in

Pakistan do combine religious curriculum with secular subjects and could produce competent militant candidates.[27] A madrasah product may be selected and even preferred by *tanzeems* if the individual confers particular operational benefits, such as Islamist and Islamic legitimacy, among fellow operatives or among the communities in which they operate.

During an economic downturn, more high-quality individuals may become unemployed or underemployed. When a person's employment status is adversely changed, the opportunity costs imposed by participating in terrorism (or other illegal activity, for that matter) are diminished relative to opportunity costs for the same person during better economic times. This may result in a higher proportion of high-quality potential militants during an economic downturn compared to periods of economic growth. By comparison, lower-quality persons have fewer opportunities in both good and bad economic conditions. Therefore, the difference in opportunity costs for participating in terrorism during times of economic downturn is less dramatic for persons of lower quality than for persons of higher quality. While both low-quality and high-quality persons may be available and willing potential recruits, *tanzeems* that impose recruitment standards select high-quality individuals from among the available source of willing manpower. Not only is this, in part, what Bueno de Mesquita means by 'quality of terror', but it also likely explains why observed militants tend to be better educated, relative to the communities from which they are recruited.[28]

Turning to studies that are ostensibly supply-side, it becomes clear that the data analyzed by Sageman, Berrebi, Bergan, and others reflects the effect of militant groups' selection for the best candidate, also known as 'selection bias'. Consequently, these studies expose the characteristics sought by *tanzeems* and the kind of recruits they are able to obtain under prevailing recruitment conditions. These supply-side studies cannot make any substantive claims about the characteristics of all persons who want to join a *tanzeem* because their data sets include only those who have successfully joined one. Furthermore, many of these supply-side studies include militants who have successfully executed an attack or who were caught in the act. This methodology imposes further sample bias by excluding those who failed to carry out an attack or whose attacks failed before anyone could have observed their preparations.

It is difficult to rectify these biases because aspiring or failed militants are rarely observed. It may be the case that poor, uneducated persons, or madrasah products are disproportionately interested in becoming militants. Groups need not hire such individuals, however, if 'higher quality recruits' (i.e. those who are more educated or accomplished in other jobs and pursuits) are available. In the case of Pakistan, even if madrasah students were more interested in joining these groups, *tanzeems* would not necessarily have to accept them when more desirable candidates were available. It is, therefore, not reasonable to conclude that *madaris* are exculpated because their students fail to be accepted by *tanzeems* under current recruitment conditions.

If this reasoning has any validity, substantially increasing education and employment opportunities may not altogether diminish the ability of *tanzeems* to operate because *tanzeems* can lower their recruitment standards. Such interventions may, however, reduce the quality of terrorists available to organizations, and concomitantly, the quality of terrorist attacks that these organizations can perpetrate. Expanding such opportunities may also diminish the support the militancy enjoys among the populations from which *tanzeems* recruit and from whom they draw ideological and material support.[29]

Madrasah–militancy connections: a new approach

The foregoing discussion suggests a different way of approaching the purported militancy–madrasah policy problem. Rather than asking whether or not *madaris* produce militants, this essay suggests that analysts should ask where particular kinds of militants are produced under prevailing conditions specific to the group in question, such as the group's theatre of operations, targets, and objectives as well as the quality of terror the group wishes to produce.

Turning specifically to Pakistan, there are dozens of militant organizations that can be categorized along several axes, including:

- Sectarian lines, both between Shia and Sunni and among different Sunni groups (e.g. Ahle-e-hadith and Deobandi)
- Political affiliation (e.g. Jamaat Islami and Jamiat-ul-Ulama-i-Islam)
- Primary theatre of operation (e.g. Afghanistan, India, and Indian-administered Kashmir)
- Ethnicity of recruits (e.g. Kashmiri and Pashtun)
- Tactics (e.g. high-risk mission, sectarian strike, suicide attack, and low-quality market bombings)
- Targets (e.g. Pakistani leadership, sectarian foes, Indian military, and Pakistani civilians)
- Connections to other organizations (e.g. al Qaeda and Taliban)

By way of illustration, one can compare the operations of groups who primarily operate in India and Indian-administered Kashmir – for example Lashkar-e-Taiba (LeT) – to those of Deobandi sectarian groups – for example Lashkar-e-Jhangvi (LeJ) and Sipah-e-Sahaba-e-Pakistan (SSP).[30] LeT is primarily interested in liberating Kashmir from India; this has increasingly entailed operations deep within India (e.g. the December 2001 attack on India's Parliament and the 2006 Mumbai metro assault, and again, the 2008 Mumbai attack on iconic hotels and buildings in the Colaba area). LeT cadres, many of whom cross into Indian-administered Kashmir at the high-altitude Line of Control (LoC), must be capable of enduring rigorous and demanding physical conditions. Militants must also carefully evade the extensive Indian counter-insurgency grid. Because militants are inserted in groups along with porters and guides, one incompetent militant puts several missions at risk and jeopardizes high-value human assets, such as porters and guides.[31] Once inserted, the LeT operatives must maintain operational security and prepare for operations. This often requires the operative to have some linguistic talent; Indians can quickly detect persons who have lived in Pakistan by their use of particular Punjabi and Urdu phrases and Pakistan-specific vocabulary. Pashto is rarely spoken in India, except by those who have settled in India from Afghanistan, and the use of Pashto may expose a person's origins. Put simply, militant commanders have an incentive not to dispatch lower-quality recruits for such missions.

During fieldwork in Kashmir in 2003, this author had the opportunity to peruse militant field notebooks that contained, along with other important mission particulars, detailed (often in English) instructions for building improvised explosive devices with openly available materials. Such content suggests that these individuals are literate, numerate, and capable of working out mathematical proportions.[32] Notably, these are not skills taught at typical *madaris*. Finally, LeT operatives tend to engage hard targets (e.g. Indian military, police, and intelligence operatives) in demanding high-risk missions.

In contrast, LeJ militants operate in Pakistan itself, where language requirements are not constraining. Getting to the theatre is obviously much easier for LeJ than for LeT. LeJ tends to target civilians in markets and Shia mosques with low-end tactics, such as grenade tosses. LeJ and a related anti-Shia organization, Sipah-e-Sahaba-e-Pakistan, have also engaged both in suicide operations and in operations against the Shia population and their religious institutions. In fact, these sectarian groups are responsible for the development and use of terror tactics in Pakistan against Shia targets. Notably, in recent years, LeJ has 'repurposed' its goals in FATA, where it has been involved in suicide attacks against Pakistani security forces.[33] Important to note is that, in general, LeJ attacks soft or low-value targets and conducts operations for which the opportunity costs of failure are low.

Analysis of these different group-specific details suggests that few LeT operatives are madrasah products;[34] madrasah products are unlikely to become operatives unless they also either attended a government or private school or otherwise confer particular advantages to LeT without some kind of non-religious education. LeT – or any group, for that matter – could use low-quality recruits from *madaris* or elsewhere for missions against soft targets, low-value targets, or against low opportunity cost targets. LeT is not currently known, however, for these kinds of operations.

In contrast, LeJ operations tend to be less sophisticated, with the exception of the recent spate of suicide attacks in FATA against Pakistani security forces. This suggests that, in principle, LeJ could employ madrasah products if others were either not available or not considered appropriate for ideological reasons. In fact, given LeJ's sectarian mission, students with some madrasah background may be preferred to those without madrasah experience, all things being equal. For more important operations (e.g. suicide operations against high-value or hard targets), better-qualified operatives may be desirable. It would be wrong to assume that all suicide attacks require high-aptitude recruits. Many sectarian suicide attacks involve soft or low-value targets (e.g. Shia mosques and religious processions) for which lower-quality recruits may suffice – provided that they are both adequately resolved to complete the mission and capable of ensuring operational security. It is also wrong to assume that all LeJ attacks against Pakistani security forces are 'hard' in the sense that many troops in FATA are not the Pakistan regular army; rather, they include personnel from the Frontier Constabulary and other less-competent paramilitary outfits.

Is there any evidence that this framework for analysis is more appropriate than contemporary approaches to the madrasah–militancy connection? Unfortunately, extant research on militancy and education and Pakistan has not proceeded along these lines, as the literature review suggests, with the exception of Fair (2011).[35] Review of LeT's mission and other activities does, however, buttress this reasoning. LeT was founded in 1987 by Zafar Iqbal and Hafiz Saeed, both professors from the Lahore University of Engineering and Technology, and an Arab scholar (Abdullah Azam) from the International Islamic University in Islamabad. (Azam was killed only two years after the organization was formed in a bomb blast in Peshawar.) Hafiz Saeed has emerged as the current leader of the LeT. Perhaps reflecting Saeed's personal background, his organization has propounded jihad and modern education alongside Islamic education, with the goal of producing 'a reformed individual who is well-versed in Islamic moral principles and the techniques of modern science and technology, to produce an alternative model of development and governance'.[36] Saeed has argued that jihad and modern education are intertwined and has reminded Muslims that when they 'gave up Jihad, science and technology also went into the hands of others'.[37]

Regarding LeJ, some scholars have found connections between *madaris* and sectarian violence although no conclusive evidence has yet been analyzed for these purposes.[38] For example Saleem Ali's study of *madaris* and sectarianism – while inconclusive – does suggest that sectarian violence is more likely to occur in localities where madrasah penetration is highest.[39] Anecdotal information derived from February 2006 interviews indicates that Pakistan government officials and religious scholars alike believed that *madaris* are culpable for the extensive sectarian violence that pervades Pakistan.[40]

To address the need for robust analysis of militancy and human capital formation in Pakistan, in 2004, this author commissioned a convenience sample of the families of 140 militants in Pakistan. The instrument collected detailed information about the militant's group affiliation, work and educational experience, and other relevant personal background as well as detailed household information. Preliminary analysis of the data does support this analytical framework and finds that militants in the sample are overwhelmingly not madrasah products, and indeed, are better educated than Pakistanis generally. The author is currently overseeing several quantitative analyses of this data set.[41] This framework is worth considering, however, both because of the importance of the research topic and because the framework does seem to resolve some of the extant disputes over the connections between *madaris* and militancy. For this reason alone, this approach merits consideration.

Rethinking the *madaris*–militancy connection

As noted, various studies of militants' backgrounds marshal little evidence of madrasah involvement in militancy. This is likely due to various selection effects, including not only the organization's own recruit selection process but also the analysts' inclusion criteria. By design, most studies of militant characteristics will certainly tend to include the more capable militants and exclude the less competent ones. Since no extant data sets collect information on persons who aspire to be terrorists, the aspiring population's characteristics cannot be observed. Thus, it is important not to discount lower-qualified persons in militant operations simply because extant studies do not observe them, and the interest of the people in joining *tanzeems* should not be precluded due to various sample biases. Moreover, while under optimal recruitment conditions, *tanzeems* likely have the luxury of making selections based on quality; should the market for high-quality recruits shrink, groups can rely upon less-qualified labour, perhaps including madrasah students.

Is there any evidence that suggests, as is often believed, that madrasah students have a greater interest in jihad than students of other kinds of institutions? While no nationally representative survey of Pakistani youth of all educational sectors has addressed this issue, the existing limited evidence suggests that madrasah students indeed have a greater taste for jihad than students in other educational streams. Tariq Rahman's path-breaking work provides important insights into the relationship between the kind of education a person receives, on the one hand, and attitudes toward and support for militancy in Pakistan, on the other. Rahman administered an attitudinal survey to 488 tenth-grade students in Urdu medium public schools and English medium private schools and to their equivalent in *madaris*.[42]

Rahman inquired about their views towards open war with India, support for various jihadi groups, and the utility of peaceful means to resolve conflicts. Rahman also asked students whether they favoured equal rights for Pakistan's religious minorities (Ahmediyas, Hindus, and Christians) and for women.[43] Rahman administered a similar survey to the students' teachers as well.[44] The aggregate responses for questions asked of students and teachers are given in Table 4.2.

Rahman's results demonstrate that madrasah students are consistently more likely to support war against India and the use of militants in Kashmir and are less likely to support equal rights for Pakistan's minorities and women. Private school (English medium) students, however, were more likely to support peaceful outcomes and minority and women's rights. Public school students and teachers, however, greatly resemble their madrasah counterparts. This finding is significant, given that analysis of the PIHS data suggests that public schools capture 70 per cent of the full-time educational market. Thus, one of the conclusions that can be drawn from this work is that even if they may not contribute significantly to the pool of observed militants, Pakistan's *madaris* may foster support for terrorism within families and communities; Pakistan's public schools, however, do so as well.[45]

Important to note is that, as with other studies, Rahman's survey also suffers from data limitations. While it is easy to attribute the observed attitudinal differences to the type of school attended, it is also possible that

71

Table 4.2 Student responses (teacher responses given in parentheses)

Question: What should be Pakistan's priorities?	% responding	Madrasah	Urdu medium	English medium
Take Kashmir away from India by an open war	Yes No DK	60 (70) 32 (22) 8 (7)	40 (20) 53 (70) 7 (10)	26 (26) 65 (65) 9 (9)
Take Kashmir away from India by supporting jihadi groups to fight the Indian army	Yes No DK	53 (59) 32 (27) 15 (11)	33 (19) 45 (68) 22 (13)	22 (38) 60 (51) 17 (11)
Support Kashmir cause through peaceful means only (i.e. no war or sending jihadi groups across LOC)	Yes No DK	34 (30) 55 (67) 11 (4)	76 (85) 18 (10) 6 (5)	72 (60) 19 (34) 9 (6)
Give equal rights to Ahmedis in all jobs, etc.?	Yes No DK	13 (4) 82 (96) 5 (NIL)	47 (27) 37 (65) 16 (8)	66 (43) 9 (37) 25 (20)
Give equal rights to Pakistani Hindus in all jobs, etc.?	Yes No DK	17 (15) 76 (85) 7 (NIL)	47 (37) 43 (58) 10 (5)	78 (62) 14 (26) 8 (12)
Give equal rights to Pakistani Christians in all jobs, etc.?	Yes No DK	18 (19) 73 (78) 8 (4)	66 (52) 27 (42) 9 (6)	84 (82) 9 (11) 8 (8)
Give equal rights to men and women, as in Western countries?	Yes No DK	17 (4) 77 (97) 6 (NIL)	75 (61) 17 (33) 7 (6)	91 (78) 6 (14) 3 (8)

Source: Table derived from data presented by Tariq Rahman, 2003, p. 29.

these attitudes reflect the student's family background and family values. In other words, *madaris* may not create pro-militancy students, but rather pro-militancy families may choose to send their children to *madaris*. This may be the case because parental choice of school type likely reflects family attitudes, with more liberal parents preferring private schools and more conservative parents preferring *madaris*, all else equal. If this is true, the observed attitudes of children in those schools may be just as much a product of the children's family environments as they are of the school environment.[46] The 2005 Andrabi study informs this question obliquely: recall that the study found that about three-quarters of the families that use *madaris* for at least one child use other kinds of schools for their other children. Presumably, if families choose *madaris* for primarily ideological motivations, it is to be expected that they would send all of their children to *madaris*. While the majority of madrasah families do not fit this description, one-quarter of madrasah households do.[47] Unfortunately, as noted above, the Andrabi study's analysis rests upon the assumption that religious education happens only in *madaris*, which is not the case. In fact, just as Pakistan's public school curriculum includes Islamic studies (*Islamiyat*), many schools run by private foundations include Islamic studies as well (e.g. the very popular and extensive Iqra Rozatul Itfal Trust chain of schools, Iqra Medina, Iqra Ryazul Itfa, and Iqra Jannatul Itfa).[48] Not clear in the household surveys is how families would categorize private Islamic schools.

Although not diminishing the value of these various studies, these empirical limitations must be kept in mind because of their policy implications: simply switching children from one medium to another (e.g. *madaris* to private schools) may not produce meaningfully different worldviews. While not providing conclusive proof of causality, Rahman's work does suggest that students in public schools and religious schools are more inclined than students in private schools to support jihad against India and even open war with India. Thus, Rahman's survey suggests that both religious and public schools may contribute to the communities of support that Islamist militancy enjoys in Pakistan.

Conclusions, implications, and recommendations

Extant research finds that madrasah products are not well represented in the ranks of the observed Islamist militants, most likely due to the efforts of *tanzeems* to select for quality among their operatives. Because of these selection effects, it would be wrong to conclude simply that *madaris* do not contribute to the problem of Islamist militancy in Pakistan. However, this essay contends that while analysts currently do not observe madrasah products in *tanzeems* for many reasons, madrasah products could become more desirable should group objectives, tactics, or preferred theatre change – or if the recruitment market changes. Nor can it be ruled out that, for some groups, some level of madrasah background may confer operational benefits (e.g. the Taliban and LeJ).

Critically, *madaris* – along with mosques and public proselytizing events (*tabligh*) – likely are important gathering places where *tanzeems*, current militants, religious ideologues, and potential recruits can interact. Some *madaris* may be important because their religious leaders issue edicts or rulings (*fatwas*) that justify the use of violence. Equally important, some religious leaders issue fatwas *against* specific kinds of violence. Indeed, some *madaris* are also known locations for militant training.[49] Limited data also support the contention that madrasah students have a somewhat greater interest in jihad than those of public schools. Yet, public school students – who comprise 70 per cent of Pakistan's enrolled students – also show comparable levels of support for violence. These factors underscore the need both to focus on the human capital requirements of specific groups and to learn where these groups' operatives are produced, rather than focusing narrowly upon *madaris*, which appear to capture a small share of Pakistan's educational market.

This analysis suggests two interrelated sets of recommendations and implications. The first is the more germane for intelligence collection and analysis and follows more directly from the framework promulgated herein. The second set pertains to US policy towards Pakistan and the threat posed by Pakistan-based terrorism to US interests. For this second set, any recommendations are more tenuous, at least in part because the central argument of this paper is that current US policy has been informed by impoverished data and analysis. Thus, data collection and analysis must precede policy formulation.

Implications for intelligence collection and analysis

Rather than arguing that *madaris* do or do not produce militants, analysts should collect background data on the operatives of key *tanzeems*, keeping in mind the impacts of various forms of selection effect. Examination of shifts in militant backgrounds over time may provide invaluable information about the recruitment market that groups face, and, concomitantly, insights into the level of support they enjoy. For example it is useful to note that in recent years, LeT operatives have tended to engage in lower-quality terror attacks (e.g. throwing grenades at tourists) rather than prosecute high-risk missions against Indian security forces, for which LeT is renowned. Holding constant the counter-insurgency capabilities of the Indian security forces, this development may be an important signal that the recruitment market for LeT has softened, that support for LeT in Kashmir has diminished, or that Pakistani security forces are circumscribing LeT's activities.[50]

Such data collection and analyses are imminently possible, as Marc Sageman's collection of militant backgrounds suggest, but require greater exploitation of regional materials, such as the Pakistani media, to populate sophisticated databases for analyses. While many terrorism databases exist, they tend both to exclude information about militant backgrounds and to rely on international accounts rather than local media accounts. Efforts to extract, organize, and analyze these kinds of data will allow analysts to capture trends in the quality of terror that groups are capable of producing, detect changes in the optimal or preferred backgrounds of their operatives, and identify recurrent nodes in militant recruitment (e.g. particular *madaris*, mosques, personalities, universities and technical institutes, and gatherings of known groups). This information is needed to ensure that counter-terrorism policies are effective and concentrate resources on the right institutions and organizations.

Even the most comprehensive data collection on militants, *tanzeems*, and their operations comprise only one part of the analytical puzzle. Efforts to better understand the supply of militancy will, at best, confer tactical advantages, in that they may identify a particular set of institutions that are pivotal to militant recruitment or training efforts. States can eliminate this cluster of institutions, but an effective *tanzeem* will evolve replacements. Unfortunately, this applies a form of selection pressure that forces groups to innovate continually in order to survive state efforts to neutralize them. Supply-side interventions, while having tactical import, also may have strategic diminishing margins of return because such efforts may bolster the popular support that these groups enjoy, creating better recruitment and funding environments for the groups.

Thus, a second, accompanying analytical effort, which focuses upon the characteristics of persons who support militancy or militant groups, is needed. Military recruitment studies consistently find that 'influencer' attitudes about enlistment and the military's public image are important determinants of a young person's decision to enlist.[51] Drawing from these robust findings, perhaps Pakistani influencer (e.g. parents, relatives, friends, and mentors) attitudes about militancy, particular *tanzeems*, and their missions may also affect the propensity of Pakistani youth to join *tanzeems*. Understanding the determinants of this support may create opportunities for strategic communications or other policy interventions to affect the

75

standing of these groups, their missions, and their causes or to engage those segments of the population where support is most intense.

Robust exposition of who supports terrorism requires the fielding of tailored data-collection instruments using nationally representative samples in key countries, such as Pakistan, to track trends in influencer attitudes.[52] Collecting these kinds of data is possible, affordable, and necessary in order to understand where support for terrorism resides. Pew, Gallup, and Zogby, all have massive data collection underway in countries of interest. Unfortunately, these studies tend to fail not only to ask questions that would permit the sort of analysis this framework calls for but also to dedicate adequate resources to ensure proper rural representation. The ability of these studies to conduct polls that do include questions about support for terrorism, however, is encouraging and suggests that such efforts are feasible.[53]

Implications for US policy towards Pakistan and beyond

As the foregoing discussion indicates, to draw expansive policy recommendations based upon this framework would be premature, and indeed, inappropriate. The current US preoccupation with *madaris* was based on impoverished empirical grounds, and, regrettably, has precluded identification of other potential threats to Pakistan and to US interests in Pakistan. It is possible, however, to proffer a few policy implications with some degree of justification.

The first pertains to those *madaris* with known ties to militancy. Pakistani authorities *do* know of key *madaris* with links to militancy because their agencies have long managed those ties (e.g. the Red Mosque). Thus, this is an intelligence, law enforcement and counter-terrorism policy concern rather than an issue of education policy. Pakistan's hesitance to act against these institutions is tied to Pakistan's steadfast commitment to employing Islamist militants under the safety of its nuclear umbrella.[54] US ability to act against them is frustrated by several factors. First, US unilateral action has become increasingly provocative. Second, US and Pakistani security and intelligence officials are increasingly coming into conflict, which will render such action ever more difficult. After the Raymond Davis affair (where a CIA contractor killed suspected ISI-sponsored men to menace him) in February 2011 and the embarrassing, unilateral US operation to kill and extract Osama bin Laden in the cantonment town of Abbotabad in May 2011, the Pakistan Army has limited its training engagement with its US counterparts. Thus, while the Pakistan Army remains unwilling to act against its assets, it is, and likely will remain, incapable of mounting effective counter-insurgency in FATA and elsewhere.[55] Moreover, in FATA, there is no police capability and throughout Pakistan, police forces tend to be corrupt, poorly trained, and in some cases, linked to militant groups.[56] While the bad news is that operating against these *madaris* and associated camps is hard, the good news is that they are few in number.

A second set of implications stems more generally from what the data suggests about education and militancy. Limited evidence suggests that both public school and madrasah students tend to support jihad, *tanzeems*, and war with India, and are more intolerant towards Pakistan's minorities and women. Thus, if Ethan Bueno de Mesquita's model is correct, creating educational and employment opportunities may not put an end to militancy because *tanzeems* can recruit from lower-quality groups. In the long term, however, these kinds of interventions may diminish the quality of terror produced, rendering *tanzeems* a mere nuisance rather than a menace to regional security. This would be a positive development.

The problem with school reform and employment generation efforts is not only that they may be beyond Islamabad's capability and resolve but also that there may be no feasible scope for the US or international efforts to persuade Islamabad to make meaningful reforms on its own. Yet, the United States and its partners must make such attempts because the opportunity costs of inaction or failure are simply too high in this unstable, nuclear-armed country facing considerable internal security challenges. The US may be best served, however, by working with multilateral organizations such as the United Nations Educational, Scientific and Cultural Organization (UNESCO) or the United Nations Development Programme (UNDP) to implement needed curricula reform, school expansion, and job creation. However, following the events of 2011, Pakistan has chosen to frustrate all US development assistance. Given the global recession and increasing Pakistani opposition to US efforts, the US would be best served by trying to do more with less and working through multilateral organizations that are not as controversial as the unilateral US programmes.

Unfortunately, Washington's varied past and current efforts to goad Pakistan into reforming its public and religious educational sectors have fostered suspicions in Pakistan about US 'colonial intentions' and may have had the perverse incentive of encouraging parents to increasingly turn to religious schools of various kinds.[57] Any efforts towards education reform must be based upon a solid understanding of the determinants of parental decisions to enrol their children in school, the type of school to be used for particular children, and the attributes of education that Pakistanis admire and seek out – including religious instruction.[58] Unfortunately, this has not been the case with respect to US educational reform programmes in Pakistan under the aegis of the United States Agency for International Development (USAID), despite the fact that the literature on educational economics in Pakistan is well developed and accessible.[59] The third set of policy recommendations stem from the data collection prescribed above. As argued, there may be diminishing margins of return to supply-side interventions aimed at deterring militant groups from recruiting, training, and operating. Demand-side interventions to diminish public support for militancy, however, remain underutilized, at least in part because there have been so few efforts to understand the determinants of this support. Yet, questions of education and militancy are only a small subset of concerns that should animate efforts to diminish public support for militancy. Extant analyses of correlates of public support for terrorism suggest that policymakers will have to do better at crafting strategic communications campaigns, and, more problematically, identifying and addressing the root causes of support for terrorism, which may include US policies in key theatres.[60] As this essay has striven to show, Pakistan's *madaris* are likely to be insignificant factors in these efforts.

Notes

1 This essay first appeared as C. Christine Fair, 'Militant Recruitment in Pakistan: A New Look at the Militancy-Madrasah Connection', *Asia Policy*, Vol. 1, No. 4 (Summer 2007), pp. 107–134. We are grateful to the National Bureau of Research and the editors of Asia Policy for permitting us to reprint this essay. It has been modified to reflect updates since it was originally authored.

2 See Ali Riaz, *Faithful Education: Madrassahs in South Asia* (New Brunswick: Rutgers University Press, 2008); Abigail Cutler and Saleem Ali, 'Madrassah Reform Is Key to Terror War', *Christian Science Monitor*, 27 June 2005; 'Pakistan: Madrassahs, Extremism and the Military', The International Crisis Group (ICG) Asia Report, no. 36, 29 July 2002; Jessica Stern, "Pakistan's Jihad Culture," *Foreign Affairs* 79, no. 6 (2000): 115–26; Jessica Stern, "Meeting with the Muj," *Bulletin of the Atomic Scientists* 57, no. 1 (January/February 2001): 42–50; and Peter Singer, "Pakistan's Madrassahs: Ensuring a System of Education Not Jihad," Brookings Institution Analysis Paper, no. 14, November 2001.

3 See Peter Bergen and Swati Pandey, "The Madrassah Scapegoat," *The Washington Quarterly* 29, no. 2 (Spring 2006): 117–125; Christopher Candland, "Religious Education and Violence in Pakistan," in *Pakistan 2005*, ed. Charles H. Kennedy and Cynthia Botterton (Oxford: Oxford University Press, 2006), 230–255; and Alexander Evans, "Understanding Madrassahs," *Foreign Affairs* 85, no. 1 (January/February 2006), 9–16. For an empirical critique of the madrasah discourse, see Anne Cockcroft, Neil Andersson, Deborah Milne, Khalid Omer, Noor Ansari, Amir Khan, Ubaid Ullah Chaudhry, "Challenging the myths about madaris in Pakistan: A national household survey of enrolment and reasons for choosing religious schools," *International Journal of Educational Development*, Volume 29, Issue 4, July 2009, pp. 342–349.

4 For a comprehensive inventory of the various popular press accounts of madrasah enrolments, see Tahir Andrabi, Jishnu Das, Asim Khwaja, and Tristan Zajonc, "Religious School Enrollment in Pakistan: A Look at the Data," John F. Kennedy School of Government Working Paper, no. RWP05-024, March 2005; and Wadad Kadi and Victor Billeh, eds., "Islam and Education – Myths and Truths," special issue, *Comparative Education Review* 50, no. 3, August 2006. Also see Saeed Shafqat, "From Official Islam to Islamism: The Rise of Daawa-ul-Irshad and Lashkar-e-Taiba," in *Pakistan: Nationalism Without a Nation?* ed. Christophe Jaffrelot (London: Zed Books, 2002/2004). Shafqat reports that up to two million students attend *madaris* in Pakistan.

5 "Pakistan: Madrassahs." In that report, the authors claimed that one-third of students attend *madaris*, having obtained this figure by dividing the total number of students attending *madaris* (estimated to be between 1 and 1.7 million children, as the Minister for Religious Affairs, Dr. Mahmood Ahmed Ghazi, reported to the ICG) by the total number of all students enrolled (obtained by adding the total number of students enrolled in primary schools, as the Ministry of Finance reported in its 2002 Economic Survey, and the total number of madrasah students). The ICG erroneously used 1.992 million as the total number of children enrolled in primary schools. Taken together [(1)/(1 + 1.992)= 0.33], these figures suggest that at least 33 per cent of all children of primary school age attend *madaris*. The ICG should have used 19.92 million for the number of children enrolled in primary school. Correcting this figure, one obtains only 4.7 per cent [(1)/(1 + 19.992)= 0.04] as the lower bound. Using 1.7 million as the enrolment for madaris suggests that 7% are enrolled in madaris as the upper bound. The ICG amended the report in July 2005 only after publication of the Andrabi et al. study of 2005, which first identified this source of error. Furthermore, it is far from obvious that this is the correct method to calculate madrasah penetration. This math presupposes that madrasah education is comparable only to primary-level education – an assumption that may not be justified.

6 While these household surveys are well-accepted instruments among economists at the World Bank and other prestigious institutions, others in the area studies and other qualitative fields have criticized these instruments as too deeply flawed to be used for serious analysis. For an example of such claims, see the 2005 revised ICG report: "Pakistan: Madrassahs," footnote 6a. For a critique of the 1998 Census, see Anita M. Weiss, "Much Ado about Counting: The Conflict over a Census in Pakistan," *Asian Survey* 39, no. 3 (July–August 1999): 679–93.

7 ndrabi, Das, Khwaja, and Zajonc, "Religious School Enrollment in Pakistan."

8 Andrabi, Das, Khwaja, and Zajonc, "Religious School Enrollment in Pakistan."

9 In 1991 for example the PIHS sample frame completely excluded the FATA, Kashmir, military restricted areas, the districts of Kohistan, Chitral, Malakand, and protected areas of the NWFP. It also excluded households that were entirely dependent upon charity for their sustenance. For the 1991 wave, Pakistan's Federal Bureau of Labor Statistics estimated that about 4 per cent of Pakistan's population was excluded from the sampling frame. See "Basic Information: Pakistani Integrated Household Survey (PIHS) 1991," The World Bank, December 1995, http://www.worldbank.com/lsms/country/pk91/pk91.pdf. In contrast, in the 2001 wave, the PIHS sample universe consisted of all urban and rural areas of all four provinces, Azad Jammu and Kashmir, the FATA, and the

Northern Areas as defined by the provincial governments. It excluded military restricted areas and protected areas of the NWFP. In total, the sample frame excluded about 2 per cent of Pakistan's total population. Information on educational choices, however, is not available in these sensitive areas. See "Sample Design of Pakistan Integrated Household Survey (PIHS) 2001–02," Pakistan Federal Bureau of Statistics, March 2005, http://www.statpak.gov.pk/depts/fbs/statistics/pihs2000–2001/pihs2001–02_6.pdf. See also Pakistan Federal Bureau of Statistics, "Pakistan Integrated Household Survey (PIHS) Round IV: 2001–2002: Basic Education," http://www.statpak.gov.pk/depts/fbs/statistics/pihs2000–2001/pihs2000–2001.html. In 1998, a limited set of questions for the Pakistan Census was used in areas such as the FATA. The short form of the census instrument does not permit a comparable analysis for FATA.

10 See Stern, "Pakistan's Jihad Culture," 115–26; Stern, "Meeting with the Muj," 42–50; Singer, "Pakistan's Madrassahs"; and *The 9/11 Commission Report: Final Report of the National Commission on Terrorist Attacks Upon the United States* (New York: W.W. Norton & Co, 2004), 367.

11 Saleem Mansoor Khaled, *Deeni Madaris Main Taleem*, [Education in Religious Schools (Urdu).] Institute for Policy Studies, 2002, 145.

12 Since this survey was released in 2001, all figures have been converted into US currency using 1 January 2001 as the reference date. Unless specified otherwise, all converted figures are in 2001 dollars.

13 For benchmarking purposes, it is useful to note that the mean household income in Pakistan, according to the 2001 PIHS, is Rs 93,684 ($1,620). When looking at income by quintiles, 40 per cent of Pakistan's families earn Rs 80,664 ($1,395) or above and 20 per cent have incomes in excess of Rs 136,320 ($2,358). Quintiles for this wave of PIHS data are available in "Household Integrated Economic Survey Round 4: 2001–02," Pakistan Federal Bureau of Statistics, April 2003, 1, http://www.statpak.gov.pk/depts/fbs/statistics/hies0102/hies0102t11.pdf. The cut-off point for annual income for the first (i.e. lowest) quintile of household income is Rs 52,692 ($911). This means that one-fifth of surveyed families in the PIHS have annual incomes at or below Rs 52,692 ($911). The cut-off for the fifth quintile is Rs 136,320 ($2,358). This means that of the sample of PIHS households, 25 per cent have an annual income of Rs 136,320 ($2,358) or greater. Breaking down annual income into quintiles demonstrates that the vast majority of Pakistani households (60%) earn between Rs 52,692 and Rs 136,320 (between $911 and $2,358).

14 Andrabi, Das, Khwaja, and Zajonc, "Religious School Enrollment in Pakistan."

15 *Madaris* are distinguished from other religious schools by the fact that *madaris* provide, in part or in full, instruction for the 'alim course'. This course of study eventually produces *ulama* (pl. of alim), or religious scholars. The alim course is in four phases, each denoted by a certificate, or *sanad*. Upon obtaining the terminal sanad, *Allimiyah*, an individual is considered to be an *alim* and can pursue further specialization. Thus, *madaris* should be distinguished from *maqasid*, or mosque schools, that teach only *nazira-e-Quran* (proper recitation of the Quran) or even *Hifz-e-Quran* (memorization of the Quran).

16 See Stern, "Pakistan's Jihad Culture," 115–26; Stern, "Meeting with the Muj," 42–50; Singer, "Pakistan's Madrassahs"; and Robert Looney, "A U.S. Strategy for Achieving Stability in Pakistan: Expanding Educational Opportunities,"

Strategic Insights 7, no. 7 (2002), http://www.nps.edu/Academics/centers/ccc/publications/OnlineJournal/2002/sept02/southAsia.html.
17 Prior to 1993, *madaris* registered under the Societies Registration Act of 1890. After 1993, madrasah administrators were no longer permitted to do so. These registrations, which often were not maintained or updated, are held within local government offices. As such, there is no database that can easily be accessed. One would have to physically collect this information from local government offices – an onerous task which few researchers outside of Pakistan could expect to do.
18 See Stern, "Pakistan's Jihad Culture," 115–26; Stern, "Meeting with the Muj," 42–50; Singer, "Pakistan's Madrassahs"; *The 9/11 Commission Report*, 367; and "Pakistan: Madrassahs."
19 See Bergen and Pandey, "The Madrassah Scapegoat"; Candland, "Religious Education and Violence in Pakistan;" Evans, "Understanding Madrassahs"; and Marc Sageman, *Understanding Terror Networks* (Philadelphia: University of Pennsylvania Press, 2004), 61–98.
20 Bergen and Pandey, "The Madrassah Scapegoat," 117–125.
21 Alan B. Krueger and Jitka Maleckova, "Education, Poverty, Political Violence and Terrorism: Is There a Causal Connection?" NBER Working Paper, no. 9074, July 2002; Alan B. Krueger and Jitka Maleckova, "The Economics and the Education of Suicide Bombers," *The New Republic*, June 2002; and Claude Berrebi, "Evidence about the Link Between Education, Poverty and Terrorism among Palestinians," Princeton University Industrial Relations Sections Working Paper, no. 477, September 2003.
22 See Sageman, *Understanding Terror Networks*, 61–98.
23 Paul Collier, "Rebellion as a Quasi-Criminal Activity," *Journal of Conflict Resolution* 44, no. 6 (December, 2000): 838–852; and Paul Collier and Anke Hoeffler, "Greed and Grievance in Civil War," World Bank Policy Research Paper, no. 2355, May 2000.
24 Stern, "Pakistan's Jihad Culture," 115–26; and Stern, "Meeting with the Muj," 42–50.
25 Ethan Bueno de Mesquita, "The Quality of Terror," *American Journal of Political Science* 49, no. 3 (July 2005): 515–530.
26 For a discussion of militant recruitment in Pakistan and the different venues in which demanders and suppliers of labour may interact and evaluate each other, see C. Christine Fair, "Militant Recruitment in Pakistan: Implications for Al Qaeda and Other Organizations," *Studies in Conflict and Terrorism* 27, no. 2 (November/December 2004).
27 See C. Christine Fair, "Religious Education in Pakistan: A Trip Report," USIP, March 2006, http://www.usip.org/events/2006/trip_report.pdf.
28 Higher-aptitude persons may be more likely to turn to terrorism when the economy is weak and jobs are in short supply. When the economy is good, high-quality persons generally have access to lucrative jobs relative to their low-quality counterparts, and the cost of leaving a good job in order to participate in a terrorist movement is relatively high. That helps explain why engineers and other technical persons with a history of underemployment get involved in terrorism. They are both available and desired by terrorist organizations, particularly during periods of economic stagnation and downturn. See

Bueno de Mesquita, "The Quality of Terror," 515–530; and Christine Fair and Husain Haqqani, "Think Again: Sources of Islamist Terrorism," *Foreign Policy Online*, January 30, 2006. http://www.foreignpolicy.com/articles/2006/01/29/think_again_islamist_terrorism.

29 There has been no work to date examining how these factors affect the support that militancy enjoys among populations, at least in part because there is inadequate information to permit such analysis. Fair and Shepherd attempted to perform this analysis using data collected from the Pew Global Attitudes Survey, but that data set was inadequate for the task. See C. Christine Fair and Bryan Shepherd, "Research Note: Who Supports Terrorism? Insights from Fourteen Muslim Countries," *Studies in Conflict and Terrorism* 29, no. 1 (January 2006), 51–74.

30 LeT was banned and quickly reformed under the name of Jamaat ul Dawa. Since the group is most commonly known by the moniker 'LeT', this essay uses that name. The same is true for Lashkar-e-Jhangvi. This group, too, has been banned several times only to reform under new names.

31 See Ilyas Khan, "The Waiting Game," *Herald* (Pakistan), July 2003; and Ilyas Khan, "Business as Usual," *Herald* (Pakistan), July 2003.

32 For a photograph of these manuals, see Peter Chalk and C. Christine Fair, "Lashkar-e-Taiba: At the Vanguard of the Kashmiri Insurgency," *Jane's Intelligence Review* 14, no. 11 (November 2002), pp. 14–18.

33 Officials from the United Nations Assistance Mission to Afghanistan claim that LeJ and others perpetrating suicide attacks in Afghanistan have ties to *madaris* in FATA. The author conducted meetings in February 2007 and October 2006.

34 This essay uses the term 'madrasah product' in preference to 'madrasah graduate' because few students actually graduate from *madaris* with any certificate. Only a very small percentage completes the *alim* course.

35 C. Christine Fair, "Lashkar-e-Tayiba and the Pakistani State," *Survival*, Vol. 53, No. 4 (August 2011), pp. 1–23.

36 See Shafqat, "From Official Islam to Islamism," 141–42.

37 Quoted in Shafqat, "From Official Islam to Islamism," 143.

38 See Christopher Candland, "Religious Education and Violence in Pakistan."

39 Saleem H. Ali, "Islamic Education and Conflict: Understanding the Madrassahs of Pakistan," August 2005, http://www.uvm.edu/~envprog/madrassah.html. Ali's study, while having potential important insights for this essay, does also have unfortunate limitations that the author does not acknowledge in his exposition. The critical problem is his sample structure. Despite the technical level of discussion in this study, the data set is derived from convenience samples, not scientifically constructed samples. In Pakistan, scientifically constructed samples are a luxury. The author fails, however, to reflect upon how the limitations of his data restrict the generalizability of his central claim that concentration of *madaris* is positively correlated with sectarian violence. To make this claim robustly, the study requires a random sample, inclusive of at least four kinds of areas characterized by high madrasah concentration (MC)/high sectarian violence (SV), high MC/low SV, low MC/low SV, and low MC/high SV. Instead, this study relies upon areas that all have high sectarian violence and high madrasah concentration. Thus, the study has inadequate variation in the two metrics that the author seeks to correlate.

40 See Fair, "Religious Education in Pakistan."

41 See Victor Asal, C. Christine Fair, and Stephen Shellman, "Consenting to Jihad," paper presented at the 148th Annual International Studies Association (ISA) Convention, March 1, 2007.
42 Because formal madrasah education (the *Alim* course or *Dars-e-Nizami* curriculum) starts after completion of *Mutavasatta*, tenth-grade equivalent madrasah students are older than their counterparts in Urdu and English medium schools.
43 Tariq Rahman, "Pluralism and Intolerance in Pakistani Society Attitudes of Pakistani Students towards the Religious 'Other'," paper presented at a conference on pluralism at the Agha Khan University Institute for the Study of Muslim Civilization, October 25, 2003.
44 In addition to asking the students and teachers specific questions about their points of view, Rahman collected basic information about each student (age, class, and gender) and teacher (gender, educational level, and the subjects taught). From both faculty and students, he obtained parental employment information (e.g. rank, title, occupational status, salary, and income) for both parents, where applicable. Few students actually provided this income information, with most indicating that their mothers do not work; thus, for students, this income information was not available.
45 There may be other problems associated with *madaris* that are beyond the scope of this inquiry. Apart from the above-noted concerns about madrasah views on minorities, women, violence, jihad, and militant groups, allegations are rife that sexual abuse and other forms of physical abuse are rampant in *madaris*. See Brian Murphy, "Pakistan Activists, Parents Want Investigation of Sex Abuse in Islamic Schools," September 15, 2005, http://www.pakistan-facts.com/article.php?story=20050918205752898; and "Boy Killed over Pakistan School," BBC News Online, September 24, 2005, http://news.bbc.co.uk/2/hi/south_asia/4278770.stm. Some Pakistani officials interviewed by this author over recent years express concern that the madrasah environment is not conducive to creating Pakistani citizens. In addition to abuse, the officials noted issues related to gender, particular interpretations of Islam, and sectarian worldviews imparted by *madaris*. These are all important issues that require further analysis.
46 To untangle these different sources of causality, Tariq Rahman would need to have interviewed the household members.
47 Andrabi, Jishnu Das, Khwaja, and Zajonc, "Religious School Enrollment in Pakistan."
48 Author fieldwork for this study in February 2006. See Fair, "Religious Education in Pakistan."
49 On October 30, 2006, two missile strikes rocked the Zia-ul-Uloom madrasah in Chinagai (Bajour Agency), a known training centre for militants based in Pakistan, but operating against the US and coalition forces in Afghanistan. See C. Christine Fair, Nicholas Howenstein, and J. Alexander Thier, "Troubles on the Pakistan-Afghanistan Border," USIP, December 2006, http://www.usip.org/pubs/usipeace_briefings/2006/1207_pakistan_afghanistan_border.html.
50 In August and September 2006, the author met in Srinagar and in Delhi with Indian political and intelligence officials, who maintain that LeT attacks in Srinagar have changed substantially. Since 2005, LeT has been less likely to mount high-risk missions against hard targets, instead using young men to throw grenades at soft targets such as tourists.

51 For this reason, the Department of Defense funds the collection and analysis of massive amounts of data to predict recruitment shortfalls or excess supply. See, for example Bruce R. Orvis, Martin T. Gahart, and Karl Schutz, *Enlistment among Applicants for Military Service: Determinants and Incentives* (Santa Monica: RAND, 1990); Bruce R. Orvis, Narayan Sastry, and Laurie L. McDonald, *Military Recruiting Outlook: Recent Trends in Enlistment Propensity and Conversion of Potential Enlisted Supply* (Santa Monica: RAND, 1996); and Bruce R. Orvis and Beth J. Asch, *Military Recruiting: Trends, Outlook, and Implications* (Santa Monica: RAND, 2001).

52 These data elements should include important information about the respondent and the household, including family sectarian background (Deobandi, Ahl-e-Hadith, Barelvi, Shia, etc.), degree of respondent and family religiosity, ethnicity and mother tongue, locality (urban or rural, province), political activism of the family and respondent, household size, numbers of sons and numbers of daughters, family connections with various political and militant Islamist organizations, and, of course, information about utilization of educational institutions (both secular and religious).

53 START (the National Consortium for the Study of Terrorism and Responses to Terrorism at the University of Maryland) has begun a multi-country study that includes Pakistan. This data set will represent a vast improvement over current data sets and should both allow exposition of the characteristics of supporters of militancy and permit evaluation of the levels of support for specific *tanzeems*, campaigns, targets, and objectives. The Program on International Policy Attitudes (PIPA) is affiliated with START and is coordinating the above-noted Pakistan survey. That instrument has not been tailored to Pakistan because it will be fielded in numerous Muslim countries. This author is working with PIPA to develop a Pakistan-specific instrument as a follow-up to the START effort. This new instrument will build off of the author's commissioned militant survey and the author's other work on support for terrorism. To date, only three studies have sought to exposit the correlates of support for terrorism in key countries. Two utilized data from the Pew Global Attitudes Survey, and the third employed data collected by the Gallup Organization. Using different models and data, the three teams came to a similar conclusion: individuals who feel threatened are more likely to support terrorism than those who do not. See Fair and Shepherd, "Research Note: Who Supports Terrorism?"; Ethan Bueno de Mesquita, "Correlates of Public Support for Terrorism in the Muslim World," USIP Center for Conflict Analysis and Prevention Working Paper, forthcoming; and Dalia Mogahed, "The Battle for Hearts and Minds: Moderate vs. Extremist Views in the Muslim World" Gallup World Poll Special Report, November 13, 2006, http://media.gallup.com/WorldPoll/PDF/GALLUP+MUSLIM+STUDIES_Moderate+v+Extremist+Views_11.13.06_FINAL.pdf.

54 C. Christine Fair, ""The Militant Challenge in Pakistan," *Asia Policy*, Vol. 11 (January 2011), pp. 105–137.

55 For a discussion of Pakistan's limited military capabilities and the trade-offs of law-and-order operations versus intelligence and militancy approaches, see C. Christine Fair and Seth G. Jones, "Pakistan's War Within," *Survival*, Vol. 51, No. 6 (December 2009 — January 2010), pp.161–188.

56 See Hassan Abbas, *Police & Law Enforcement Reform in Pakistan: Crucial for Counterinsurgency and Counterterrorism Success*, Report, Institute for Social Policy and

Understanding, April 2009. http://belfercenter.ksg.harvard.edu/publication/18976/police_law_enforcement_reform_in_pakistan.html.

57 During interviews with analysts, government officials, and parents in Pakistan, interlocutors expressed concerns that the United States is seeking to de-Islamify Pakistan's educational systems. These fears are well-founded. Author interviews with high-level officials in the US Department of State confirmed this objective.

58 Forthcoming work by this author details the determinants of parental choice with particular focus upon preferences for some degree of religious education. To accommodate preferences of parents who want their children to garner employable skills while also obtaining religious instruction, new private schools have entered the educational market to provide secular and religious education simultaneously. In other cases, famous *madaris* have opened public and even private schools, teaching secular subjects in an Islamic environment. See Fair, "Religious Education in Pakistan."

59 This assessment derives from author interviews with persons at USAID and the US Department of State. Officials and analysts interviewed by this author were unaware of the extant literature. Matthew J. Nelson reports a similar set of findings in his recent research. See Matthew J. Nelson, "Muslims, Markets, and the Meaning of a 'Good' Education in Pakistan," *Asian Survey* 46, no. 5 (September/October 2006), 690–720.

60 Christine Fair, Neil Malhotra, Jacob N. Shapiro, "Democratic Values and Support for Militancy: Evidence from a National Survey of Pakistan," SSRN Working Paper, June 13, 2011. http://papers.ssrn.com/sol3/papers.cfm?abstract_id=1829322; Graeme Blair, C. Christine Fair, Neil Malhotra, Jacob N. Shapiro, "Poverty and Support for Militant Politics: Evidence from Pakistan," SSRN Working Paper, http://ssrn.com/abstract=1829264; Jacob N. Shapiro, C. Christine Fair, "Why Support Islamist Militancy? Evidence from Pakistan," International Security, Vol. 34, No. 3 (Winter/2009/2010), pp. 79–118.

5

DESTABILIZING ELEMENTS
The Punjabi militant threat to Pakistan

Stephen Tankel

Introduction

On 15 June 2014, the Pakistan military launched a long-awaited offensive, titled Operation Zarb-e-Azb, against militants in North Waziristan. Air strikes preceded the ground phase, which proceeded at a cautious pace and was telegraphed far enough in advance so that militants of all stripes were probably able to escape before the offensive truly got underway.[1] Previous military offensives in the Federally Administered Tribal Areas led to retaliatory attacks in Pakistan's heartland, Punjab province, and its capital, Islamabad. Between 2008 and 2010, there were 143 terrorist attacks in Punjab and 25 in Islamabad alone.[2] Although Operation Zarb-e-Azb raised fears that history would repeat itself, terrorist attacks across the rest of Pakistan fell in the months following the launch of the offensive.[3] At the time of writing, it was too early to tell whether that trend would continue. A terrorist attack against Pakistani security forces at the Wagah border on the outskirts of Lahore suggested that anti-state militants had some fight left.[4] Although the Pashtun-populated Tehrik-e-Taliban Pakistan (Movement of Pakistani Taliban or TTP) claims responsibility for the great majority of attacks in Pakistan, anti-state Punjabi militants have played a critical role in enabling strikes against Pakistan's heartland.

The evolution of the jihadist insurgency in Pakistan's Federally Administered Tribal Areas (FATA) and neighbouring Khyber Pakhtunkhwa, and the Pashtun militants leading it have merited significant attention.[5] Far less focus has been given to the role Punjabi militant organizations and their splinters have played in bringing the insurgency to Pakistan's heartland.[6] This chapter defines Punjabi militants groups as those that were established in Punjab province during or soon after the anti-Soviet jihad in Afghanistan and which grew powerful during the 1990s as a result of state patronage. Some of these organizations had their origins in the Sunni Islamization efforts occurring at the time and the contestation of those efforts by Pakistan's minority Shia population.[7] Punjabi groups historically have drawn members from the Punjab, though not exclusively. The term 'Punjabi group' is the result of both these groups' historical geographic base and the predominant ethnic identity of their members. Since 9/11, some Punjabi group members have turned on the state and recruited others from Punjab province to join the insurgency. For many years, federal and Punjabi provincial government officials, as well as the Pakistan military, denied the threat from Punjabi militants despite evidence to the contrary.[8] Instead, officials typically blamed the onslaught of attacks in the country's heartland on the TTP, often suggesting it acted with the support of a 'foreign hand' – code for India. In addition to Pakistan's serial denials, the fluidity that characterized Punjabi militancy made understanding its dynamics even more difficult. This chapter aims to fill in some of the missing pieces as well as to qualify the threat Punjabi militants pose to Pakistan.

Contextualizing the Punjabi militant milieu

Many of Pakistan's militant groups belong to the Deobandi sect. The largest Punjabi militant groups emerged from or were tied to the Deobandi Jamiat Ulema-e-Islam (Assembly of Islamic Clergy, or JUI) as well as the robust madrassa (religious school) system affiliated with it. The most notable Deobandi militant groups to emerge during the 1980s and 1990s included:

- Harkat-ul-Jihad-al-Islami (HuJI)
- Harkat-ul-Mujahideen (HuM), which splintered from HuJI[9]
- Jaish-e-Mohammed (JeM), which broke from HuM
- Sipah-e-Sahaba Pakistan (SSP), which was launched to counter Shia influence and
- Lashkar-e-Jhangvi (LeJ) initially formed as the militant wing of SSP before (nominally) splitting from it.

Lashkar-e-Taiba (LeT) was the biggest and most significant group to emerge from the Ahl-e-Hadith movement.[10] Unlike Barelvis and Deobandis, who follow the Hanafi school of jurisprudence, the Ahl-e-Hadith are Salafist in orientation and emphasize adherence only to the Quran and 'authentic' hadith. They reject *taqlid*, the imitation of one of the schools of Islamic jurisprudence, and they are a small Sunni minority in Pakistan. Strong divisions existed between the LeT and the Deobandi groups. Although an Ahl-e-Hadith group, LeT also recruited Deobandis (as well as Barelvis), who, soon after joining, were expected to convert to Ahl-e-Hadith Islam.[11] This list is not exhaustive and accounts only for the largest Punjabi groups extant prior to 9/11. In the 1990s, the Pakistan Army and Inter-Services Intelligence Directorate (ISI) deployed LeT, JeM, HuM, and HuJI to advance the country's national interests in Indian-administered Kashmir, where an insurgency had erupted in 1989. Pakistan also supported numerous other groups in Kashmir, both indigenous and Pakistani.[12] During the same period, SSP and LeJ members dedicated themselves to protecting the majority Sunnis' domestic interests from Shia agitation in Pakistan, and primarily were active in Punjab province and Karachi. JeM cadres also engaged in sectarian violence in Pakistan, which the security establishment allowed on the condition that the group remained focused primarily on fighting in Kashmir. In addition to sharing a similar sectarian bent, JeM members also shared the same profile as (and close personal connections) with those belonging to SSP and LeJ.[13] After the Taliban swept to power in Afghanistan in the mid-1990s, that country became another place where the major Deobandi groups came together. All of the major Deobandi groups trained in territory under Taliban control and contributed cadre to fight alongside Taliban soldiers against the Northern Alliance as well.[14] In addition to training in Taliban-controlled territory and providing foot soldiers for the movement, some Deobandi militant leaders served in the Taliban administration and others had offices in Kandahar.[15]

LeT was part of the same jihadist galaxy as the Deobandi groups, but moved in a separate orbit as a result of its Ahl-e-Hadith identity, which was antithetical to Deobandi Islam, and its narrower focus on fighting only in Indian-administered Kashmir.[16] LeT's first training bases in Afghanistan were in Paktia and Kunar provinces.[17] The group continued to use the latter as an area for training after the Taliban came to power but relocated its primary training infrastructure to Pakistan-administered Kashmir and Mansehra, with smaller camps elsewhere in Pakistan.[18] According to one member who joined the group in the mid-to-late 1990s, the ISI blocked many LeT members from traveling independently to Afghanistan during that time.[19] If true, this might have been done either as part of a divide-and-control strategy intended to keep LeT members from mixing too closely with Deobandi militants and, hence, preserve the group's purity, or out of concern that LeT members would assist their fellow Salafis in Northeast Afghanistan, who were fighting against the ISI-supported Taliban. Both may have been contributing factors. Although contact and cooperation occurred between LeT and the Deobandi groups in Indian-administered Kashmir, it was limited in Afghanistan, where LeT cadres did typically not fight alongside the Taliban or administer camps in its territory.[20] Thus, during the latter years of the decade, when all of the Deobandi groups were increasing their ties to one another as well as to the Taliban, LeT remained a group apart within the jihadi milieu in terms of both its sectarian identity and its operations.

During Nawaz Sharif's second term as prime minister, from February 1997 through October 1999, support for the Kashmir jihad declined slightly and the state cracked down significantly on the sectarian groups – SSP and LeJ – making progress in degrading their networks in Punjab.[21] The response authorities encountered was a harbinger of things to come in terms of the future problems the security establishment would confront in its bid to divide state allied militants from anti-state ones. In 1998, LeJ leaders fled to Afghanistan, where they received sanctuary.[22] The Taliban, which continued to receive support from the Pakistan military and ISI, rejected Islamabad's extradition demands. This became a source of friction between the two.[23] In January 1999, LeJ went on the offensive and attempted to assassinate Sharif.[24] The plot failed and Sharif survived, though his grasp on power soon ended. Ten months later, in October 1999, General Pervez Musharraf toppled Sharif's government in a bloodless coup. Sharif had initiated a peace process with India and begun scaling back the Kashmir jihad. Musharraf reversed course and increased support to those militants fighting in Indian-administered Kashmir.[25] Like his predecessor, however, Musharraf viewed the sectarian groups negatively. He banned both the SSP and LeJ in Pakistan in August 2001. A month later, al-Qaeda attacked the US homeland, and Pakistan faced a stark choice: submit to US demands to break with the Taliban and assist in the invasion of Afghanistan and fight with al-Qaeda, or side against America.

Pakistan's concept of national security at the time rested on three pillars: 'resisting Indian hegemony in the region and promoting the Kashmir cause; protecting and developing the nuclear programme; and promoting a pro-Pakistan government in Afghanistan'.[26] Musharraf chose to provide enough assistance against the Taliban and al-Qaeda to meet US demands – a decision influenced by the calculation that doing so was necessary to protect the Kashmir jihad and Pakistan's nuclear deterrent.[27] At the same time, the Musharraf regime sought to prevent the US from decimating the Taliban, and provided the Taliban safe haven in Pakistan.[28] Moreover, the cooperation Pakistan agreed to with the United States did not include action against those militants focused on fighting in Indian-administered Kashmir or attacking India; and it sought to differentiate these so-called freedom fighters from al-Qaeda and other foreign elements.[29] Pakistan later increased its support to the Taliban and other regional actors, including the

Haqqani network, which continued to wage an insurgency against the coalition forces (International Security Assistance Force – ISAF) in Afghanistan at the time of writing.[30]

The evolving Punjabi militant milieu

The Musharraf regime cooperated with the United States against al-Qaeda in the wake of 9/11. It also escalated the pre-9/11 crackdown on LeJ, which had a history of violence within Pakistan and lacked geopolitical utility against India. Although this crackdown was legitimate, LeJ also served as a convenient scapegoat for the anti-US and anti-Pakistani violence that some militants from the historically Kashmir-focused Punjabi groups began to engage in following 9/11.[31] Crackdowns on LeJ built on those initiated against it during the late 1990s and led to the group's fragmentation. Many LeJ members subsequently deepened their ties with al-Qaeda and later began launching attacks against the state.[32] The fact that these Punjabi militants, predominantly from the Deobandi militant groups, quickly became involved in attacks against the state should have signalled to the Pakistani security establishment that its selective approach overlooked the shared connections among them, the linkages between them and Taliban, and al-Qaeda's attempts to cultivate disaffected jihadists who viewed Pakistan's decision to side with the US as betrayal. Instead, the regime went to great lengths to preserve its jihadist assets for use against India. It had banned HuM under US pressure in November 2001, and then, LeT and JeM in January 2002 after the latter's attack against India's Parliament.[33] But these three groups (HuM, LeT, and JeM) were forewarned so that they could protect their infrastructure and in early 2002, the ISI facilitated their re-emergence under new names.[34] Although thereafter technically deemed 'banned outfits' in Pakistan, these state-allied groups continued to enjoy official sanction. Despite the crackdown on LeJ, its parent organization, SSP, also remained tolerated for domestic political purposes. In addition to its political utility, SSP has roots in society and sectarian support that includes those in lower ranks of the police and bureaucracy.[35] SSP has continued to carry out its activities under a series of new names.[36] Despite repeated relabelling since 9/11, these groups are generally still referred to by their original names – a practice this chapter follows.

Although the Musharraf regime sought to protect all of the major Punjabi groups, save LeJ, their relations with the state were nonetheless strained after 9/11. Initially, Punjabi militants who turned against the state targeted US interests and members of Pakistan's Christian community, but before long, the Pakistani establishment itself had become a target.[37] In December 2003, members of the Pakistani Air Force motivated by Maulana Masood Azhar, JeM's amir, attempted to blow up President Musharraf's motorcade. Two weeks later, a Jaish member, who the leadership later maintained had split from the group by this time, made a similar attempt not far from where the first attack took place.[38] Concerns about the involvement of low-level military personnel and police officers in JeM activities contributed to a crackdown in which the authorities detained hundreds of individuals, primarily associated with JeM, HuM, and HuJI. Many were held without trial.[39]

In addition to arresting or eliminating problematic militant elements, the ISI also attempted to pressure state-allied amirs to keep their cadre in line.[40] Maulana Azhar turned in a portion of his rank-and-file to escape arrest.[41] LeT leaders distanced their organization from al-Qaeda, and may have betrayed some al-Qaeda members to the authorities.[42] ISI handlers appear to have believed that because they 'had the amirs with them the situation was in check'.[43] In other words, Pakistan aimed only to eliminate problematic elements, not to dismantle the Punjabi militant infrastructure. Yet, the amirs' willingness to accede to state directives actually drove more members away, particularly in the cases of JeM and HuM.[44] Pakistan's response had unintentionally contributed to the atomization that began to occur among the state-allied Deobandi groups.[45] Some of the Deobandi militants who escaped the intermittent crackdowns or split with their organizations remained in Punjab. Others took shelter in Pakistan-administered Kashmir, the Northwest Frontier Province Areas (NWFP), known since 2009 as Kyhber-Pakhtunkwah (KP), and FATA.[46] Many of those who went to the FATA linked up with al-Qaeda, LeJ members who fled there after 9/11, and those from SSP who had left to join their sectarian colleagues.[47] Before long, additional splinter groups began to emerge.

In 2004, India and Pakistan initiated the Composite Dialogue to address the many thorny bilateral issues between them. This initiative corresponded with a sustained reduction in activity for Kashmir-centric militant outfits. Even LeT, which, through 2004, remained more active in Kashmir than the Deobandi groups and had yet to experience any significant pressure, was pressed to reduce its militant activities thereafter, according to several of its members. Some militant groups were beginning to receive additional breathing space in spring 2005, but the Musharraf regime came under increased pressure following the 7/7 (2005 London) attacks to curtail militant infiltration into Kashmir. This led to the beginning of a sustained reduction in militant activity in Kashmir for India-centric LeT, which had remained more active in Kashmir than the Deobandi groups and had yet to experience any significant pressure, from the Pakistan government.[48]

Once again, however, rather than dismantling these groups, the security establishment was making efforts to control them and limit their activities. Thus, many inactive militants were confined to training camps in the event their services were required in the future.[49] Rather than wait for such a day, however, some militants began migrating to FATA, where recruitment for the insurgency in Afghanistan was escalating.[50] The destruction of training infrastructure in Pakistan-administered Kashmir during the 2005 earthquake and the release of those Punjabi militants jailed in the 2003–4 crackdown following the failed Musharraf assassination attempts contributed further to this militant migration.[51] As with previous migrations, many of those who travelled to FATA linked up with Punjabi militants already there, who, by this time, had strengthened their ties with al-Qaeda and pro-Taliban Pashtun tribesmen.

Meanwhile, al-Qaeda's presence in Waziristan, coupled with escalating Taliban raids into Afghanistan, led to US pressure on Islamabad to launch a series of incursions into FATA. The incursions went poorly, failing to halt cross-border activity or permanently dislodge foreign militants. Instead, they catalyzed a rebellion led by pro-Taliban Pashtun militants and reinforced the perception among a growing number of Punjabi militants as well as a generation of new recruits that the Pakistani state was an extension of America. A series of peace agreements signed in the wake of failed incursions emboldened those anti-state militants based in FATA, who escalated the tempo and audacity of attacks against military, civilian, and tribal officials. Their growing strength, coupled with the Taliban's resurgence in Afghanistan, invigorated the Pakistani jihadist community. By 2006, as the Kashmir conflict was showing visible signs of decline, Pakistan's failed military incursions into the FATA and subsequent peace agreements had emboldened anti-state militants there. An insurgency against the state was accelerating swiftly.[52]

In July 2007, Pakistani security forces launched an assault against the Lal Masjid (Red Mosque) in Islamabad and the two *madaris* attached to it. The Lal Masjid had been a well-established ISI asset, and one of its *madaris*, Jamia Fareedia, historically attracted students from the North West Frontier Province and FATA, many of whom were sympathetic to militancy.[53] The operation was a military success, but is widely viewed as turning a primarily FATA-based proto-insurgency into a full-blown insurgency that soon threatened to envelop the country. By this time, many Punjabi militants who were predisposed to viewing the Pakistani state as an enemy already had migrated to FATA. In addition to those hardened militants already based in FATA and yet another wave that migrated there after the raid, some estimates suggest as many as 5,000 students from Punjabi *madaris* headed to Waziristan at the time as well. Collectively, many of these men contributed to the violence that soon beset Pakistan.[54] Terrorist attacks increased significantly after the Lal Masjid raid. Critically, the insurgency also spread to Punjab and Islamabad. The FATA-based Tehrik-e-Taliban Pakistan (TTP), which unified formally in December 2007, became the face of the insurgency in Pakistan and militants operating under its umbrella claimed credit for most attacks. But anti-state Punjabi militants provided the capability to strike Pakistan's heartland.

The Punjabi militant threat to Pakistan

Some of the most notable militants involved in anti-state violence came from the major Deobandi groups, all of which had splintered by the time of the Lal Masjid raid.[55] Some of these militants came together to form the Punjabi Taliban.[56] Hassan Abbas defined the Punjabi Taliban as a loose conglomeration of (current and former) members of banned militant groups of Punjabi origin, most notably LeJ, SSP, and JeM, who developed strong connections with the TTP, al-Qaeda, and other militant organizations in FATA and Khyber Pakhtunkhwa.[57] The Punjabi Taliban network enabled these anti-state militants to pool resources and improve coordination. The various actors feeding into this network often maintained their individual names for recruiting and fundraising purposes, and many continued to pursue multiple agendas.[58] Moreover, they are part of a wider network of anti-state Punjabi militants comprising splinter groups, small cells of individuals that emerged as a result of fragmentation, and a new generation of militants.

This mélange of Punjabi splinters, emerging outfits, and established mercenaries worked independently in some instances, and other times, in concert with one another, the TTP, and al-Qaeda. Generally speaking, the TTP proffered a safe haven, training camps, or space to establish them in FATA, and provided them money; al-Qaeda has helped with planning, financing, and technical assistance for attacks.[59] In return, Punjabi militants provided manpower and logistical networks to strike Punjab's cities. The capability to launch attacks throughout the country, especially against the capital and major cities in Punjab, gave the FATA-based TTP another means to impose costs on the state in response to military incursions.[60] Because bigger entities such as the TTP contracted out attacks, this created space for new, daring, and innovative militants to flourish by leveraging connections to a 'known' actor in order to bring in more money and recruits.[61]

Crucially, connections among state-allied militant organizations and their splinters meant anti-state militants are able to leverage the infrastructure belonging to state-allied groups and the religious parties associated with them for seemingly unsanctioned operations in Pakistan. According to provincial police officials responsible for counterterrorism, many attacks in Punjab involved at least some measure of cooperation from locals. As one police official in the Bahawalpur Region explained, 'A person from DG [Dera Ghazi] Khan might be used in Multan for an attack planned and funded by persons in the FATA, but he will coordinate with local influential people often from a "banned organization"'.[62]

Mosques and *madaris* associated with establishment groups have functioned as hideouts, transit points, staging grounds, and storage depots for attacks against Pakistan.[63] For example in one instance, Punjabi militants connected to the TTP, JeM, and HuJI used the Madrasa Usmania Shadan Lund in Multan to store weapons and ammunition in advance of a failed attack on a government office building. At least two militants involved in this plot also were involved in the attack on the Sri Lankan cricket team bus, for which the Madrasa Usmania Shadan Lund was again used as a storage depot for weapons later transported to Lahore.[64] In particular, mosques and *madaris* associated with LeJ and SSP in Punjab are believed to have operated as 'networking centers for the Punjabi Taliban'.[65] These mosques and *madaris* also provide a means of recruiting 'within the system'. LeJ's ability to regroup owed partially to the fact that it could tap into Deobandi *madaris* and mosques associated with SSP, which escaped a sustained crackdown.[66]

Once recruited, militants might float around inside the system on their own, including going from state-allied organizations to anti-state ones. According to police officials, individual recruits from the Punjab are often indoctrinated in a mosque or madrassa simply to do jihad, rather than for a specific purpose or to fight against a singular enemy. As Shaukat Javed, the Inspector General of the Punjab police until 2010, explained:

> It's difficult to quantify how many people are joining for what reason because when we probed people we arrested about why they joined whatever outfit, inevitably they talked about some mullah who inspired them to do jihad. Sometimes it's for sectarian reasons or maybe Afghanistan. But often they're just told jihad is important. Then someone contacts them and arranges

for travel to FATA. So the group you join (and hence against whom a recruit wages jihad) depends on the Mullah who inspires you and the talent spotter who facilitates travel to FATA.[67]

Anti-state Punjabi militants built up a presence in Miram Shah in North Waziristan before the Pakistan military finally launched a clearing operation in 2014. This enabled greater portability among militant cadre *and* greater coordination among militant leaders in which one group might provide money; a second, logistics; a third, reconnaissance; a fourth, a vehicle; a fifth, explosives; and a sixth, a bomber, though many bombers were recruited and detailed by the TTP.[68] As a result, the authorities often broke up cells in which they found individuals from several different groups. Some of these men did not even know who was organizing them, according to several security officials.[69] Historical connections among Deobandi organizations and the rise of new groups born as a result of splintering or fragmentation amplified this phenomenon.

It is important to consider these dynamics within the wider context of the realignments that occurred within the militant milieu from roughly 2004–05 onwards. Afghanistan became a focal point for many major Pakistani militant groups and a host of smaller networks and splinter groups. As the insurgency against coalition forces and the Afghan government grew from 2004 onwards, these groups' participation increased.[70] LeT maintained a significant focus on India, which, by the middle of the decade after 9/11, received less attention from other Punjabi groups. India's perceived malevolent involvement in Afghanistan contributed to the integration of these two loci in the minds of some militants, however, and after 2008, there was an escalation of attacks on Indian targets in Afghanistan by Pakistan-based actors.[71] Sectarian attacks in Pakistan increased from the middle of the decade onwards, following a lull, during which LeJ members were either on the run or launching attacks against official targets.[72] In addition to these three focal points, which existed before 9/11, revolutionary jihad against the state emerged as a new locus of activity. Finally, although most militants remained preoccupied with local and regional factors, al-Qaeda's global jihadist ideology, which includes striking US and allied targets wherever they may be found, also influenced the militant environment by the latter years of the decade. Al-Qaeda also stoked the revolutionary jihad against Pakistan and promoted jihad in Afghanistan, providing ideological as well as operational support. Several important trends emerged as a result of these developments.

First, the over-representation of LeJ members in anti-state violence infused the insurgency against Pakistan with sectarianism. In just one example of this phenomenon, many of the attacks against the Army and Frontier Corps that took place in FATA after the Lal Masjid raid resulted in militants singling out Shia members for beheading.[73] Although militants associated with LeJ remained at the forefront of sectarian violence, their ideology influenced many of those waging jihad against Pakistan. A number of TTP commanders were previously affiliated with SSP and LeJ, which contributed to the intermingling of revolutionary and sectarian activities. On the one hand, militants associated with SSP/LeJ exploited Talibanization in FATA and KPK, while, on the other hand, sectarian attacks became 'an extension of the TTP war against cities'.[74]

Second, revolutionary jihad became a major dividing line for militants, cutting between outfits and within them. However, this dividing line is a permeable border and one commonly crossed since the latter years of the last decade. As one Jamaat-e-Islami member observed, the state may not have declared it as against Islam, but 'Pakistan's leaders and army [began] acting unIslamically so some people who go to wage jihad against America will realize they must fight Pakistan too because Pakistan is helping America'.[75] Further, because separateness and togetherness co-existed among and within groups, Punjabi militants who disagreed with one another over activity in one locus might cooperate (or compete) in another.

Third, the integration of old loci and emergence of new ones, coupled with the increasing interconnectivity of the militant milieu at the grassroots level contributed to and was exacerbated by what could be termed a 'flea market effect'. All of the established organizations had, and continue to have, mullahs from different areas in their ranks, each with clout in his location. Smaller entities may follow these clerics or others who are independent of or only tangentially connected to established organizations, splinter groups, or emerging outfits. Many of these clerics contribute to the debate among Sunni militants and mullahs in Pakistan regarding the most important target for jihad: the Pakistani government and military, the Shia, India, or the United States. In the case of the US, the debate extends to whether militants should focus exclusively on fighting America in Afghanistan or also attempt to attack it elsewhere in South Asia.

Al-Qaeda ups the ante

On 3 September 2014, al-Qaeda's amir, Ayman al-Zawahiri, announced the creation of a new al-Qaeda affiliate in South Asia. Al-Qaeda in the Indian Subcontinent (AQIS) was two years in the making, according to Zawahiri, and its formation reflects critical changes in al-Qaeda and the Punjabi militant milieu.[76] Since 2008, US drone strikes have decimated the al-Qaeda organization in Pakistan, killing numerous leaders and high-level operatives and leaving only a handful of senior Arabs alive.[77] These strikes also created a hostile environment for surviving al-Qaeda leaders, while developments in the Middle East, including the civil war in Syria, made that the region a more attractive base for operations.[78] The depletion of al-Qaeda's senior ranks in Pakistan coincided with the growing strength of al-Qaeda affiliates in other locations, most notably al-Qaeda in the Arabian Peninsula or AQAP. In August 2013, Ayman al-Zawahiri appointed AQAP amir, Nasir al-Wihayshi as al-Qaeda's general manager for global operations.[79] Before al-Wihayshi was killed by a US drone in the summer of 2015, it was conceivable that he would have assumed the top slot if Zawahiri were killed or captured. Even with al-Wihayshi dead, it is possible that at some point 'core AQ' could shift entirely from South Asia back to the Arab world.[80]

As Arab al-Qaeda members in South Asia died or fled, Pakistanis, including powerful Punjabi militants, filled the void.[81] Al-Qaeda ties to Punjabi militant groups stretch back decades.[82] Since the eruption of the insurgency in Pakistan, al-Qaeda has provided planning, financing, and technical assistance to various anti-state Punjabi militants, including, but not limited to, the Punjabi Taliban.[83] This likely contributed to al-Qaeda's influence over these Punjabi militant actors. Indeed, al-Qaeda reportedly was known to arbitrate among them, when necessary.[84] In recent years, notable Punjabi militants joined al-Qaeda, including the now-deceased Ilyas Kashmiri and Badr Mansur, who split from HuJI and HuM, respectively.[85] Maulana Asim Umar, who leads AQIS, had a strong affiliation with HuM.[86] In short, although the organizational contours of AQIS were still taking shape at the time of writing, historical ties suggest anti-state Punjabi militants might play a prominent role in the new organization.

In the video announcing AQIS, al-Zawahiri, Asim Umar, and the AQIS spokesman, Osama Mahmood, outlined the new group's mission as the re-conquest of al-Hind, an area that encompasses all of India, most of Pakistan, Bangladesh, and parts of Myanmar. As more Pakistanis joined al-Qaeda, its media operations focused more on Pakistan and India.[87] AQIS likely intended its inaugural message to appeal to Punjabi militants, in particular, for whom jihad against India has always resonated strongly. In another video released earlier in 2014, Asim Umar, the AQIS amir, called on Kashmiri Muslims to join al-Qaeda's ranks and accused the Pakistani government of forsaking their cause.[88]

The focus on India is not simply rhetorical. Before his death, Ilyas Kashmiri sought to expand al-Qaeda's attack capabilities in India. His efforts included recruiting Abdur Rehman Syed, a former Pakistani army officer and LeT member who launched an outfit called Jund-ul-Fida [Army of Fidayeen]. Syed's outfit operated under Kashmiri's command and was intended to carry out operations primarily in India.[89] There are also reports that some members of the Indian Mujahideen network sheltering in Pakistan attempted to connect with al-Qaeda to conduct joint operations in India.[90] At the time of writing, there are no indications that AQIS has managed to build its network in India, Bangladesh, or Myanmar. AQIS may aspire to attack India but since its formation, it has been active only in Pakistan. Al-Qaeda's South Asian affiliate announced its presence by attempting to seize a Pakistani frigate, the PNS *Zulfiqar*, reportedly as part of an elaborate plot to use it to launch missiles at US warships in the region.[91] The plot failed, but illustrated that AQIS had managed, not for the first time, to recruit Pakistani naval officers to assist with a terrorist operation.[92] These events do not constitute evidence of widespread jihadist sympathies in Pakistan's armed forces, but they are, nevertheless, troubling. How deeply AQIS has penetrated the Pakistan military is unknown, but it is almost certain that the group will continue seeking to execute ambitious attacks in Pakistan.

Conclusion

AQIS may be a manifestation of some of the changes that have occurred within the Punjabi militant milieu, but it is only part of the wider Punjabi militant threat to Pakistan. Anti-state Punjabi militants have the potential to execute attacks against an array of high value targets in Pakistan's heartland. These attacks can be more destabilizing than those in the FATA, and their impact can also be significantly corrosive to a narrative of state control. In addition to these high-profile attacks, the sectarian ideology advanced by a subset of Punjabi militants is equally, if not more, corrosive. Sectarian strife cuts deep and has expanded from Sunni–Shia conflict to include Deobandi–Barelvi violence. This has created a ratcheting effect, whereby various Islamist actors are racing to the extremes in order to avoid being out-muscled.

Myriad structural and systemic deficiencies hamper Pakistani counter-terrorism efforts, which are further hindered by the integrated nature of the militant milieu in which anti-state militants are sometimes able to leverage Pakistan's tolerance of state-allied groups. In other words, the triage policy that Pakistan pursues for strategic purposes, which targets some militants while protecting others, can have malignant operational consequences. Moreover, because militant entities that disagree with one another over activity in one locus might cooperate in another, this creates a bottom-up pressure on militant leaders, many of which are experiencing factionalism, freelancing, and attrition among members to varying degrees. This illustrates the challenges that derive from an environment in which multiple militant agendas and organizations are present. Chief among these challenges is the attenuation of control – for militant leaders and their official sponsors. Moreover, because relationships among the various groups in Pakistan are characterized by separateness and togetherness, this creates challenges for analysts seeking to make sense of the militant threat and practitioners attempting to arrest it.

The state's unwillingness or inability to arrest staunch religiously motivated violence reflects its lack of moral authority and weakness in the face of a drift towards intolerance spearheaded by jihadist groups – anti-state and state-allied – who have arrogated power and preach exclusionary ideologies. This can discourage private citizens from providing intelligence against anti-state militants or from alerting the authorities when extremists seek to exert their influence through extra-legal means. It also can lead officials to conclude that attacks against minorities, women, and other popular targets are acceptable or, at least, to be tolerated. This further influences the breakdown of law and order, which then has the cyclical effect of encouraging further extremist action. Left unchecked, these groups will continue weakening Pakistan's ability to cope with the many other challenges it faces.

Notes

1 Saeed Shah, Safdar Dawar, and Adam Entous, 'Militants Slip Away Before Pakistan Offensive', *Wall Street Journal*, 17 July 2014. Michael Kugelman, 'The Haqqani Threat to the US-Pakistan Détente', *The Diplomat*, 31 July 2014. Phil Stewart, 'U.S. tells Pakistan: Do not let Haqqani fighters resettle', Reuters, 25 July 2014.
2 *PIPS Security Report 2008*, (Pak Institute for Peace Studies, January 2009). *Pakistan Security Report 2009*, (Pak Institute for Peace Studies, January 2010). *Pakistan Security Report 2010* (Pak Institute for Peace Studies, January 2011).
3 'Taliban Tumult', *The Economist*, 24 October 2014.
4 Waqar Gillani and Salman Masood, 'Bomber Kills At Least 50 Along Border In Pakistan', *New York Times*, 2 November 2014.
5 See for example C. Christine Fair, 'Pakistan in 2011: Ten Years of the "War on Terror"', *Asian Survey*, 2012, 52 (1): 100–113; C. Christine Fair and Seth Jones, 'Pakistan's War Within', *Survival*, 2009–2010, 51 (6): 161–188; Z. Hussain, *The Scorpion's Tail* (New York: Free Press, 2010); Hassan Abbas, (ed), *Pakistan's Troubled Frontier* (Washington, DC: Jamestown Foundation, 2009); A. Mir, *The Fluttering Flag of Jehad* (Lahore: Mashal Books, 2008).
6 Notable exceptions include: Hassan Abbas, 'Defining the Punjabi Taliban Network', *CTC Sentinel*, 2009, 2 (4): 1–4; A. Mir, *Talibanisation of Pakistan: From*

9/11 to 26/11 (New Delhi: Pentagon Press, 2009); Amir Mir, 'Punjabis Here, Pushtuns There, Taliban Everywhere', *Middle East Transparent*, 25 October 2009; M. Hussein, *Punjabi Taliban: Driving Extremism in Pakistan* (New Delhi: Pentagon Press, 2012).

7 On the rise of Sunni sectarian groups see, for example S. V. R. Nasr, 'Islam, The State and the Rise of Sectarian Militancy', in Christophe Jaffrelot, (ed), *Pakistan: Nationalism without a Nation* (London: Zed Books, 2004), 85–114.

8 The authorities only publicly began acknowledging the threat from Punjabi militants in late 2009, following a series of devastating strikes in Lahore and a daring attack against the Pakistan Army's General Headquarters (GHQ) in October. That month, Interior Minister Rehman Malik finally admitted Punjabi militants were 'operating jointly in Pakistan' with al-Qaeda and the Tehrik-e-Taliban Pakistan. Matt Wade, 'An Unholy Trinity', *The Age*, 21 October 2009.

9 The two briefly reunited to form Harkat-ul-Ansar (Movement of Partisans or HuA), and then separated again.

10 This is not an exhaustive list and accounts only for the largest Punjabi groups extant prior to 9/11. Numerous other smaller groups existed as well, as did front organizations and splinter groups in the Kashmir theatre. Nevertheless, it is accurate to assert that prior to 9/11, these entities constituted the major Punjabi militant organizations.

11 C. Christine Fair, 'Militant Recruitment in Pakistan: Implications for Al-Qa'ida and Other Organizations', *Studies in Conflict and Terrorism* 2004, 27 (6): 489–504; S. Tankel, *Storming the World Stage: The Story of Lashkar-e-Taiba* (New York: Columbia University Press, 2011), 84; Mariam Abou Zahab, 'I Shall Be Waiting for You at the Door of Paradise: The Pakistani Martyrs of the Lashkar-e Taiba', in Aparna Rao et al. (eds), *The Practice of War* (New York: Berghahn Books, 2008), 142.

12 Numerous works have detailed the involvement of indigenous and Pakistani militants in the Kashmir conflict and Pakistan's support for them. See, for example S. Bose, *Kashmir: Roots of Conflict, Paths to Peace* (Cambridge, MA: Harvard University Press, 2003); A. Jamal, *Shadow War: The Untold Story of Jihad in Kashmir* (Brooklyn, NY: Melville House, 2009); L. Puri, *Militancy in Jammu and Kashmir: The Uncovered Face* (New Delhi: Promilla, 2008); M. A. Rana, *Jihad in Kashmir and Afghanistan* (Lahore: Mashal Books, 2002).

13 Mariam Abou Zahab, 'Pashtun and Punjabi Taliban: The Jihadi-Sectarian Nexus', in *Contextualising Jihadi Thought*, (eds) Jeevan Deol and Zaheer Kazmi (UK: Hurst, 2011), 370.

14 National Commission on Terrorist Attacks upon the United States, *The 9/11 Commission Report: Final Report of the National Commission on Terrorist Attacks Upon the United States* (New York: W.W. Norton, 2004).

15 HuJI contributed three government ministers and twenty-two judges to the Taliban's administration and its amir, Qari Saifullah Akhtar, served as an adviser to Mullah Mohammed Omar.

16 LeT did engage in sporadic sectarian violence in Afghanistan during the 1980s and against Shia and Barelvi Muslims in Pakistan during the early 1990s. However, it eschewed such activities in Pakistan from the mid-1990s onwards, after becoming the ISI's favoured proxy in Indian-administered Kashmir. Within Kashmir, the group continued to engage in sectarian violence against local

DESTABILIZING ELEMENTS

Barelvis, though not with the same intensity with which it fought against the Indian security forces. For more on LeT's sectarian activities, see: Tankel, *Storming the World Stage*, 42.

17 Markaz-al-Dawat-wal-Irshad, 'A Brief Introduction to the Markaz and the Lashkar', no date; Zahab, 'I Shall be Waiting for You at the Door of Paradise', 137.
18 Tankel, *Storming the World Stage*, 30; Zahab, 'I Shall Be Waiting for You at the Door of Paradise', 137.
19 Jamaat-ul-Dawa official, interview by author, Islamabad, Pakistan, 2011.
20 Tankel, *Storming the World Stage*, 30, 108–109.
21 The Crime Investigation Department of the Punjab police at the provincial level and Intelligence Bureau at the federal level led the crackdown.
22 Riaz Basra and Akram Lahori, both wanted by the Pakistani authorities, reportedly took shelter at a Harakat-ul-Mujahideen camp in Khost.
23 Khost was technically under Taliban control, but in reality, was the fiefdom of Jalaludin Haqqani. He was part of the Taliban government, but enjoyed significant autonomy. In any case, both the Taliban and Haqqani received support from the Pakistani state, and so, the refusal to hand over wanted fugitives is notable. 'Request for Extradition of Pakistani 'Terrorists', CTC Harmony Database, AFGT-2002–000079.
24 Zahab, 'Pashtun and Punjabi Taliban', 371, fn. 7.
25 Alexander Evans, 'The Kashmir Insurgency: As Bad As It Gets', *Small Wars and Insurgencies*, 2000, 11 (1): 69–81.
26 A. Rashid, *Descent into Chaos: The United States and the failure of Nation Building in Pakistan, Afghanistan and Central Asia* (London: Penguin, 2008), 219.
27 President Pervez Musharraf, President [sic] Address to the Nation, September 19, 2001, http://presidentmusharraf.wordpress.com/2006/07/13/address-19-september-2001/.
28 Sumit Ganguly and Paul Kapur, 'The Jihad Paradox: Pakistan and Islamist Militancy in South', *International Security*, 2012, 37 (1): 111–141.
29 *The 9/11 Commission Report*, 331.
30 A. Giustozzi, *Koran, Kalashnikov and Laptop: The Neo-Taliban Insurgency in Afghanistan* (London: Hurst, 2007), 21–28; V. Brown and D. Rassler, *Fountainhead of Jihad: The Haqqani Nexus, 1973–2012* (London, UK: Hurst, 2013), Ch. 5.
31 Zahab, 'Pashtun and Punjabi Taliban', 372–373.
32 Ibid.; Ashley J. Tellis, *Pakistan and the War on Terror: Conflicted Goals, Compromised Performance*, Washington, DC: Carnegie Endowment for International Peace, 2008; Mohammad Amir Rana, 'Structural Violence', *Dawn*, 25 January 2012; Huma Yusuf, 'Sectarian Scourge', *Dawn*, 31 January 2012.
33 SSP was re-banned in January 2002 as well.
34 LeT became Pasban-e-Ahl-e-Hadith and its above-ground wing, Markaz-al-Dawa-wal-Irshad became Jamaat-ul-Dawa. Jaish-e-Mohammed renamed itself Khuddam ul-Islam. Harkat-ul-Mujahideen changed its name to Jamiat ul-Ansar.
35 Abbas, 'Defining the Punjabi Taliban Network' ; Zahab','Pashtun and Punjabi Taliban', 382; Amir Mir, 'Punjab Govt May Not Act against LeJ PML-N Has Seat Adjustments with Defunct SSP', *The News*, 22 February 2013; Declan Walsh, 'Extremists Pursue Mainstream in Pakistan Election', *The New York Times*, 5 May 2013.

36 President Musharraf legitimized the SSP when he allowed Azam Tariq, the SSP chief (at the time) to contest elections from prison in October 2002 as an independent candidate, provided Tariq support the regime. In exchange for doing so, Tariq also obtained the release of many SSP militants as well as a more lenient approach towards SSP overall. Abou Zahab, 'Pashtun and Punjabi Taliban', 372.
37 Amir Mir, 'The Maulana's Scattered Beads', *Outlook India*, 1 September 2003.
38 Mir, *Talibanization of Pakistan*, 110. P. Musharraf, *In the Line of Fire: A Memoir* (New York: Free Press, 2008), 244–257; Rashid, *Descent into Chaos*, 230–231.
39 Zahab, 'Pashtun and Punjabi Taliban', 73.
40 Stephen Tankel, *Domestic Barriers to Dismantling the Militant Infrastructure in Pakistan* (Washington, DC: USIP, September 2013).
41 Mir, *Talibanization of Pakistan*, 110–111.
42 Amir Mir, journalist with *The News*, interview by author, Lahore, Pakistan, 2011. Jamaat-ul-Dawa official, interview by author, Islamabad, Pakistan, 2011. Mir, *Talibanization of Pakistan*, pp. 110–111.
43 Journalist with *Geo News*, interview by author, Islamabad, Pakistan, 2011.
44 Only LeT managed to avoid splintering and maintained internal cohesion relative to the Deobandi groups, though some of its members split from the group as a result of their leaders' willingness to obey ISI dictates.
45 Mir, *Talibanisation of Pakistan*, 108–111; Mir, 'The Maulana's Scattered Beads'.
46 Abou Zahab, 'Pashtun and Punjabi Taliban', 373–374.
47 Ibid.
48 For more on constraints placed on LeT and other groups fighting in Kashmir from 2004 onwards see, Tankel, *Storming the World Stage*, 176–80.
49 M.A. Rana, *The Seeds of Terrorism* (London: New Millennium, 2005), 28.
50 Giustozzi, *Koran, Kalashnikov and Laptop*, 334–35.
51 Most headed to Waziristan, but the sectarian groups also had a presence in Lower Kurram and Orakzai. LeT began reclaiming a foothold in Bajaur and Mohmand, where it had historical connections. On the sectarian groups, see Abou Zahab, 'Pashtun and Punjabi Taliban', 373–374. On LeT see, Tankel, *Storming the World Stage*, 197.
52 'Testimony of David Coleman Headley to the Indian National Investigative Agency', 3–9 June 2010.
53 Hassan Abbas, 'The Road to Lal Masjid and Its Aftermath', *Terrorism Monitor*, 2007, 5 (14): 4–7; Manjeet Pardesi, 'The Battle for the Soul of Pakistan at Islamabad's Red Mosque', in C. Christine Fair and Sumit Ganguly (eds) *Treading on Hallowed Ground: Counterinsurgency Operations in Sacred Spaces* (New York: Oxford University Press, 2008), 97.
54 Abou Zahab, 'Pashtun and Punjabi Taliban', 380.
55 Ibid, 373-4. Abbas, 'Defining the Punjabi Taliban Network'; Mir, *Talibanisation of Pakistan*, 108–109; Tankel, *Storming the World Stage*, 123, 128.
56 The name was first used to refer to ethnic Punjabis from HuJI who joined the Taliban regime in Afghanistan in the mid-1990s. The term resurfaced when Musharraf banned those groups, including HuM, LeT, JeM, and SSP, which have a support base in Punjab. Then, in 2007, the FATA-based militant leader Maulvi Nazir, with state support, challenged Uzbek foreign fighters residing in South Waziristan. Maulvi Nazir attracted recruits from the banned Punjabi

groups for this purpose, leading some to call him a leader of the 'Punjabi Taliban'. Abbas, 'Defining the Punjabi Taliban Network'; Nasreen Ghufran, 'Pushtun Ethnonationalism and the Taliban Insurgency in the North West Frontier Province of Pakistan', *Asian Survey*, 2009, 49 (6): 1092–1114.
57 The designation does not apply to all members of LeJ, SSP, and JeM, instead referring only to those individuals or factions who shifted to FATA or collaborate closely with other anti-state militant groups based there.
58 Abbas, 'Defining the Punjabi Taliban Network'.
59 Tariq Pervez, former Director General of the Federal Investigative Agency and currently Director of the Initiative for Public Security, interview by author, Islamabad, Pakistan, 2011. Senior official in the Research and Analysis for Punjab Police Counterterrorism Division, interview by author, Lahore, Pakistan, 2011; Senior counterterrorism official with the Punjab Police, interview by author, Lahore, Pakistan, 2011; Amir Mir, "Punjabis Here, Pushtuns There, Taliban Everywhere', *Middle East Transparent*, 25 October 2009; Abbas, 'Defining the Punjabi Taliban Network'.
60 Abbas, 'Defining the Punjabi Taliban Network'; Ghufran, 'Pushtun Ethnonationalism'.
61 Senior counterterrorism official with the Punjab Police, interview by author. Senior official in the Research and Analysis Wing for the Punjab Police, interview by author. Intelligence Bureau (IB) official, interview by author, Islamabad, Pakistan, 2011. Tariq Pervez, interview by author. Mir, interview by author. 'Attack on Sri Lankan Cricket Team at Lahore, Police Report, Case FIR No. 252, 3 March 2009. 'Interrogation of Amanullah (aka Asadullah, aka Kashif)' Police Report, no date. 'Testimony of David Coleman Headley to the Indian National Investigative Agency'. See also, Mir, 'Punjabis Here, Pushtuns There, Taliban Everywhere'; Abbas, 'Defining the Punjabi Taliban Network'.
62 Senior police official in Bahawalpur Region, interview by author, Bahawalpur, Pakistan, 2011.
63 Shaukat Javed, former Inspector General of Punjab police, interview by author, Lahore, Pakistan, 2011; Punjabi police counterterrorism squad officer, interview by author, Lahore, Pakistan, 2011; Senior official in the Research and Analysis for Punjab police Counterterrorism Division, interview by author; 'Attack on Sri Lankan Cricket Team at Lahore'; 'Interrogation of Amanullah (aka Asadullah, aka Kashif)'.
64 'Attack on Sri Lankan Cricket Team at Lahore'; 'Interrogation of Amanullah (aka Asadullah, aka Kashif)'.
65 Abbas, "Defining the Punjabi Taliban Network"
66 Ibid. Senior counterterrorism official with the Punjab Police, interview by author.
67 Shaukat Javed, former Inspector General of Punjab police, interview by author.
68 Senior official in the Research and Analysis for Punjab Police Counterterrorism Division, interview by author. Senior counterterrorism official with the Punjab Police, interview by author; Abbas, 'Defining the Punjabi Taliban Network'; Mir, 'Punjabis Here, Pushtuns There, Taliban Everywhere'.
69 Senior official in the Research and Analysis for Punjab Police Counterterrorism Division, interview by author. Senior counterterrorism official with the Punjab Police, interview by author. Senior police official in Bahawalpur Region,

interview by author. Second senior police official in Bahawalpur Region, interview by author, Bahawalpur, Pakistan, 2011. 'Attack on Sri Lankan Cricket Team at Lahore'; 'Interrogation Report of Amanullah (aka Asadullah, aka Kashif)'.

70 Giustozzi, *Koran, Kalishnikov and Laptop*, 34–35; Zahab, 'Pashtun and Punjabi Taliban', 373–374; Brown and Rassler, *Fountainhead of Jihad*, 138–141.

71 Praveen Swami, 'Kabul Attack: US Warning Was Accurate', *The Hindu*, 3 August 2008; Mark Mazzetti and Eric Schmitt, 'C.I.A. Outlines Pakistan Links with Militants', *New York Times*, 30 July 2008; Lynne O'Donnell, 'Eight Killed in Suicide Attack near Kabul Hotel', Agence France-Presse, 14 December 2009; Karin Brulliard, 'Afghan Intelligence Ties Pakistani Group Lashkar-i-Taiba to Recent Kabul Attack', *Washington Post*, 3 March 2010;
  Alissa Rubin, 'Militant Group Expands Attacks in Afghanistan', *New York Times*, 15 June 2010; Jason Motlagh, 'Pakistani Insurgent Group Expands in Afghanistan', *Time*, 10 September 2010.

72 Rana, 'Structural Violence'; Yusuf, 'Sectarian Scourge'.

73 Brigadier Mohammad Feyyez, commander of a Pakistan army brigade in N. Waziristan from 2006–2008, interview by author, Lahore, Pakistan, 2011. See also: Abou Zahab, 'Pashtun and Punjabi Taliban', 376.

74 Abou Zahab, 'Pashtun and Punjabi Taliban', 374–377.

75 Irfan Shahzad, Research Coordinator at JI's Institute for Policy Studies, interview by author, Lahore, Pakistan, 2011.

76 Ellen Barry, 'Al Qaeda Opens New Branch on Indian Subcontinent', *New York Times*, 4 September 2014.

77 For more on AQ leaders killed in Pakistan see, New America Foundation, *Drone Wars Pakistan: Leaders Killed* at http://securitydata.newamerica.net/drones/pakistan/leaders-killed, (last accessed 30 October 2014).

78 In late September 2014, US airstrikes were directed against senior al-Qaeda members who moved into Syria and formed the Khorasan Group. Josh Levs, Paul Cruickshank, and Tim Liste, 'Source: Al Qaeda group in Syria plotted attack against U.S. with explosive clothes', CNN, 23 September 2014.

79 As one analyst observed, Wihayshi's promotion suggests that 'core al-Qaeda' is expanding geographically. 'Al-Qaeda's Center of Gravity 'Shifting' from Pakistan to Yemen', Agence France- Presse, 14 August 2013.

80 Arif Rafiq, 'The New Al Qaeda Group in South Asia Has Nothing to Do With ISIS', *The New Republic*, 5 September 2014.

81 Stephen Tankel, 'Going Native: The Pakistanization of al-Qaeda, *War on the Rocks*, 22 October 2013.

82 Tankel, *Storming the World Stage*, 107–9.

83 Tariq Pervez, interview by author; Senior official in the Research and Analysis for Punjab Police Counterterrorism Division, interview by author; Senior counterterrorism official with the Punjab Police, interview by author; Mir, 'Punjabis Here, Pushtuns There, Taliban Everywhere'; Abbas, 'Defining the Punjabi Taliban Network'.

84 Tariq Pervez, interview by author; 'Testimony of David Coleman Headley to the Indian National Investigative Agency'; 'Letter from Osama bin Laden to Hakimullah (Mehsud); Bill Roggio, 'Commander Killed in Drone Strike "Funneled Pakistani Jihadists" to Al Qaeda', *Long War Journal*, 9 February 2012.

85 Both men were reportedly killed by the time of writing.
86 Ali K. Chishti, 'Target: Karachi', *The Friday Times*, 26 September 2014.
87 For more on AQ media statements see, IntelCenter, *Al-Qaeda Speakers Left Standing: 8 June 2013* at http://intelcenter.com/reports/WordClouds/AQ-Speakers-LeftStanding/ (last accessed 30 October 2014).
88 Rafiq, 'The New Al Qaeda Group in South Asia Has Nothing to Do With ISIS'.
89 Tankel, *Storming the World Stage*, 203.
90 Rajesh Ahuja, 'Bhatkal says IM looking for tie-up with al Qaeda', *Hindustan Times*, 20 September 2013.
91 Thomas Joscelyn, 'Al Qaeda in the Indian Subcontinent claims 2 attacks in Pakistan' *Long War Journal*, 13 September 2014.
92 The 2011 al-Qaeda attack on Pakistan Naval Station Mehran was carried out after naval intelligence refused to release members of the navy arrested because of their links to al-Qaeda. As discussed earlier in this chapter, members of the Pakistani Air Force motivated by Maulana Masood Azhar, JeM's amir, were involved in one of the two December 2003 assassination attempts against then-President Musharraf. On al-Qaeda's recruitment in the Pakistan navy in 2014 see, Praveen Swami, 'First claim by al-Qaeda subcontinent wing: Pakistan Navy men ours', *The Indian Express*, 12 September 2014. On al-Qaeda's recruitment in the Pakistan navy in 2011 see, Syed Saleem Shahzad, 'Al-Qaeda had Warned of Pakistan Strike, *Asia Times*, 27 May 2011.

6

THE BATTLE FOR KARACHI
Changing patterns of a permanent civil war

Laurent Gayer

> Everyone in the city,
> while attending to business every day, is afraid of getting hit by a stray bullet.
> (. . .) Now when we look at the dead,
> tears no longer come to our eyes.
> Instead of pain, our hearts
> are filled with smoke (. . .).
> Zeeshan Sahil, 'Ek Din' (One Day) (1995).[1]

The walls of Qasba Colony speak for themselves. 'The blood of those killed will not be shed in vain' (*Khun rang laega*), proclaims a graffiti at the 'border' between two strife-torn *mohallas*, while bullet marks in the metal shutters of local stores and in the facades of residential homes bear witness to the heavy fighting that took place here in the early days of July 2011. In the Pathan-dominated locality of Kati Pahari facing Qasba Colony's Sector E, ten-feet-high concrete slabs have been erected at the entrance of the most exposed alleys. A group of party workers affiliated with the Awami National Party (ANP), one of the parties to the conflict, explains that these merely serve a defensive purpose, although they could also make pretty good *morchas* (shooting posts), once the fighting resumes. The recently built memorial to the 'martyr' Alamgir – a 21-year-old Pathan resident of Kati Pahari, who was shot in the head and chest while on his way to the mosque to offer *namaz* – is another reminder of the intensity of the violence which erupted here in July 2011 between the armed militants of the two parties competing for the control of this strategic area: the Pathan-dominated ANP and the Muttahida Qaumi Movement (MQM), a party representing Karachi's Urdu-speaking populations, locally known as *Mohajirs* (migrants/refugees, a reference to the Indian roots of this population, whose elders migrated from India to Sindh after Partition).

Qasba Colony is one of Karachi's most volatile localities. Standing at the edge of Orangi, Karachi's largest *katchi abadi* (squatter settlement), and in the shadow of the 'cut mountain' of Kati Pahari, it is emblematic of Karachi's tryst with ethnic, political, and criminal violence since the mid-1980s. The Khasa Hills on both sides of Kati Pahari are the exclusive abode of the Pathans (Pakistani Pashtuns), who have recreated here a living environment reminiscent of their mountainous villages in the Northwest. Their small houses cling to the flank of the hill, overseeing the *Mohajir* localities situated below. This overhanging position may well be a hurdle on an everyday basis: it's a strenuous climb to the top of the hill, and water has to be pumped up by private electric pumps. But when fighting erupts, as it regularly does, there is simply no better spot in Karachi to position snipers. This is precisely what happened in December 1986, when Pathan gunmen linked to the arms and drug mafia occupied the top of the hills and showered Qasba Colony with bullets, before launching raids on the terror-struck locality and neighbouring Aligarh Colony, where they slaughtered men, women, and children indiscriminately. Twenty-five years later, Qasba Colony remains at the epicentre of Pathan–Mohajir violence in Karachi. A series of deadly clashes erupted between 2007 and 2011, culminating in four days of intense street battles in the early days of July 2011. If this violence seemed to be a repetition of the incidents of the mid-1980s, a closer look suggests otherwise. Whereas *Mohajirs* were at the receiving end of the violence unleashed by Pathan criminal elements in 1986, this is no longer the case. In the meantime, the *Mohajirs* have brought to power the MQM, whose strong-arm tactics have drastically affected the balance of power between the city's ethnic communities in favour of the *Mohajirs*. The bullet-ridden metal shutters of Pathan stores in Kati Pahari are here to attest to the fire power of the MQM, which acquired additional weapons in recent years.[2] According to the Pathan residents of Kati Pahari – one of whom described his locality as 'more dangerous than Waziristan' – the MQM has formed 'death squads' in every locality where it operates. During outbursts of violence, these frequently masked militants are deployed in a different locality from that where they reside, so as to prevent their personal ties from interfering with their task.[3] Rather than setting neighbours against neighbours, Karachi's turf wars, therefore, seem to be waged by battle-hardened youths with no ties to their 'enemy', be it other armed militants or 'non-political people' (*ghair tanzim log*), targeted on the basis of their ethnicity.

The unprecedented powers given to the MQM under the regime of Pervez Musharraf (1999–2008) helped it get an upper hand in the governance of the city – an institutional position of dominance that the party leadership has used to its fullest potential, by deploying local state agencies to redesign the city at will and enfeeble its rivals in the process. Again, no other place in Karachi exemplifies this better than Kati Pahari. Officially, a passage across the Khasa Hills was carved here in 2007–2008 to open up the factories and mills of SITE Town while connecting better Orangi to the rest of the city. But many Pathan residents of Qasba and Orangi believe that the 'mountain' was, in fact, 'cut' to evict them and facilitate the expansion of the MQM in this contested area, by connecting it with the MQM stronghold of North Nazimabad, on the other side of the ridge. Since 2007, however, the MQM's hegemony over Karachi has been violently challenged by the ANP, which has been able to carve a place for itself in Karachi as the powerful spokesman of an increasingly vocal Pathan minority, a growing section of which has made Karachi its home for good and intends to defend its own right to the city. The leadership of the MQM, which represents and projects itself as the custodian of Karachi, has been trying to contain this development by invoking the threat of a 'talibanization' of Karachi, by forcing Pathan shopkeepers to close down their businesses and by sponsoring attacks against ANP workers and Pathan civilians.

In addition to these turf wars, Karachi has seen several terrorist attacks since 2001. But if diplomatic missions, Pakistani military bases, Shia processions, and more recently, Sufi shrines have been repeatedly targeted by Jihadi and sectarian organizations during the last decade, Karachi has so far been spared the campaign of terror unleashed against other Pakistani cities (Peshawar, Quetta, and to a lesser extent, Islamabad and Lahore) in recent years. On the whole, it is estimated that these conflicts have costed the lives of 15,000 to 20,000 people between 1985 and 2011, with approximately 10,000 having been killed between 2007 and 2013, following the resumption of inter-party violence after an eight year lull (1999–2007).[4]

Despite the enduring nature of this state of violence – which anthropologist Stanley Tambiah has equated to a 'continuous civil war'[5] – important variations need to be accounted for when retracing Karachi's history of violence. This chapter, therefore, attempts to challenge two common assumptions about political and criminal violence in Karachi: first of all, that the city would be drifting towards chaos, making it ungovernable and threatening Pakistan's, if not global, stability in the process[6]; second, that the more things change, the more they remain the same in a city ostensibly mired in its conflicts.

Trouble every day: the routinization of violence in Karachi

'Today, so many people are dying that [whenever someone is killed], we are less affected than if a flea was creeping over our ear' (*Ab itne log mar jate* *hain, to logon ke kan par jun tak nahin ringti).* This is how Mohammad Afzal, a 55-year-old Urdu-speaking bookseller at Karachi's Urdu Bazar, conveyed to me his sense of the routinization of violence in the city.[7] Far from being an oddity, this naturalization of everyday violence in Karachi can also be discerned in the verses of Zeeshan Sahil, quoted at the beginning of this paper, and it reappeared in many interviews I conducted over the years in the city. In the same vein, this is what Asif*[8], a middle-aged Urdu-speaking resident of Orangi Town, replied after I asked him if he saw some end in sight to the violence affecting his locality: 'No, I don't see peace coming in the future... it will be very difficult... because most people don't have any affection for each other *(koi ek dusre ko pasand karte hi nahin, zyadatar)*... so tensions will remain and the next generation will have to live with that'.[9]

For most residents of Karachi, including the barricaded city elites, violence has become part of the natural order of things. This is not to say that violence has become acceptable to the *Karachi-wallas*, but simply that they cannot imagine a future without it. In the context of Colombia, sociologist Daniel Pécaut observed a similar phenomenon of banalization of everyday violence, which he attributes to two mutually constitutive phenomena: '[One is] the lack of novelty characteristic of most political interactions and, [two], the lack of any imagined novel future'.[10] Pécaut's observations are worth considering when pondering over Karachi's own history of violence, as they point to the interconnections between the routinization of violence in the eyes of city residents and the nature of political interactions between the parties and organizations competing for control of the city. Indeed, in Karachi, as in Colombian cities, violence has become a structural element of these interactions from the 1980s onwards. Even the protagonists of the battles for local supremacy acknowledge this. As Uzair Baloch, the head of the Lyari-based People's Amn Committee (cf. infra), declared in front of an assembly of traders in February 2012, 'Politics was once just about lying. Now it is the politics of corpses'.[11]

The violent restructuring of everyday political interactions

The militarization of Karachi's politics predates the ethnic riots of the mid-1980s as well as the rise of MQM at the helm of city politics and actually started on the city campuses at the end of the 1970s. At that time, the control of these campuses was disputed by Islamist and 'progressive' student organizations, who would occasionally engage into brawls, but with no serious consequences, as Fahim Zaman Khan, a former Karachi mayor and progressive student activist recalls, 'At the end of the 70s, when someone pulled out a knife, it was really a big deal',[12] he noted. The patterns of student violence started changing with the inflow of firearms on Karachi campuses, as a consequence of the Afghan Jihad. Modern weaponry (Sten guns and revolvers, and later on, Kalashnikovs, locally known as *klashnis*) was introduced on the campus by the militants of the 'Thunder Squad', the armed wing of the Islami Jamiat-e-Tulaba (IJT, the student wing of Jamaat-e-Islami). This student militia was apparently formed in the late 1950s to counter rival, left-wing student organizations in the universities of Punjab and Karachi. However, it is only in the 1970s that it evolved into a proper strike force, after it attracted young veterans of the Bangladesh civil war, who had joined the al-Badr and al-Shams Islamist militias fighting on the side of the Pakistan Army.[13] Thunder Squad militants probably acquired their firearms in the markets of Khyber Agency, and maybe directly from some *mujahidin* factions (such as Gulbuddin Hekmatyar's Hizb-i-Islami, who received a delegation of IJT members in Peshawar as early as 1975). This weapons procurement spree was tolerated, if not encouraged, by the regime of General Zia-ul-Haq, which aimed to reduce the influence of left and pro-PPP forces on campuses. The inclusion of the Jamaat-e-Islami in Zia's government also guaranteed political protection to Islamist student activists when they tampered with the law. Leftist and pro-PPP student organizations initially had more difficulties in accessing weapons. Among the rivals of the IJT, the Peoples Student Federation (PSF – the student wing of the PPP) was the first organization to acquire firearms. In 1979, a group of PSF students managed to get hold of weapons that were meant for the IJT. As one of the participants to this arms raid, Akram Qaim Khani, recalls:

> I was going on a motorbike with a friend of mine in my area [Shah Faisal Colony] and suddenly we saw a university students' union van. At that time, the union was run by the Jama'at-e-Islami. It was very surprising because the *Jama'atis* never dared to enter our area. Then I saw one *badmash* [goon] called Sayyid in the van. So I told my friend: 'Maybe they are planning to do something to us, to attack us. There must be something wrong, we must follow them'. So we followed them in the colony and they parked the van in front of a house and Sayyid and another *badmash* came out of the car and they had two large *boris* [big bags] that looked very heavy. Then they dumped these two bags in that house. [. . .] I decided that we should check on them in the morning. I gathered all our friends, maybe 20, 30, in my house, and in the early morning, we surrounded their house. At eight o'clock, Sayyid came back with the van and they started uploading the bags. When they were about

to upload the second one, Tipu [the most well known PSF militant] came and, you know, he had no patience in him. I had told everyone 'Let them complete their job and then we'll do something'. But after the first batch [was uploaded in the van], he shouted "Oh, Sayyid!" He was carrying a gun – we only had one gun, with maybe 20 bullets – and he started firing at Sayyid. Sayyid ran away and the other man ran away and we captured all those bags. They were full of pistols, Sten guns, knives... Hundreds of them... That is the day we became rich in Karachi, when we realized that we could conquer all Karachi. Jama'at was missing from Karachi University for a month. Not a single of them went outside because they knew that we had guns now. It was the first time that we saw so many guns. Then the thinkers, the political people (like him) realized that something is happening. How come they have that much [weapons] and are bringing that much revolvers in Karachi University? Nearly 500 revolvers and Sten guns? What is happening? Everybody realized that things in Karachi were about to change.[14]

The violent legacy of the MQM

It is in this context of gradual militarization of student politics that the future founders of the MQM had their first taste of politics – a bitter experience that left an indelible mark on these political activists and informed their own muscular politics after the launch of the MQM in 1984. The autobiographies of two founding members of the All Pakistan Mohajir Students Organization (APMSO, launched in 1978), and later of the MQM, Altaf Hussain and the late journalist Saleem Shahzad, are particularly revealing in this regard. Both of them emphasize how *Mohajir* student activists were unable to carve a place for themselves on Karachi's campuses after they faced the armed opposition of IJT activists. For Saleem Shahzad, the firepower (*aslahah taqat*) of the IJT could not be matched by the APMSO, making the 'policy of violence' (*tashaddud ki polici*) an unrealistic option for the latter. It carried the risk of having the APMSO expelled from educational institutions by the better armed IJT, whose activists occupied the main mosque at Karachi University and used it to store their weapons.[15] Altaf Hussain also acknowledges that the APMSO could not compete with better armed organizations as it had no weapons at its disposal. This left *Mohajir* activists at the mercy of Thunder Squad militants, who occasionally ransacked their stalls and roughed them up.[16] IJT's opposition to APMSO culminated on 3 February 1981, when Thunder Squad militants assaulted *Mohajir* activists during a convention for newcomers at Karachi University.

Following this incident, the IJT effectively denied entry to APMSO members at Karachi University. The situation had become so critical that on 4 February, Altaf Hussain gathered his companions at a private residence in the *Mohajir*-dominated locality of Federal B Area and announced the suspension of all the activities of the APMSO. Male and female activists were then dispatched to Landhi, Korangi, Malir, Azizabad, and Nazimabad – all neighbourhoods with a large *Mohajir* presence – to publicize the 'Mohajir cause'.[17] The armed opposition of the IJT, therefore, prepared the ground for the transformation of the APMSO into a political party. Yet, the successful transition of Altaf Hussain and his companions from student to party politics would be incomprehensible without bringing the 1985–86 'riots' into the picture. It is in response to these 'ethnic riots' that the MQM imposed itself as the voice and shield of the *Mohajirs*, as attested by the attendance of its first mass gathering at Nishtar Park (August 1986), and a year later, by its first electoral success in local elections. The loss of lives and material destructions brought by the 1985 and 1986 riots gave a new resonance to the ethnic discourse that, a few years earlier, had only brought ridicule to *Mohajir* activists, while the military build-up of their organization gave greater credibility to their offer of protection.

Karachi's ordered disorder

The lasting contribution of conflict and violence to the social and political fabric of Karachi suggests that there could prevail a fragile yet sustainable 'ordered disorder', to use Bertolt Brecht's expression about the 1930s Germany.[18] This violent ordering of Karachi encompasses mechanisms of social control, rituals of political interaction, and patterns of economic accumulation born out of armed conflict and reproducing themselves through it. As in other chronically violent cities such as those of Colombia since the 1980s, it is difficult to disentangle 'political' from 'criminal' violence in such a configuration. The competition over land and *bhatta* (protection money) has been fuelling these conflicts, with an ever-increasing number of protagonists competing over illicit markets (cf. infra). But despite this criminal component, Karachi's unending battles are primarily political – a point consistently emphasized by Pakistani scholars[19], by Pakistan's Human Rights Commission,[20] as well as by the magistrates of Pakistan's Supreme Court.[21]

The crystallization of this peculiar configuration owes much to the politics of the MQM. Since its creation in the mid-1980s, the MQM has been Karachi's dominant political and paramilitary force, pretending to play the democratic game while deploying its violent ways to counter its political rivals and ensure compliance within its own ranks. Recent episodes of ethnic and political violence confirm that the MQM remains a multifaceted organization that, like other hybrid nationalist movements, makes simultaneous use of violence, disruption, and political convention.[22] And although its militants are involved in small-scale turf wars against political rivals or criminal groups, the MQM is not merely fighting for a turf but for control over the local state and its different organs – the city government, the police, the courts, the universities and colleges, and so on. The MQM's involvement in Lyari's (one of the eighteen constituent towns of Karachi) conflicts, for instance, seems to be informed by its hegemonic ambitions, as the party has an eye on the PPP's only secure seat from Karachi in the National Assembly.

Democracy and militancy here go hand in hand: power is derived from the party's electoral results, but these results are conditional on martial strength, which is freely used not only to constrain the choices of voters but also to influence them through certain favours such as jobs, housing, or physical protection against rival armed groups. The violent ordering of Karachi is not merely a matter of coercion, but also of redistribution of power and economic resources. Karachi has its own polity predicated on armed clientelistic structures that legitimate the interactions between every protagonist of the battles over the city and its constituents, with all these rival organizations proposing protection packages, extending from personal safety to economic incentives and opportunities. However, 'ordered' does not necessarily equate with 'orderly' and this configuration has seen some degree of stability for very short periods of time only – namely, from 1999 to 2007, a period which corresponds to the 'guided-democracy' regime of Pervez Musharraf, under which the MQM was authorized by the most powerful of all patrons – the army – to rule uncontested over Karachi. Beyond this short period of time, Karachi has been subjected to frequent outbursts of violence, including bomb attacks, target killings, and ethnic riots that increasingly resemble small-scale civil wars. This synchrony of democracy and militancy comes as a challenge to dominant theories about interconnections between violence and democratization, which suggest that 'struggle both precedes and accompanies democratization',[23] eventually to recede once democracy matures. Such a prediction seems highly unlikely in the case of Karachi, where ordered disorder thrives in a democratic environment that remains fragile, but that allows electoral contests, political change, and a relative autonomy of civilian government, at least as far as domestic politics is concerned. Denying this democratic dimension to Karachi's conflicts would also obviate their mechanisms of containment. Indeed, if explosions of collective violence are frequent in Karachi, they are also limited in time and space. If democratic politics inform these clashes, it also contains them. Between 2008 and 2013, for example the three major protagonists of the city's politics – the MQM, the ANP, and the PPP – were partners in coalition governments at the centre and in Sindh. As a result, none of them could allow levels of violence to escalate to a general conflagration that would have compromised their participation in the government – or risk the dismissal of the government, by the military that continues to exercise control over the country. Thus, if the level of control of these parties over their armed cadres is open to question, one cannot fail to notice that, to date, local clashes have never escalated to a city-wide conflagration. These clashes never last more than three to four days, after which the political leadership intervenes to restrain its militias, while authorizing security forces to deploy themselves in strife-torn localities.

This peculiar mode of government relies upon concealed interactions between 'political entrepreneurs' and 'violent specialists', to use Charles Tilly's terminology.[24] Parallel to official circuits of governance, the 'gray zone' of Karachi's politics runs deep. As Javier Auyero suggests in his study of Argentina's food riots of December 2001, this 'gray zone of politics' is the product of clandestine connections between established political actors and private individuals or organizations involved in criminal activities.[25] In Karachi, this is exemplified by the recent upsurge of target killings orchestrated by rival parties and perpetrated by the local variant of Colombian *sicarios*: young, male, professional killers specializing in pillion-riding drive-by shootings. Other important protagonists of Karachi's 'gray zone of politics' have been the campus *badmashs* (goons) of the late 1970s, who introduced a new, violent style of politics on college campuses, as well as the Baloch *dacoits* (bandits) of Lyari, who have rented their protection to successive generations of politicians, from military rulers such as Ayub Khan in the 1960s to PPP leaders more recently.

However oxymoronic it may seem, the idea of an 'ordered disorder' is helpful to clarify the Karachi conundrum: that of a megalopolis and economic hub confronted with endemic political and criminal violence since the mid-1980s, with no end in sight to this violence, but also with no prospect of a complete breakdown of the economy or the local state machinery. Karachi works, in all the senses of the term, despite this chronic state of violence. Strike calls by political parties and transporters, the routinization of extortion by political activists and security agencies,[26] the rise in 'dacoities' (robberies), as well as the ethnic and political polarization of the bureaucracy has created major hurdles for local entrepreneurs and foreign investors. Thus, the 1990s saw a flight of Karachi's industrial and financial capital to cities such as Lahore, which had the reputation of being safer. More recently, the increase in extortion and the rise in attacks on businessmen (such as on industrialist Kalid Iqbal, who was murdered in broad daylight in August 2011) have further eroded the confidence of the business community. The cost of these disturbances has been increasing over the years and a recent study by the Karachi Chamber of Commerce and Industry put the cost of every new day of strike around $190 million. Assuming that Karachi would register 35 days of strikes on average yearly, the same study then put the yearly cost of these disturbances at $6.7 billion or almost 3 per cent of the national GDP. Even if these figures seem slightly inflated (the yearly number of city-wide strikes is probably closer to 15), there is no doubt that political disturbances have a huge cost for the local economy, but also for that of Pakistan at large. But if political and criminal violence have undoubtedly taken their toll on the city's economy – particularly on the manufacturing sector – they are yet to challenge significantly Karachi's centrality in Pakistan's economy and finance. Economic actors, both local and foreign, have learnt to cope with frequent outbursts of political violence – an indication of the sustainability of Karachi's 'ordered disorder'. In fact, more than these episodic peaks of tension, what truly hinders the operations of economic actors in Karachi is the rapid deregulation of the city's protection rackets that has been associated with the rise of extortion.

But Karachi not only works *despite* violence: its peculiar politics and political economy also work *through* multiple forms of collective violence, which have simultaneously served as an instrument of ethnic consolidation, of territorial control, of economic accumulation, and of political bargaining. In Charles Tilly's terms, collective violence shows a strong 'salience' in Karachi's politics: the infliction of damage, whether actual or potential, dominates these political interactions. This propensity for violence in Karachi's politics is not limited to interactions between political rivals, but can also be found between partners in provincial or central coalition governments, who regularly plan and conduct coordinated attacks against each other. Not all collective violence in Karachi is organized, as the riots following the killing of religious personalities or the rough justice dispensed by lynch mobs against suspected robbers suggest. However, the most lethal episodes of collective violence show a high degree of coordination, whether they take the shape of 'coordinated attacks' against political rivals and their ethnic community, or, in Tilly's term, that of 'broken negotiations'. Karachi's episodic outbursts of violence (*hangamas*) primarily result from such 'broken negotiations', i.e. from the pursuit of political bargaining through coordinated collective violence.[27] The MQM, in particular, has used this form of violent bargaining off and on to extract concessions from its partners in the provincial and federal governments. To take only one recent example, since 1995, Karachi witnessed its worst episode of violence during the summer of 2011, after the MQM withdrew from the coalition government in Sindh. This round of violence was concentrated on the western part of the city in its first phase (June/July) before spreading to its southern neighbourhoods (in August). However, it swiftly receded once the MQM received assurances from its coalition partners and re-joined the government.

Local orders of violence, circumscribed to specific localities, may not be entirely congruent with trends governing the city at large. Local antagonisms and alliances may contradict the 'master cleavage' of the conflict, producing their own ontology of political violence in the process[28]. In the case of Liaquatabad, for instance, Nichola Khan shows that kinship ties often transcend political loyalties and that marriages between families of MQM and Jamaat-e-Islami supporters are not unknown. And while APMSO and IJT militants fought pitched battles on the city's campuses, in Liaquatabad, they were more prone to socialize with each other. This local sociability extended to a number of services that clearly contradicted the 'master cleavage' of the MQM-Jamaat conflict, such as providing information on impending attacks, assistance in weapons procurement, or access to legal aid in case of arrest.[29] In the opposite direction, however, local conflicts may have a spillover effect. This is, for instance, what happened a few years ago, after armed clashes erupted between ANP and Sindhi nationalist activists in the strife-torn locality of Rabia City, in Gulistan-e-Jauhar. A stronghold of the ANP, gunshots rang out in this apartment complex after Sindhi nationalists hosted the flag of their party there in January 2009. Fearing that this was the prelude to an attack on their office in Rabia City apartments, local ANP activists kidnapped and tortured one of their rivals, which led to armed clashes between the two groups, killing three political workers. Subsequently, violence spilled over to other localities of Karachi, such as Shah Faisal Colony and the old vegetable market (Sabzi Mandi).[30]

The changing face of Karachi's 'permanent civil war'

Violence has become an integral feature of Karachi's politics and woven into the social fabric of the city. To argue that social order reproduces itself through violence does not mean that it does so identically, however. As the conflict intensifies, new variables come into play, displacing original motivations and opportunities. In Karachi as elsewhere, this 'metamorphosis of effect into cause'[31] is key to the perpetuation and escalation of collective violence.

As a contested hegemon, the MQM has had to cope with an ever increasing number of competitors, from dissidents (the Haqiqis) from its own ranks to mainstream political parties (the PPP, and, more recently, the ANP) to sectarian groups (Sunni Tehrik, Ahle Sunnat wal Jama'at), to Jihadis (the Tehrik-e-Taliban Pakistan), to more recent militias with links to the underworld (the Peoples Amn Committee of Lyari). Not only are there more actors involved today than in the mid-1980s, but the scope of their activities has widened, from mainstream politics to more dubious practices of wealth accumulation (through extortion and land grabbing, in particular). Even the PPP has recently joined the fray, by using the PAC as its own military wing, while getting involved in land grabbing.[32] The spreading of illicit activities across the political spectrum does not simply amount to a process of criminalization of Karachi's politics, which would translate into, in Tilly's words, atomistic forms of 'opportunistic violence'. The rise in extortion is primarily the result of an economy of scale, as the presence of armed men within political or religious groups makes it possible to apply violence to one context (political strife) and then to another (illicit activities) for a limited additional cost – a phenomenon witnessed in other situations of armed conflict, such as that of Northern Ireland.[33] The motives behind land-grabbing are more complex and cannot be reduced to the logic of economic gain, as *qabza* (capture) also applies to political projects. As a recent report in the *Herald* magazine suggested, 'Land also has a political role to play in a city as polarized as Karachi. Here land means housing, housing means inhabitants, and inhabitants mean potential votes'.[34]

As a result of these developments, Karachi's protection rackets have become increasingly disordered, with an ever-increasing number of racketeers – including bogus ones, posing as collectors for political, religious, or criminal groups – competing with each other, unhindered by mechanisms of cartelization.[35] This deregulation of the business of protection has important consequences for 'customers', as it makes protection more expensive and yet less reliable, effectively turning it into a form of extortion. Wajid Durrani, Sindh's Inspector General of Police (IGP), acknowledged this in front of the Supreme Court in August 2011, when he candidly testified that Karachi residents had no problem with paying *bhatta* (protection money), but that they resented having to pay several protectors, as they have been compelled to do in recent years. The competition over *bhatta* is also making extortion more violent, as demonstrated by the attack on Shershah scrap market in October 2010, in which 15 traders were killed. This problem is becoming increasingly acute, as such competing offers of protection do not only emanate from rival political parties, but also from different officials within the same party: in matters of protection, 'unfair' competition often begins at home.[36] As a Karachi-based builder, who plans to shift his activities to Saudi Arabia in the near future, explained:

- It has become impossible to do business in this city. I work in the construction sector and it's been two years that I cannot conduct any project. The single reason for this is extortion, which has reached unprecedented levels [*inteha par hai*]. I have to spend so much money just to ensure the feasibility of a given project. And *bhatta* has become so sophisticated: instead of being direct, it is now largely indirect. Let me give you an example. The last project I conducted involved the construction of a building to which I decided to add one more floor, which was not included in the original plan [*nakhsa*]. In this case, the normal procedure consists in requesting permission from the relevant government office.... There, they told us, 'You won't get the permission but it's ok, you can go on with your project. We will just ask you to give us two million rupees'.
- At this point, I inquired: Were they affiliated with any political party?
- Yes. [Lowering his voice.] They belonged to the MQM. This department is full of them and we had to pay them. Then we went to the local sector office of the MQM, where the sector-in-charge told us, 'Yes, we will make your project feasible'. For such a 20 million rupees project, they would generally ask for 1 to 3 million rupees. Then, when the project was almost completed, the elder brother of [names a prominent political personality] submitted a petition against the project at the High Court, which argued that this was an illegal construction and that it should be demolished.... He told us that we had to give him three million rupees and that he would withdraw the petition. After much bargaining, he agreed to bring down this sum to 1.5 million rupees.... In order to save us some trouble [*jan churane ke liye*], we gave the money, and within an hour, the petition was withdrawn [laughs].... I invested 20 million rupees in this building and all I earned from this operation was a big headache.... After this, I put all my activities in Karachi on hold. Because in addition to this [the aforementioned practices of extortion], there are also people [party activists] who come to you asking for donations for x, y, z function, and the minimum contribution is 100,000 rupees ... and such functions take place every week...[37]

The same entrepreneur also made it clear that episodic outbursts of violence were less of a hurdle than the increasing cost of protection, as 'riots only last two to three days [and then recede]'. In other words, more than

Karachi's endemic violence, it is the deregulation of its protection rackets which is currently threatening its economy, forcing leading local entrepreneurs to shift their activities to other parts of Pakistan (such as Lahore or Islamabad) or abroad (Dubai, Saudi Arabia, Bangladesh, and so on). While the number of protagonists of Karachi's battles and the scope of their activities expanded, their violence mutated and spread to new areas. The current cycle of violence started in May 2007, when the MQM tried to prevent the Chief Justice of Pakistan's visit to Karachi at a time when he was in open conflict with President Musharraf. The gun battles that ensued between the MQM and the ANP cost the lives of around 50 people and marked the beginning of a bloody conflict between the two parties. It is in this context that target killings resumed in the city, with the MQM bearing the brunt of these attacks. Dead bodies stacked in gunny bags – a practice which the MQM borrowed from the police in the 1990s – also reappeared across the city. As in the past, these corpses would often be tied up and bear torture marks. More often than not – and this is a more recent trend – they would also be beheaded or castrated. These increasingly gory murders seem to be the answer of Karachi's 'violent specialists' to the routinization of violence in the city. As murder alone no longer catches the attention of the public, assassins and their political patrons have shifted to terror tactics to 'tip the scales' – a trend also witnessed in Colombia in the late 1980s.[38] In recent years, the belligerents have had access to increasingly modern weapons, some of which are rumoured to have been hijacked from containers destined for NATO forces in Afghanistan,[39] which is contributing to the escalation of the city's turf wars. The last major round of violence, during the summer of 2011, is a case in point. Even by Karachi standards, the street battles that erupted in the early days of July were of unprecedented intensity. In the worst affected localities, such as Banaras and Qasba Colony, those residents who were not chased away by armed fighters, looters, or arsonists were forced to stay indoors for four consecutive days, often without electricity, food, and water, only to escape through the holes they dug into the walls of their homes so as to find a safe passage to their neighbors'. The escalation of Lyari's gang wars since 2013 provide another illustration of this trend: while rival groups used to battle it out with assault rifles, they are increasingly resorting to RPGs and indigenous rockets (*awans*), with devastating consequences for residents and bystanders. The increasing ruthlessness of the city's armed fighters can also be gauged by the fact that even ambulances are now being targeted, while hospitals are pressured to select patients on the basis of their ethnicity[40], and occasionally turn into battlegrounds, where armed militants do not hesitate to 'finish off' their rivals.[41]

Many of these armed fighters are intermittent combatants, who are only occasionally sent to the frontline. But their ever-increasing firepower, the expertise developed by recruiting more battle-hardened militants ('the shooters', in MQM's parlance), as well as their own experience of combat, partly compensate for this amateurism. Iqbal (not his real name) is one of these Sunday fighters, but otherwise, a regular MQM party worker in one of the party's contested turfs. In recent years, he has been sent to the frontline on several occasions; and while he insists that most temp-warriors like himself turn out to make poor combatants, he also points to the military organization behind these turf wars. When I asked him if any of his companions were ever killed or wounded during these street battles, he recalled the following incident, which took place in August 2011 during clashes with what he identified as 'the drug mafia', with reinforcements from the ANP and a certain 'law and order agency':

> I was using a sniper rifle... I always use a sniper rifle and try to take a position on rooftops... One of our companions – a brave one, very well trained – was carrying a PKM Russian automatic light machinegun. We were accompanied by two Kalashnikov holders, who were giving him covering fire. He was inside the enemy area. Then in one street, one sniper was holding his position and as soon as he put his leg out, he was shot in the leg. It was a sniper rifle, so the bullet passed through his leg. Then we had to recover his automatic weapon so I shot many rounds from the rooftop to provide cover fire [to the rescue team].[42]

Another emerging trend in the city's conflicts is the multiplication of arson attacks against shops and homes. This trend emerged after the attacks on Shia processions in December 2009, which led to a wave of attacks using phosphorus bombs that destroyed one of the city's largest markets. In the meantime, violence has expanded to areas that, until then, had remained relatively safe, such as the old vegetable market of Sabzi Mandi and several localities in the middle-class colony of Gulshan-e-Iqbal. Last, but not least, new turf wars have begun, in which the MQM is only marginally or indirectly involved, through the use of proxies. In New Karachi, for instance, it is primarily two Sunni sectarian groups, the (Deobandi) Sipah-e-Sahaba and the (Barelvi) Sunni Tehrik, which confront each other, while in Lyari, the MQM has been providing support to the recently formed Kutchi Rabita Committee (KRC) against the gangsters of the PAC, who, for their part, have been patronized by PPP leaders such as Zulfiqar Mirza, the rabidly anti-MQM former Home Minister of Sindh.

Conclusion

For the last three decades, Karachi has been subjected to various forms of collective violence. This cycle of violence started on the city's campuses at the end of the 1970s, before escalating in the mid-1980s after criminal groups provoked ethnic riots between Pathans and *Mohajirs*. These riots – which were, in fact, episodes of organized violence patronized by local mafias – infused a sense of insecurity among Urdu-speaking *Mohajirs*, which paved the way for the MQM's rise at the helm of city politics. Once in power, instead of mending its violent ways, the MQM systematized a form of violent government that was meant to ensure its domination of *Mohajirs*, as much as to counter its political rivals. The presence of armed men within its ranks also facilitated the expansion of its use of violence from political control to wealth accumulation, through extortion and land-grabbing in particular.

Although the MQM played a central role in the routinization of violence in Karachi, the city's state of endemic warfare is irreducible to the strategies of local politicians. It originated in rapid changes in the technologies of student warfare (the inflow of firearms in the wake of the Afghan Jihad) and in episodes of collective violence (the ethnic riots of 1985–86) that were beyond the control of these politicians and were initially a source of bewilderment for them. Political entrepreneurs did adjust as best as they could to these changes, but their attempts to ritualize collective violence for political ends and to expand the use of violence from one context (political warfare) to another (capital accumulation) had unanticipated effects. The current deregulation of Karachi's business of protection, which challenges the hegemony of the MQM while threatening the city's economy, is suggestive of such incremental changes, born out of conflict itself. As in Colombia, the situation of 'generalized violence' resulting from the overlapping of multiple forms of organized and random violence has acquired over the years 'its own logic, its own modes of conflict and systems of transaction'.[43] In Karachi, this translated into an 'ordered disorder' structuring the interactions between the ever-increasing number of political, religious, and criminal groups claiming ownership over the city, as well as the relations of these collective actors with the populations they aim to protect, control, and represent. If the MQM played a central role in the advent of this 'ordered disorder', it is no longer in control of it, and its violence is now largely reactive, aiming to counter rivals whose political clout and firepower have dramatically increased over the last few years. At this stage, even if the MQM's leadership decided to give up violence as a political and economic tool, it seems highly improbable that Karachi's armed conflicts would recede. Organized violence has gradually 'democratized', with an ever-increasing number of protagonists competing for control over the city at large or over certain sections of it. The routinization of violence – that is its 'banalization' in the eyes of the city's residents – is as much an outcome as a factor of these transformations: for these populations, political and criminal violence has become part of the natural order of things, however painful this may be. As a result, very few Karachiites still believe in a future of peace, their pessimism hindering the very possibility of non-violent forms of political mobilization and contributing, in turn, to the perpetuation of the city's 'ordered disorder'.

Notes

1 Zeeshan Sahil, 'Ek Din' (Urdu), in *Karachi aur Dusri Nazamen* (Karachi and Other Poems), Karachi: Aaj, 1995, p. 124.
2 Interview with an MQM activist involved in the street battles of 2011, Karachi, December 2011.
3 Interviews with Kati Pahari residents, Karachi, December 2011.
4 These figures are only approximations. The most reliable source is the data compiled by the Citizens Police Liaison Committee (CPLC), on the basis of First Investigation Reports (FIRs) filed in the city's police stations. However, this data has three major shortcomings: it does not cover the early years of these conflicts (as the CPLC was launched in 1990), it does not disaggregate 'political' and 'criminal' murders, and it does not cover deaths which remain unreported by the police.
5 Stanley Tambiah, *Leveling Crowds: Ethnonationalist Conflicts and Collective Violence in South Asia*, Delhi: Vistaar, 1997, p. 193.
6 See, for instance, the recent cover story by *Time* magazine: Andrew Marshall, 'To live and die in Karachi', *Time*, 179, no. 2, 2012: 24–29.
7 Interview, Karachi, December 2011.
8 Names followed by an * have been changed due to security concerns.
9 Interview, Karachi, December 2011.
10 Daniel Pécaut, 'From the Banality of Violence to Real Terror', in Kees Koonings and Dirk Kruijt (eds.), *Societies of Fear: The Legacy of Civil War, Violence and Terror in Latin America*, London/New York: Zed Books, 1999, p. 147.
11 Quoted in 'Lyari strongmen break bread with traders over extortion', *The Tribune*, 2 February 2012,14.
12 Interview, Karachi, July 2009.
13 Nadeem F. Paracha, 'Among equals', *Smokers Corner*, 18 September 2011. http://www.dawn.com/2011/09/18/smokers-corner-among-equals.html.
14 Interview, London, 2009.
15 Saleem Shahzad, *Sha'ur ka Saffar* (Urdu) (A Journey of the Mind), Edgeware: MQM International Secretariat, 2006 [2005].
16 Khalid Athar, *Safar-e-Zindagi: MQM ki Kahani, Altaf Hussain ki Zabani Mein* (Urdu) (The Journey of Life: The Story of MQM in the Words of Altaf Hussain), Karachi: Jang Publishers, 1988, pp. 34, 42.
17 Ibid., p. 85.

18 Quoted in Michael Taussig, 'Terror as Usual: Walter Benjamin's Theory of History as a State of Siege', *Social Text*, 23, Autumn-Winter 1989, p. 7.
19 Haris Gazdar, 'Karachi Battles', *Economic & Political Weekly* (17 September 2011): 19–21.
20 Human Rights Commission of Pakistan, *Karachi: Unholy Alliances for Mayhem*, 2011.
21 Judgment by Iftikhar Muhammad Chaudhry CJ, Suo Moto Case 16 of 2011.
22 Cynthia L. Irvin, *Militant Nationalism: Between Movement and Party in Ireland and the Basque Country*, Minneapolis/London: University of Minnesota Press, 1999, p. 4.
23 Charles Tilly, *The Politics of Collective Violence*, Cambridge: Cambridge University Press, 2003, p. 44.
24 Ibid.
25 Javier Auyero, *Routine Politics and Violence in Argentina: The Gray Zone of State Power*, Cambridge: Cambridge University Press, 2007.
26 Entrepreneurs have to pay between 200 to 50,000 rupees daily to political parties as '*bhatta*' (protection money); this practice routinized under the Chief Ministership of Jam Sadiq Ali (1990–2) and seems to be increasingly deregulated, with petty criminals currently competing with political parties; cf. Moosa Kaleem & Khwaja Akbar, 'That dreaded call for money', *The Herald*, June 2011, pp. 27–29.
27 Tilly, *The Politics of Collective Violence*.
28 Stathis N. Kalyvas, 'The Ontology of "Political Violence": Action and Identity in Civil Wars', *Perspectives on Politics* 1, no 3 (Sep. 2003), pp. 475–494.
29 Nichola Khan, *Mohajir Militancy in Pakistan: Violence and Transformation in the Karachi Conflict*, Milton Park/New York: Routledge, 2010, pp. 131–133.
30 Mansoor Khan, 'Karachi: the fire within', *The Herald* (Karachi), Feb. 2010, 31–32.
31 Fernando Coronil, Julie Skurski, 'Introduction: States of Violence and the Violence of States', in Fernando Coronil, Julie Skurski (eds.), *States of Violence*, Ann Harbor: University of Michigan Press, 2006, p. 2.
32 Khan, 'Karachi: the fire within', 32.
33 Diego Gambetta, *The Sicilian Mafia: The Business of Private Protection*, Harvard: Harvard University Press, 1993, p. 252.
34 Khan, 'Karachi: the Fire Within', p. 33.
35 On the distinction between 'orderly' and 'disordered' markets of protection, see Diego Gambetta, *The Sicilian Mafia*, chaps. 8, 9.
36 Ibid., p. 176.
37 Interview with a Karachi-based builder (name withheld for security reasons), Karachi, December 2011.
38 Pécaut, 'From the Banality of Violence...'.
39 A persisting rumor has been doing the rounds in Karachi in recent years, suggesting that arms containers destined for NATO forces in Afghanistan would have been hijacked by some of the belligerents of Karachi's battles (the MQM in particular, who held the Federal Ministry of Shipping in the government of Yusuf Reza Gilani). It seems rather doubtful that a significant quantity of American weaponry was hijacked at the Karachi port, though, as NATO forces avoid letting lethal weapons transit across the most volatile areas of Pakistan. In

fact, as the interview with a fighter of the MQM quoted above shows, the most recent weaponry acquired by the party seems to be of Russian origin.
40 Human Rights Commission of Pakistan, *Karachi*.
41 Saher Baloch, 'In Karachi, hospitals are as dangerous as its streets', *Dawn.com*, 01 June 2013.
42 Interview with an MQM party worker (name withheld), Karachi, December 2011.
43 Pécaut, 'From the Banality of Violence. . .', 145.

7

MILITARY RULE

Facilitating factors and future prospects

Steven Barracca

As in many developing countries, subordinating the military to civil rule remains a vexing problem in Pakistan. Arguably, this struggle is characterized by the frequency of military coup d'états. Since achieving independence in 1947, Pakistan's army has seized power on three occasions, replacing significant episodes of civilian rule with extended periods of military rule. These coups occurred in 1958, 1977, and 1999. All told, in its 65 years as an independent state, the armed forces have ruled the country directly for over half that time, and it has maintained a tutelary role over civilian regimes since 1988. The most recent instance of the army assuming direct control resulted from the coup of 12 October 1999, when General Pervez Musharraf brought an end to eleven turbulent years of civilian leadership and ushered in a nine-year military interregnum.

To observers less familiar with Pakistan's history, the military's continued dominance over the country's political life might appear somewhat anomalous in light of global trends. For instance, analysts who study civil–military relations in Latin America have heralded the post-Cold War era as a 'post-coup era'. According to this view, the demise of Cold War justifications for reliable anti-communist dictatorships, the growth of global economic integration and norms of democracy, and stronger international regimes to enforce these norms, are all making successful putsches and military regimes less common.[1] This claim is supported by statistics. During the twentieth century, Latin America had 167 successful military coups, with an average of 16 in each decade between 1900 and 1989. In contrast, in the last decade of the century, there were only two instances where civilian rulers were replaced by military regimes through the use or threat of force.[2]

This is not to say that Latin American politics is a sea of tranquillity in the wake of the third wave of democratization. On the contrary, since 1980, there have been over a dozen cases of 'interrupted presidencies', where popularly elected executives were forced from office before the end of their constitutionally mandated term. These episodes occurred against a common political backdrop of economic crisis, social turmoil, and institutional conflict. Moreover, in virtually all cases, the military played a central role in removing the chief executives. However, what is significant about these cases of 'presidential breakdowns' is that in none of the ten countries in which they occurred did the military use the occasion to seize power and establish a military regime. Instead, the generals rapidly turned power over to an interim civilian government until new elections could be held. In short, rather than evidence of the military's continued dominance in Latin American politics, analysts have interpreted these cases as evidence of the military's diminished interest in direct rule and a stronger commitment to preserving the democratic constitutional order.[3]

To this comparison, an objector might reply that Pakistan is not Argentina and South Asia is not Latin America. That is true. Yet, the persistence of praetorianism in Pakistan also stands out when viewed against what might be considered more apt comparisons. Consider the cases of Turkey and Indonesia, two countries that the Pakistani elite have historically looked to as models for how a polity can combine secular or moderate Islamic states with civilian-led 'guided democracy', all under the watchful eye of a strong military.[4] In all three countries, the military has played an extensive role in direct and indirect rule over the past half-century. The three countries also share in common histories of acute ethno-political violence, regional separatist movements, and more recently, Islamic terrorism. Yet, over the past decade, Turkey and Indonesia have made greater progress, subordinating the military to civilian oversight. Since Turkey's Justice and Development Party came to power in 2002, the government of Prime Minister Tayyip Erdogan has shifted the balance of political power away from the armed forces towards elected officials. This is particularly evident since 2007, when the government moved forcefully against a series of alleged coup plots, resulting in the resignations of top commanders and the arrest and trial of some 200 military personnel, including senior officers. While there is debate about whether the government manufactured these conspiracies to undermine the military, the consensus among analysts is that the political power of the Turkish armed forces has diminished as a result.[5]

Tentative progress can also be seen in the case of Indonesia. Over the 32-year dictatorship of President Suharto, the armed forces firmly ensconced themselves in the country's political and business affairs. However, since the transition to electoral democracy in 1999, elected civilians have governed the country without interruption, and observers view the probability of a military coup as extremely remote. Although subordination of Indonesia's military to civilian rule is far from institutionalized, good personal relations between the top brass and two-term President Susilo Yudhoyono, along with the ability of the armed forces to protect its institutional interests from behind the scenes, have worked to limit the army's intervention in politics.[6]

So, where does Pakistan stand in all of this? For reasons I hope to make clear in this chapter, all serious observers of Pakistan expect that the army will continue to play a dominant role in the country's politics for the foreseeable future.[7] In other words, achieving the subordination of the military to civilian rule is not a realistic goal in the intermediate term. However, in light of developments in civil–military relations in other parts of the world, perhaps a more realistic hope is that Pakistan's military will refrain from establishing direct rule, preferring instead to restrict its role to one of indirect influence. Perhaps, like its counterparts in Latin America, Turkey, and Indonesia, the Pakistani military will conclude that, based on past experience, the costs of governing outweigh the benefits. These costs include weakening military readiness by focusing the leadership's attention on domestic political issues and away from its core missions of training and national defence, undermining institutional unity due to the politicization of decision making, exposing the ranks to greater opportunities for corruption, and tarnishing the public image of the armed forces.

To understand what factors might incline Pakistan's military to opt for a behind-the-scenes role over direct rule, two recent cases of failed coups in Latin America are particularly illuminating. These are the military putsches in Ecuador in January 2000 and Venezuela in April 2002.[8] In both episodes, coup coalitions with military support successfully seized power with plans to establish an interim regime of extended duration for the purpose of reorienting the country's political and economic model. Yet, in both cases, the military quickly abandoned those plans and chose instead to restore the constitutional order – within 24 hours in Ecuador and after 48 hours in Venezuela. In contrast, in Pakistan's coup of 1999, the military established itself in power for nearly a decade. What explains these different outcomes? What factors entered into the calculations of the coup plotters and influenced their choices? Moreover, in light of Pakistan's return to electoral democracy in 2008, what are the prospects that the Pakistani military will opt for direct rule again? These are the main questions to be addressed in this chapter.

Factors affecting coup outcome

The literature on coups suggests that three major factors are particularly significant in influencing a military's decision to seize power and consolidate long-term rule. These are popular support and mobilization, cohesion within the armed forces, and pressure from foreign powers.

First is the variable of popular support. Aside from the military itself, mass publics arguably have the greatest potential impact on the success or failure of a coup.[9] If armed insurgencies or mass demonstrations in the form of general strikes, road blockades, and seizures of government buildings and media outlets make governing impossible, the military may not be willing to use the deadly force necessary to end the resistance.[10] Since mass resistance to a coup can greatly increase the costs of governing for the armed forces, it is reasonable to assume that the military considers public opinion and mobilization in both its decision to seize power and whether to hold on to power once it has been seized. These propositions find support in the two South American cases. In Ecuador, opinion polls conducted the week of the coup showed broad support for removing the unpopular president, Jamil Mahuad, but equally strong opposition to military rule. In Venezuela, public support for the coup that removed President Hugo Chávez was divided along class lines, and the military knew that opponents of the coup had a capacity to launch widespread public protests. In both cases, the military factored public opinion into their decisions to restore constitutional order.[11]

Divisions within the military are a second factor with great potential to undermine the consolidation of power in the wake of a coup.[12] The reason for this is straightforward. One of the great advantages the armed forces enjoy in successfully executing a putsch is a monopoly over the legitimate use of force. Even in cases of armed insurgencies, where the military's monopoly of force is contested, the army typically enjoys an edge in terms of weaponry, training, intelligence, and strategy. However, when schisms within the armed forces emerge during or after a coup, these advantages can be lost as one faction of the military faces the prospect of fighting against equally matched fellow soldiers. These divisions can result from many factors, including disagreements over the preservation of the chain of command, changes in the country's economic and political model, the use of lethal force against citizens, and the likelihood and impact of foreign economic sanctions or military intervention.

Again, these factors were significant in the South American cases where the militaries of both countries were divided over the coups. In Ecuador, the putsch was launched by junior officers seeking to establish a more socialist regime along the lines of Hugo Chávez's Venezuela. The more conservative senior officers, who turned against the coup, opposed a radical break from the country's political and economic system and resented that the junior officers had violated the military chain of command. In Venezuela, the armed forces were divided into pro- and anti-Chávez factions. When the best-trained and best-equipped army brigade mobilized to restore Chávez to power, officers who initially supported the putsch decided to withdraw their support from the coup coalition.[13]

The third major factor affecting coup outcomes is the threat of international retaliation. An important reason cited for the decrease in the number of successful military coups in the developing world in the post-Cold War era is greater pressure from major Western powers for countries to democratize and stay democratic. However, the effectiveness of foreign pressure depends on two factors. The first is leverage, which varies depending upon the degree to which a country is linked to states and multilateral institutions that are committed to supporting democratic governments. These linkages take many forms, including cultural ties, economic integration, and military and political alliances.[14] However, for power to be effective, it must be accompanied by a second factor, a willingness to use it, which is something that cannot be taken for granted. Realist approaches to international relations argue that normative commitments, like multilateral agreements to defend democracy, are likely to be trumped by the material and security interests of individual states.[15]

Once again, this factor played an important role in determining coup outcomes in the South American cases. In Ecuador, the Clinton administration determined that it did not have any overriding national security interest in the outcome of the coup. So, it chose to cooperate with the multilateral effort of the Organization of American States (OAS) to oppose the putsch and defend democracy. Meetings between American diplomats and the military, in which the US threatened economic sanctions, were particularly important in turning the military high command against the coup. In the case of Venezuela, the regional response was more divided. The OAS denounced the coup, but the Bush administration tacitly supported it because Chávez was viewed by Washington as the chief opponent of US interests in Latin America. Yet, in the end, the Bush administration chose not to actively participate in orchestrating or defending the coup due to higher geostrategic priorities. Specifically, Washington did not want to damage its relations with countries in the region at a time when it was seeking allies for the recently launched War on Terror.[16]

This examination of recent coups in Ecuador and Venezuela demonstrates that armed forces are less likely to opt for direct rule when there is strong public or international opposition and when the military is internally divided. If the converse holds, this would mean that the intervention of the armed forces in removing civilian politicians would be more likely to result in extended periods of military rule when public resistance is weak, the military is united in the cause, and foreign powers lack the capacity or willingness to oppose the move. The following sections demonstrate that these factors have facilitated Pakistan's three coups. The analysis also situates those events within the boarder historical context of civil–military relations in Pakistan.

Pakistan's founding and the strategy of state-building

The prominent role of Pakistan's army in politics has deep historical roots in the country's founding. When the fledgling nation emerged from the Partition of India, it confronted serious internal and external obstacles to state-building, and the military came to be viewed as the only institution capable of handling these perceived existential threats.[17] The numerous internal challenges included a weak economy, grappling with six to eight million refugees, and dealing with the unprecedented administrative challenge of governing a country divided into two wings (East and West Pakistan), separated by 1,000 miles of hostile Indian territory.

But the paramount internal obstacle to state-building was the lack of elite consensus about the nature of the Pakistani state. Particularly divisive were issues of regional autonomy, the economic and political model, and the role of Islam. Having enjoyed histories with varying degrees of political independence, three of the country's major ethnic groups – the Balochis, Sindhis, and Pathans – were either opposed or weakly committed to the idea of a united Pakistan. This left the Punjabis and *Mohajirs* to provide the political energy for state-building, an effort that has yet to fully succeed. Over the years and continuing into the present, regionalism gave rise to periodic armed insurgencies in Baluchistan, Sindh, and the Northwest Frontier Province (re-named Khyber Pakhtunkhwa in the Eighteenth Amendment to the Constitution approved by the Pakistani Senate by a unanimous 90 votes on 15 April 2010) aimed at outright independence, greater autonomy, or simply, a greater share of the state's resources. In all cases, the army has been called upon to suppress the ethno-regional uprisings in order to maintain order and hold the state together.

Elite divisions extended to other fundamental questions of domestic politics as well. As Cohen summarizes it, 'In West Pakistan, the newly arrived Mohajirs favored a more or less secular state, laissez-faire economy and liberal politics. By contrast, Muslim Leaguers from the NWFP, Punjab, Baluchistan, and Sindh tended to favor Islamization, a state-managed economy and a go-slow policy toward land reform'.[18]

In the country's first attempt at civilian rule between 1947 and 1958, these divisions produced a highly factious and dysfunctional politics. Few politicians could see past their provincial interests or personal ambitions to work towards a broader conception of the public good. Attempts at democratic governance were further frustrated by the untimely death of the country's founder, Muhammad Ali Jinnah, and also by a lack of strong political parties. The Muslim League, the primary institutional expression of the independence movement, lacked roots in West Pakistan. The parties that did exist were regional, personality-driven, and clientelistic, devoid of the attributes necessary for constructing broad programmatic legislative coalitions, based on popular consent. This helps explain why in its first seven years of independence, Pakistan had eight prime ministers and why it took the country nine years to adopt a constitution.

In addition to internal challenges, Pakistan faced external threats from its inception. To the west was Afghanistan, which voted against Pakistan's inclusion in the United Nations at the time of independence. The source of bilateral tension was the Afghan government's rejection of the Durand line as the boundary between the two countries. This artificial border, established by a 1893 treaty, divided Baloch and Pathan tribes, and to varying degrees over time, Afghan governments gave verbal and material support to irredentist movements that challenged the territorial integrity of Pakistan. To this day, the writ of Pakistan's central government does not extend into the Federally Administered Tribal Areas (FATA) on the country's north western frontier with Afghanistan. This has allowed the region to serve as a sanctuary for an assortment of militant and terrorist groups, including al-Qaeda and the Afghan and Pakistan Taliban.

To the east was India, which Pakistan came to define as its chief nemesis. At the time of Partition, centuries-old tensions between Muslims and Hindus, accentuated by the British Raj, were inflamed by ethnic violence perpetrated by both sides. But from Pakistan's perspective, a particularly bitter pill was India's lack of adherence to the terms of Partition with respect to the division of assets of the former colony, India's alleged collusion with the British to manipulate the territorial boundary between the two states, and New Delhi's efforts to get princely states to accede to India.[19] Falling into this last category was the dispute over Jammu and Kashmir, which has been the major ongoing source of conflict between the two states. Motivated by the belief that this Muslim-majority territory ought to be united with a Muslim state, Pakistan has initiated three wars against India (1947, 1965, and 1999), and has maintained a low-grade insurgency in Kashmir since 1989.

Faced with these internal and external threats, Pakistan's early political leadership gradually coalesced around a strategy of nation-building based on what Haqqani calls the 'policy tripod'.[20] First, officials sought to foster a national Islamic identity to serve as the glue uniting a population divided by language, ethnicity, and divergent political and economic interests. Second, India was portrayed as an implacable enemy of Pakistan, a conflict rooted in what state propaganda depicted as the Hindu's nearly 'pathological' hatred of Muslims, and the desire of India's leadership to see Pakistan dismembered or weakened.[21] Third, to counter the threat from India, the militarily and economically weak Pakistan sought foreign alliances with the West in order to procure weapons and development assistance. From the very start, the United States was deemed the most suitable great-power patron and by the mid-1950s, the US was providing weaponry and economic support in exchange for Pakistan's participation in the Central Treaty Organization (CENTO) and the Southeast Asia Treaty Organization (SEATO), two military alliances formed to serve as bulwarks against Soviet expansion.

The principal mechanism for implementing the policy tripod is what Haqqani calls 'the mosque-military alliance'.[22] This refers to a partnership formed over the years, in which military rulers use religious parties and groups as instruments for achieving domestic and foreign policy aims in exchange for the country's deepening Islamization. Often serving as the nexus in this alliance is Pakistan's intelligence agencies, the most important of which are Military Intelligence (MI), focused on defence matters, the Intelligence Bureau (IB), concentrating on domestic political activities, and most notably, the Inter-Services Intelligence (ISI), which provides foreign intelligence and overall coordination. In terms of the *modus operandi* of this alliance, four tactics have been the most common. First, the MI and IB have assisted in the organization and funding of Islamic political parties – such as the Jamaat-e-Islami (JI) – in order to fragment the parliament and destabilize civilian governments. Second, the intelligence agencies have mobilized religious groups in street protests in order to put pressure on and undermine civilian governments. Third, the ISI has provided organizational, operational, and financial assistance to jihadi groups operating in Kashmir (since the 1960s) and in Afghanistan (since the 1970s). Fourth, the military uses its ties with Muslim clerics and educators to propagate the state ideology of Islamic nationalism and hostility towards India. This includes persuading clerics to issue fatwas in support of government policies, including foreign jihads and opposition to political parties, especially those of the secular left.

While the mosque–military alliance has served certain interests of its members, Haqqani argues that it has given rise to 'three interlinked problems that have dogged Pakistan's internal politics over the past fifty years: part of the state apparatus used religion and religious groups for a political purpose. The extent of the religious groups' influence and the sentiment unleashed by them could not be controlled. And the military stepped in to deal with the symptoms of the chaos generated by the religious-political agitation, without any effort to deal with its causes'.[23] An early glimpse of the negative ramifications of the policy tripod came into view under Pakistan's first military regime that seized power in 1958. Under the leadership of General Muhammad Ayub Khan, the government established an alliance with the United States to spur Pakistan's economic and military development, which, in turn, emboldened the government to launch a costly war in Kashmir in 1965.

The 1958 coup

By the late 1950s, there was a widespread loss of public confidence in Pakistan's civilian rulers. Coming after a decade of chronic political instability, the year 1958 found the country in the midst of a deep economic crisis, the army was fighting ethnic separatists in Baluchistan, and East Pakistan appeared ungovernable as its regional government witnessed the downfall of four ministries within six months. When a political brawl in East Pakistan's provincial assembly resulted in the death of the deputy speaker, this provided the pretext for the county's first military coup. It began with the country's President Iskander Mirza declaring martial law on 6 October. While Mirza intended to keep hold of the reins of power, he was outmanoeuvred by the Chief of Army Staff (COAS) Ayub Khan, who forced Mirza's resignation and took power himself on 27 October. The putsch ushered in a decade of reform aimed at economic development and the establishment of what General Ayub Khan called a guided-democracy under the supervision of the military – a contradiction in purpose, if ever there was one. Viewing the country's civilian politicians as incompetent and a threat to national security, Ayub constructed an oligarchic regime based on the tripartite alliance of the country's military commanders, civil service elites, and feudal landowners. With the subsequent addition of an industrial elite – often linked to the feudals – this establishment has ruled Pakistan to the present day, whether the regime had a civilian or a military face.[24]

Looking at the factors that facilitate the consolidation of military rule, all three were in place for the 1958 coup. First, the putsch was greeted with broad support from a public that was tired of fleckless politicians. This included the civil service, which seemed eager to work with a military regime that would free its technocrats from having to engage in endless political wrangling with local power brokers to get things done.[25] It also included the judiciary, which was quick to give legal cover to the coup, based on the Doctrine of Necessity, the juridical precept that 'that which otherwise is not lawful, necessity makes lawful', and that the public welfare and the safety of the state is the supreme law.[26] These same legal grounds were used by the Supreme Court to justify coups in 1977 and 1999. The army's transition to power was also assisted by cohesion within the military. Ayub Khan, who had been COAS since 1951, was well-respected throughout the officer corps, and he used his seven years in the post to surround himself with loyalists who all agreed that Pakistan was not ready for democracy.

The coup also received support from the two foreign powers that had the most leverage over Pakistan: Britain, and, especially, the United States. Mirza and Ayub had been contemplating the coup for some time, and they confided in British and US diplomats about the plans in order to gauge foreign reaction. In President Mirza's conversations with the British High Commissioner, the diplomat made no effort to change the president's mind. He only encouraged him to declare his peaceful intentions towards India, a recommendation that Mirza ignored.[27] Clearly, the British were more preoccupied with preserving peaceful relations between their former colonies than they were in the maintenance of democracy in Pakistan.

As for the Americans, General Ayub indicated to the US Ambassador to Pakistan, James Langley, that 'only dictatorship will work in Pakistan'. In response, Secretary of State John Foster Dulles asked Langley to convey to Ayub and Mirza that 'the U.S. favored democratic government over authoritarian government, [but that] there may be certain exceptions that can be justified for limited periods'.[28] As Nawaz suggests, the coup plotters interpreted this as a green light from the US – a green light that was not to be the last. Indeed, the 1958 coup made clear what would become the ongoing US agenda for the country: 'a pro-Western Pakistan, a stable Pakistan, a prosperous Pakistan, and a democratic Pakistan were all desirable, but in that order'.[29] Based on this logic, Dulles saw Ayub as a stable link in his chain of containment on the Soviet's southern flank, and the preservation of a flawed democracy was a lesser priority.

During Ayub's decade in power, there were a number of significant developments that would have long-term effects on civil–military relations. First, Ayub centralized control over the media and the school curriculum. This enabled his regime and subsequent governments to more effectively inculcate the population with the state ideology, based on Islamic nationalism and confrontation with India. Second, contrary to the commonly held view that Ayub was a secularist, the president actually sought to use a basic, non-sectarian Islam as an ideological tool for state-building and advancing national security.[30] While Ayub banned Islamist groups and parties that criticized his regime, these years saw members of the military and civil service cultivating closer relations with religious scholars – a trend that would grow in the future.[31] A third important development was that, in the early 1960s, Pakistani military strategists began seriously formulating a doctrine of irregular warfare as a tool in the country's defence.[32]

This strategy for low-intensity warfare was soon employed offensively in August 1965, when Pakistan's army sent infiltrators into Kashmir, hoping to ignite a wider uprising. Just as in the first Indo-Pakistan War in 1947, 'Religious symbols and calls to jihad were used to build the morale of soldiers and the people', linking Pakistan's military closer to its Islamist ideology.[33] In the end, the war ended in a stalemate, just as the first war had, but not without some lasting damage to US–Pakistan relations. With the US cutting off arms to both states involved in the conflict, Pakistan's civilian and military rulers now viewed the US as an untrustworthy ally, and one that they were justified in deceiving to further their own national interest. Thus, Zulifikar Ali Bhutto, Ayub's foreign minister, initiated discussions with China for a strategic alliance against their common enemy, India.

The 1977 coup

By the late-1960s, a stagnant economy and the lack of democratic freedoms were fomenting a growing opposition to the Ayub Khan regime. Based on an economic report suggesting that 22 leading families in the country controlled most of the country's private industrial and financial assets, more and more people were expressing dissatisfaction with the lack of trickle-down growth under Ayub's economic model. Left-wing opponents of the regime found a home in the Pakistan People's Party (PPP). Established in 1967, the party was founded by Bhutto, the former foreign minister in Ayub's cabinet. Bhutto had distanced himself from the regime after the unpopular Tashkent Accords were signed in 1966, bringing the Second Kashmir War to a settlement that neither side found satisfactory. Emphasizing populist themes about inequality of wealth and the need for income redistribution, Bhutto began to mount a challenge to Ayub from the left.

In March 1969, shortly after President Ayub Khan became incapacitated from a heart attack, COAS Agha Yahya Khan seized power in a palace coup and declared martial law. In public, the military committed to return the country to democracy by holding free and fair elections in December 1970. However, behind the scenes, the military–intelligence complex schemed to promote the electoral prospects of religious parties in order to prevent a decisive victory by the two major parties, the PPP in West Pakistan and the Awami League in East Pakistan. The Awami League had successfully galvanized support in the east wing by tapping into Bengali resentments over cultural discrimination and the fact that the province was not receiving its fair share of the country's political power and economic benefits, even though it contained slightly over half of Pakistan's population. Help for the Islamists came from the IB, which gave organizational and financial assistance to the Jamaat-e-Islami, Jamaat Ulema Islam, and Jamaat Ulema Pakistan. The IB also persuaded clerics to issue a fatwa 'declaring secularism and socialism as *kufr* (disbelief)', an edict clearly intended to undermine support for the socialist PPP and the secular Awami League.[34]

Despite the government's efforts to splinter the vote, the efforts were not enough to prevent strong showings for the major parties. The PPP won a solid plurality of the vote in the west wing, and the Awami League won by a landslide in the east, giving it a legitimate claim to lead the new government. However, Bhutto and the military refused to accept a government controlled by Bengalis. This led to a prolonged political standoff, which ultimately precipitated civil war in East Pakistan, military intervention by India, and the independence of the east wing (Bangladesh) in December 1971.

After Pakistan's humiliating defeat, the military forced Yahya Khan to resign. In order to rebuild the shattered country and restore the army's tattered image, the military transferred power to Bhutto, the only civilian politician deemed to have sufficient national prestige to move the country forward. From the perspective of civil–military relations, the Bhutto years were significant for a number of reasons. First, the prime minister cultivated relations with China, Europe, Saudi Arabia, and the Gulf states in order to procure military and economic aid. This effort to diversify alliances had the objective of decreasing dependence on the United States, which had come to be viewed as an unreliable partner after Washington's refusals to side more firmly with Pakistan in its wars against India.

Second, Bhutto initiated a nuclear weapons programme in 1972 in order to maintain parity with India, which was soon to test its own bomb. Bhutto's quest to go nuclear also served the prime minister's aim of weakening the military by decreasing its conventional forces while still maintaining an army strong enough to counter the perceived Indian threat. Ironically, after Bhutto was deposed in a coup, the military would take control over the nuclear weapons programme, thus enhancing its power vis-à-vis civilian politicians and increasing its leverage with the United States. Third, through the ISI, Bhutto began supporting Islamist militias in Afghanistan to counter the growing Soviet influence in that country. Here, Bhutto was perusing the longstanding ambition of Pakistani military strategist to establish a sphere of influence in Afghanistan in order to give Pakistan 'strategic depth' in case of full-scale war with India.[35] Bhutto rose to political prominence with the backing of students, factory workers, sharecroppers, and the intelligencia. Indeed, he 'could legitimately claim that he had come to power with the largest support base' of any leaders since Jinnah in 1947.[36] Yet, over the course of six years, he lost the support of many, and eventually, was removed in a coup on 5 July 1977, led by COAS Mohammad Zia ul-Haq. The trigger for the putsch was popular unrest, resulting from the government's use of fraud to pad the PPP's victory in the national elections of March 1977. As in 1958, the military's ability to consolidate power after seizing it was facilitated by popular support, military cohesion, and acceptance by foreign powers.

How did the popular Bhutto manage to antagonize so many in such a short period of time? First, in 1972, he earned the ire of the nation's large business owners when he nationalized 31 large businesses encompassing ten major sectors of the economy, including basic metals, electrical equipment, chemicals, natural gas, shipping, and banking. This, along with union unrest, resulted in declining private investment and fewer job opportunities for the urban middle class. In 1976, Bhutto further angered agricultural interests that were already concerned about land reforms, when he nationalized cotton, rice, and flour mills.

In addition to business, Bhutto antagonized bureaucrats and the political elite. As in India, Pakistan's civil service was viewed as one of the country's better functioning institutions. Yet, to get around entrenched interests, the prime minister 'eliminated the civil service and replaced it with a District Management Group, weakening the 200-year-old civil service tradition'.[37] As for politicians, Bhutto made the political error of alienating the leaders and activists of his own party by establishing alliances with the country's industrial and landed elite. He also earned the enmity of the opposition parties when he created the Federal Security Force (FSF) to maintain domestic order. While the original goal in creating the FSF was to minimize the role of the military by keeping it out of domestic security affairs, the agency was ultimately used to seize private property of regime opponents, spy on the opposition, and intimidate members of the media. It was even linked with a series of political murders, one of which Zia would use to convict and execute Bhutto in 1979.[38]

Finally, the prime minister was opposed by the more politically active religious groups in society. Among these was the Jamaat-e-Islami (JI), which was putting pressure on Bhutto for a more Islamic system of government. The JI was also critical of the Prime Minister for his lack or personal piety, which they saw as damaging the state's Islamic ideology.[39] With the encouragement of the intelligence agencies, these grievances led the JI to take a leading role in organizing the street protests in Lahore that eventually gave the army justification for seizing power. While Bhutto did retain support among the peasantry, especially in his home province of Sindh, strong patron–client relations kept the rural masses from mobilizing. It is likely that regional power brokers in the countryside did not organize protests based on Zia's promise to hold fresh elections within ninety days.[40] And by the time it was clear that Zia had no intention of keeping to this schedule or of relinquishing power, there was less motivation to protest what had become a *fait accompli*.

There were also no visible signs of factionalism within the military over the decision to remove Bhutto. This consensus was the result of the military's fear that efforts to suppress the electoral protests could undermine the institutional cohesion of the army. Some 200 people were killed in clashes between protestors and security forces in the three months preceding the coup, and Bhutto had to ask for the military's help in quelling the protests. When officers began disobeying orders to shoot demonstrators, the military commanders were concerned that a prolonged exposure of the troops to agitation might erode military discipline.[41] And while there was likely some reluctance among the army's core commanders to assume direct rule, these concerns would have been alleviated by Zia's promise to hold fresh elections in three months.

A final factor that facilitated the military's consolidation of power was the lack of retaliation by foreign powers. Two of Pakistan's most important allies, China and Saudi Arabia, were no threat to intervene based on those states' longstanding policies of non-interference in the domestic politics of other countries. In the US, Jimmy Carter, who had become president only months before, was not strongly committed to helping Bhutto. In general, the prime minister's anti-American rhetoric, confrontational approach with India, and efforts to develop ties with communist countries, did not earn him much affection in Washington. Moreover, given that Carter had made nuclear non-proliferation a major focus of his foreign policy, his administration had even less reason to support the man who was bent on developing the 'Islamic bomb'.[42]

The watershed Zia years

While Zia spoke of his desire for a quick return to electoral democracy, he reneged on those promises and retained power until his death in a suspicious plane crash in August 1988. Presiding over Pakistan's longest period of military rule, 'Zia went farthest in defining Pakistan as an Islamic state, and he nurtured the jihadist ideology that now threatens to destabilize much of the Islamic world'.[43] More specifically, Zia's regime had a major and lasting impact on civil–military relations in four broad areas.

First, based on a sincere belief that Islamic revival would provide the cure for the country's many social and political ills, he set out to deepen the country's Islamization – something that had only been pursued half-heartedly and opportunistically by previous governments. This programme sought to introduce changes to many spheres of society. In the armed forces, religious education was introduced into military training. In the judicial system, a parallel system of Sharia courts was established, along with greater efforts to adopt Sharia law. In the government and bureaucracy, more positions were assigned to religious leaders and members of religious groups. The educational system and the media underwent purges of secularist producers, journalists, and professors, who were replaced by those holding fundamentalist religious views. Zia's government also funded and promoted a host of Islamic groups, including the JI and the Tableegi Jamaat. The total effect of this programme was to embolden Islamists and increase intolerance for those that challenged the state ideology. Not only were Christians a target, but also Shia and Sufi Muslims, who increasingly became the victims of sectarian violence. Also coming under greater threat were the country's secular liberal elite, limiting space for that ideological alternative.

A second important consequence of the Zia years was the government's accelerated efforts to acquire nuclear weapons. While Zia did not live to see it, Pakistan acquired a deployable nuclear weapon by the early 1990s, and since then, has produced an estimated 100 bombs. Among the many important implications of this development, two stand out. First, not only does Pakistan see nuclear weapons as a way to counteract India's dominance in conventional forces, but obtaining these weapons was part of a strategy to give cover to low-intensity jihadi groups, including those operating inside Kashmir, and Sikh terrorists operating inside India. This, in turn, allows Pakistan to put pressure on governments such as those of India and Afghanistan to negotiate without provoking full-scale conflict.[44] Second, acquiring nuclear weapons made Pakistan a more important geostrategic concern for the United States, which has long made nuclear non-proliferation a top policy priority, but especially so in an age of Islamic terrorism. By joining the 'nuclear club', Pakistan was able to garner more attention from Washington and increase its leverage in bilateral relations.

A third impact of the Zia years are the long-term consequences of Pakistan serving as the staging ground for the anti-Soviet war in Afghanistan. After Soviet troops rolled through the Hindu Kush in 1979, Pakistan became a magnet for *mujahideen* and jihadi groups from throughout the

Middle East, Central Asia, and North Africa. These forces were eagerly funded and supplied by Saudi Arabia, the Gulf states, and the United States, the later channelling some $2 billion into the war between 1979 and 1988. Among the many consequences of the war, the most troublesome was that it deepened the alliance between Islamists and Pakistan's military–intelligence complex. During the 1980s, the ISI grew in power and significance as it served the major role in organizing and funding various militias fighting against the Soviets. The ISI continues to perform this role today. Recent US National Intelligence Estimates indicate that the ISI provides intelligence and financial support to the Afghan Taliban, including the Haqqani network operating out of North Waziristan. Haqqani's militia is actively involved in attacking NATO troops in Afghanistan, and was responsible for attacks on the American embassy and NATO headquarters in Kabul on 13 September 2011. The ISI also gives cover to Lashkar-e-Taiba, which conducted the terror attacks on Mumbai in 2008, which killed 200 people.[45]

Finally, the covert support of Pakistan's intelligence services for Islamist militants has worsened the security situation inside Pakistan over the past twenty years. Both Pakistan and the United States have learned the hard way that nurturing jihadi fighters is a dangerous game because those furies are hard to control. The lawless environment in Pakistan's tribal regions that made it such an effective recruiting and training ground for the Afghan Taliban and al-Qaeda has, in recent years, spawned militants that are seeking to overthrow the Pakistani state. Chief among these is the Tehrik-i-Taliban-Pakistan (TTP). Also known as the Pakistan Taliban, the TTP is an umbrella group formed in 2007 to coordinate various militant factions operating in the north western tribal areas.

It was an affiliate of the TTP that shocked Pakistan in 2009, when militants took over the Swat Valley. In military operations to retake the area, and in other operations against the Pakistan Taliban in the FATA, Pakistan's army has suffered significant losses. The military reports that since 2001, it has lost 3,000 men and suffered 13,000 casualties. This does not include the estimated 19,000 Pakistani citizens that have lost their lives since 2003 in terrorist attacks. Beyond the grave human cost, the deteriorating security situation in Pakistan is significant for its impact on civil–military relations because the army uses the precarious security state at home and in neighbouring Afghanistan to justify its continuing heavy hand in politics.

Yet, even before Pakistan's stability began to erode after 9/11, the military did not trust elected officials to handle the country's domestic security and foreign policy. This was evident between 1988 and 1999, when

Pakistan returned to nominal civilian rule, but the military played the role of king-maker. During this ten-year interlude of electoral democracy, Benazir Bhutto and Nawaz Sharif alternated in the office of prime minister, each serving for two terms that were cut short by the army's meddling. Although the prime ministers had the constitutional authority to determine foreign policy, the military continued to call the shots over affairs with India and Afghanistan. This is why Prime Minister Bhutto, who was interested in improving relations with India, succumbed to pressure from the army chiefs to continue covert support of militants in Kashmir. The civilian governments during this period also continued to support the Taliban in Afghanistan.

The 1999 coup

Despite its ability to determine foreign policy from behind the scenes, the military eventually grew tired of indirect rule and launched its most recent coup on 12 October 1999. This putsch ousted the elected Prime Minister Nawaz Sharif and replaced him with the COAS, General Pervez Musharraf. While the trigger for the coup was Sharif's dismissal of Musharraf, it was the accumulation of political, economic, and military crises that created the context in which the military intervention would receive broad support. On the political front, the coup was motivated by Sharif's attempts to centralize political power in his hands, undermine democratic checks and balances, and harass critics of his regime. The prime minister also presided over a declining economy. In 1998, Pakistan was on the brink of defaulting on its international debt. While good relations with the IMF and international investors were requisite for economic recovery, Sharif inopportunely picked a fight with these institutions over electricity power projects, destroying the confidence of foreign investors. The resulting economic downturn, along with escalating sectarian strife, lawlessness, and government corruption fuelled regular anti-government demonstrations in the months before the coup.

Another significant factor setting the stage for the coup was Sharif's tense relations with the military over the Kargil War fiasco. In May 1999, the prime minister authorized an army plan to activate paramilitary and regular army forces in an offensive in Kashmir. The military initially viewed the operation as a success after Pakistani forces captured the strategic heights in the Kargil district. However, by July, the success of the Indian counter-offensive and pressure from the Clinton administration led Prime Minister Sharif to call for a withdrawal of forces. In the wake of the conflict, in which an estimated 4,000 Pakistanis died, Sharif disavowed his support for the operation and blamed Musharraf and the generals for the humiliating defeat. From the perspective of the military, Sharif was damaging the public reputation of the military, destroying the country's fragile democratic institutions and mishandling the economy. Not surprisingly, rumours of a putsch were circulating widely at the time of the coup.[46]

Public support for the coup made it easier for Musharraf to consolidate military governance. News accounts of the putsch uniformly describe the action as receiving overwhelming public support.[47] This was a response to Sharif's corruption and authoritarianism, his mishandling of the economy and the Kargil conflict, and a growing sense of lawlessness in the country. Moreover, as Sharif's tenure was marked by a repression of critics in civil and political society, the coup was welcomed by leaders from across the political spectrum.[48] Indicative of the depth of public disgust with Sharif, not a single member of his own political party, the Pakistan Muslim League (PML-N), condemned the putsch or spoke in defence of the prime minister.

To be sure, democracy activists in political and civil society spoke out for the need to restore civilian rule quickly; however, Musharraf likely understood that the broader public did not share this sense of urgency – at least, not initially. The public's willingness to give military rule another try was a by-product of widespread disillusionment with the previous eleven-year period of democratic rule in which power oscillated between the PPP and PML-N, and the only constants were gross mismanagement, corruption, and ruling party efforts to persecute the opposition.

There was also a high degree of consensus among the army's corps commanders for the coup and the need for a longer period of military rule.[49] This unity can be explained by a number of factors. Aside from a shared belief among the generals that Sharif was destroying the country's democratic institutions and economy, they also drew together because of the damage the prime minister was inflicting on the military institution itself. Specifically, Sharif was perceived to be politicizing and dividing the military high command through controversial firings and appointments.[50] He also created a rift within the military by attempting to emasculate the ISI. A second factor that soured relations between the prime minister and the armed forces was the debacle over the Kargil conflict and making the military the scapegoat for this failed offensive.

Yet, the greatest point of consensus among the corps commanders was their opposition efforts to remove Musharraf from his position as Chief of Army Staff. By August of 1999, rumours had been swirling among the military brass that the prime minister was thinking of replacing Musharraf. However, the nine corps commanders met on 18 September and agreed to a contingency plan that would block these attempts.[51] When the prime minister did sack Musharraf less than a month later, the military knew what to do. When word got out that Sharif was not allowing Musharraf's plane to land in Pakistan as he was returning from a meeting in Sri Lanka, the army worked in unison to execute a textbook coup. Moreover, when Sharif attempted to replace Musharraf with a crony, four-star General Ziauddin Khawaja Butt, not a single senior officer was willing to accept his command.[52]

The case of the 1999 coup also confirms the importance of foreign powers in influencing coup outcomes. Western countries denounced the coup and had significant leverage over Pakistan.[53] Most significantly, Pakistan had a foreign debt of more than $30 billion and rapidly diminishing foreign currency reserves. The country's economic recovery was dependent on the IMF releasing a $280 million tranche of a $1.6 billion aid package, and the US and EU had influence over this decision. However, for two main geostrategic reasons, the Western powers were not willing to use this leverage. First, in May 1998, Pakistan tested five nuclear bombs, removing any doubt among Western powers as to whether Pakistan had become a nuclear state. This development, along with the fact that Pakistan contained a domestic hardline Islamist movement, left the West very concerned that this nuclear capability might fall into the wrong hands. Accordingly, it adopted a position of guarded tolerance towards Musharraf, viewing the 'Liberal Autocrat' as the best means for preventing nuclear technology from falling into the wrong hands.[54]

A second reason Western powers chose not to exercise their leverage was the Sharif government's support for the Taliban regime in neighbouring Afghanistan, which had granted al-Qaeda a safe haven, from which it carried out the twin bombings on US embassies in East Africa in August 1998.[55] The United States and EU viewed the Musharraf coup as an opportunity to reorient Pakistan's relations with Afghanistan so that they were more in line with the West's security interests. So, while the West had leverage to oppose the coup, it lacked the will to take anything but symbolic measures of opposition. This was the same logic that led the US to give tacit approval to Pakistan's previous coups in 1958 and 1977.

Future prospects

In the period following Musharraf's eight-year rule, there have been some hopeful signs for Pakistan's democracy. In 2008, the country returned to electoral democracy with the election of a PPP government and its leader, Asif Ali Zardari, as president. Although his administration struggled under the weight of devastating floods, energy shortages, and insurgent violence, there were notable accomplishments. In 2010, Zardari signed the 18th Amendment to the Constitution, which returned the country to a parliamentary system and ended the president's ability to appoint heads of the military, select the prime minister, and dissolve the National Assembly. This change was viewed as a significant advance in civil–military relations because it rendered void previous legal provisions that enabled the military to function as king maker by pressuring presidents to dissolve and appoint governments. Also not to be overlooked, the Zardari administration became the first civilian government to complete its full term in office and hand over power to another democratically elected government in the most recent national elections in May 2013. This contest returned Nawaz Sharif to the premiership for the third time, with the PML-N gaining a solid majority of seats in the legislature.

These developments naturally give rise to speculation as to whether Pakistan has turned a corner in breaking out of what observers describe as 'the vicious circle'.[56] This is the historical pattern in which ineffective and unstable civilian government provokes reformist military rule, which further stunts the development of civilian democratic institutions and values, thus creating justification for more military intervention. While the assessments of experts vary in detail, there is consensus that disrupting this cycle won't be easy. Long-term success will require that the political elite pursue a broad array of measures to build the country's democratic institutions and culture.

Recent scholarship has endeavoured to evaluate the country's progress since 2008 across a broad spectrum of reforms.[57] Rather than repeat these findings, I approach the prospects of future military rule from the framework that has been laid out in this chapter. Specifically, this analysis has sought to draw attention to the idea that those factors that enable and tempt the military to rule directly are different from the factors that determine whether it will chose to do so. Popular attitudes towards military rule, cohesion within the military, and pressure from international actors are all factors that can singularly, or in combination, induce the military to limit itself to a behind-the-scenes role. So, where does Pakistan currently stand in terms of these three factors?

Perhaps the biggest factor currently working against the military assuming direct control is that it knows there would be strong public opposition. With Musharraf's rule still a recent memory, and a degree of public pride in Pakistan's recent electoral achievements, Pakistanis would not easily accept a return to a military regime. Contributing to this attitude is the fact that the public image of the military has suffered in recent years due to its cooperation with the US in the unpopular war in Afghanistan,[58] and the killing of Osama bin Laden, who is widely revered in Pakistan as the implacable enemy of the anti-Islamic West, by the US Navy Seals in the garrison town of Abbottabad in May 2011.

Of equal, if not greater, significance than general public opinion is the extent to which the leaders of Pakistan's political parties have a greater commitment to defending democratic rule. Of particular concern here are the Islamist parties, which the military and intelligence agencies have historically been able to mobilize in street protests, which become a pretext for the army in bringing down civilian governments. As the analysis below will reveal, there are troublesome signs on this front.

The next factor to examine is military cohesion in support of military rule. Many observers have noted the remarkable amount of loyalty that soldiers give to the Pakistani military. Some have even described the institution as being like its own tribe or political party. The explanation for this goes beyond the common socialization experience that soldiers in all armies undergo during their training. Rather, the particularly intense degree of loyalty in the Pakistani military can also be attributed to how well the institution takes care of its own. It does this by operating an extensive welfare system for both its currently active and retired members. Benefits include the military's own healthcare system, special schools and tuition stipends for the children of servicemen, discounted food and consumer goods, and access to subsidized land, which can be resold at a handsome profit. Moreover, the military effectively runs the Fauji Group, a commercial conglomerate with assets in 2009 worth $1.48 billion. Among the businesses under its commercial wing are textiles, fertilizers, cement, cereal, electricity plants, and security services. From the perspective of garnering loyalty, these firms are significant, in that they allow the military to employ some 4,500 ex-servicemen, including retired generals with good paying jobs.[59] In sum, with the benefits given to active-duty servicemen, ex-soldiers and their families, the armed forces provide its members with an assurance of material security throughout life. The impact this has on a soldier's sense of loyalty should not be understated, given that opportunities for social and economic advancement outside the military are limited in Pakistan.[60]

Not surprisingly, the military jealously guards these perks and uses their considerable political clout to resist efforts to cut them. So these benefits, and the loyalty they generate, are likely to continue into the foreseeable future. Yet, against these forces, there are at least two factors at play in Pakistan today with the potential to undermine military cohesion. First are changes in recruitment patterns for soldiers over the past two decades. Whereas traditionally, new recruits largely came from a small number of tribes in rural communities in Punjab and among Pathans in the Northwest

Frontier Province, today's army has made some strides in becoming more reflective of the country's diverse ethnic population. Demographically, the military tends to be more urban, lower-middle class, and with increasing numbers of recruits from the traditionally underrepresented provinces of Baluchistan and, to a lesser extent, Sindh. If these recruitment patterns continue, they could potentially weaken institutional cohesion if the members of a more diverse army become less willing to use force against civilian protesters or armed groups that come from their own ethnic or kinship groups.[61]

A second and more immediate source of potential factionalism in the military comes from US pressure on the Pakistan military to fight the Afghan Taliban. Reflecting public opinion in the country, members of Pakistan's military are generally sympathetic with the Afghan Taliban and have little stomach to engage them militarily.[62] This is not because they are supportive of the type of rule the Taliban wants to implement. Rather, they see the ethnic Pathan Taliban as reliable allies in Pakistan's efforts to prevent Indian-allied, non-Pathan nationalities from ruling Afghanistan. Moreover, most soldiers do not see the Afghan Taliban as a threat to Pakistan, and feel that they are only being called upon to attack them in the FATA because Pakistan's military and civilian elite are financially dependent on the United States and beholden to do their bidding. During the Musharraf–Bush period, when the US was committed to a military defeat of the Afghan Taliban, these attitudes in the military provided the greatest potential for divisions in the armed forces. However, the likelihood of this scenario has receded under the Obama administration due to its greater emphasis on negotiations with the Taliban and a phased withdrawal of US troops.

The final factor for consideration is the ability of international pressure to facilitate or hinder the consolidation of military regimes in the wake of a coup. One recent assessment of US–Pakistan relations since 9/11 describes the countries as 'locked in a hostile embrace'.[63] At its root, the hostility derives from the fact that Washington and the generals who control Pakistan's foreign policy perceive their national interests to be fundamentally opposed. Whereas the US has sought to prevent Taliban rule in Afghanistan, either through military defeat or moderating them politically, Pakistan has supported them. Since the 1990s, the US has fostered a closer partnership with India and is sympathetic with its national security concerns, while Pakistan continues to support insurgents and terrorists aimed at undoing India's interests in Kashmir and Afghanistan.

Yet, despite these sources of conflict, the countries need each other. Pakistan still depends on the US for $2 billion in annual subsidies; it counts on the US to be its advocate with international financial institutions; and Pakistan relies on the US for access to American weapons system, even though it has diversified its arms suppliers. As for the US, it depends on Pakistan as a staging ground for its continuing war in Afghanistan, where the country's ports and highways are important for supplying NATO forces. The US relies on Pakistan for permission to use its airspace for its drone operations. It depends on Pakistani intelligence for information about al-Qaeda; and it counts on the military to keep Pakistan's nuclear weapons secure and out of the hands of terrorists.[64]

Looking at this list, it is hard to say which country is more dependent on the other. It is not even clear that if the United States wanted to support Pakistan's civilian constitutional order against a military coup (an unlikely prospect at present), that Washington would have sufficient leverage to do so. What can be said with greater confidence is that the United States, arguably, has less leverage over Pakistan today than it did thirty years ago. This is for three main reasons. First, the US and its ally, India are the targets of international terrorist groups, and Pakistan has become a breeding ground and safe haven for these organizations and their sympathetic supporters. Second, Pakistan's intelligence agencies have assets on the ground that the US cannot easily duplicate, and thus, Pakistan is in a better position to either help the US in its counter-terrorism activities or to turn a blind eye. Third, since Pakistan became a nuclear weapons state in the 1990s, the US believes it can better ensure the security of these weapons by cooperating with the Pakistani military in that effort.

There are those who argue that the US has an opportunity to leave this dysfunctional relationship when it completes its withdrawal of troops from Afghanistan by the end of 2016. But even after US military operations in Afghanistan come to a close, Washington will still have an interest in maintaining effective working relations with Pakistan's military due to the security interests mentioned above.

In light of this assessment of the three factors, one cannot rule out Pakistan's military assuming direct rule again. The army is likely to maintain a high degree of cohesion in the immediate future, and due to its security interests in the region, it is unlikely that the United States would risk cooperative relations with Pakistan's military by taking strong measures against a coup. Yet, presently, with its estimation that the public would strongly oppose another bout of military rule, the generals appear to have opted instead to work actively behind the scenes to control the Zardari and Sharif governments through assorted means. These include manipulation of party politics, the judiciary, and the media.[65] The military pursues this strategy in order to maintain leverage over civilian officials for the purposes of defending their perceived institutional interests.

In relations between President Zardari and the military, there was little love lost. Not only did Zardari have a track record of corruption and incompetence, his party (the PPP) has historically been the most resolute of the major parties in trying to subordinate the military to civilian rule and challenge the military's policy of supporting low-intensity insurgencies under the nuclear umbrella. So, there were grounds for believing that the military would seek to intimidate the president and keep him under control.

A centrepiece of the military's strategy in achieving this objective is manipulating the judiciary. Here, the generals' principal ally is the Chief Justice Ifikhar Muhammad Chaudhry. Chaudhry and Zardari have a history of political conflict. Soon after becoming president in 2008, Zardari opposed reinstating Chaudhry as Chief Justice after he had been sacked by President Musharraf. Then, in December 2009, in apparent retaliation (and with the probable blessing of the military), Chaudhry declared unconstitutional the National Reconciliation Ordinance (NRO). This was the agreement made in 2007 between President Musharraf and Benazir Bhutto, paving the way for her to return to the country and to the premiership in the 2007 elections. In exchange for giving Musharraf this face-saving way to transition out of power, the ordinance dropped legal charges against Bhutto, her Husband Zardari, and other members of the PPP.

With the revocation of the NRO and the court's ruling that Zardari does not enjoy automatic political immunity, the way was opened for Zardari and his allies to be prosecuted. A bold step in this direction came in June 2012, when the Chief Justice ousted Prime Minister Yousaf Raza Gilani on the grounds that Gilani was ignoring court orders to reopen investigations into corruption charges against Zardari dating back to the 1990s. Then, in January 2013, Chaudhry arrested Gilani's replacement, Prime Minister Raja Pervez Ashraf, on charges of corruption. The military's motives in taking these actions were reputed to be the creation of a caretaker government that could be more easily managed in the months leading up to the May 2013 national elections.

The 'Memogate' scandal also generated suspicion that the military was trying to undermine the Zardari government through the intelligence agencies, the press, and the judiciary. This scandal began in October 2011, when the wealthy Pakistani American, Mansoor Ijaz published an editorial in the *Financial Times*. In it, Ijaz claimed that shortly after the US raid on Osama bin Laden's compound in May 2011, he was asked by 'a senior

Pakistani diplomat' to deliver a memo to US Chairman of the Joint Chiefs of Staff, Admiral Mike Mullen. The document 'asked for U.S. assistance to stave off a coup and in return offered to reverse Pakistan's decades-long policy of jihad under an expanding nuclear umbrella'.[66] Without solid proof to back his story up, Ijaz claims that the memo was either drafted or dictated to him by Husain Haqqani, who was then Pakistan's Ambassador to the United States. Ijaz's critics maintain he was an operative in a plot by Pakistan's intelligence services and military to discredit the Zardari government. Soon after publication of Ijaz's editorial, stories appeared in the Pakistani press, labelling Haqqani a traitor and an 'American Agent'.[67] Denying that he was the source for the memo and seeking to clear his name, Haqqani returned to Pakistan. On 23 November, former Prime Minister Sharif filed a petition at the Supreme Court, demanding a judicial commission investigate the origins of the memo. After the court agreed to the inquiry, Haqqani was placed under house arrest. Potentially facing capital charges of treason, Haqqani claimed that the military was waging 'psychological warfare' against the government of President Zardari.[68] In the end, Haqqani resigned the ambassadorship in an attempt to diffuse the scandal.

In addition to utilizing the judiciary and intelligence services, the military has manipulated party politics as well. The main protagonists have been Imran Khan and Tahir ul-Qadri. In the run-up to the 2013 election, the military was seeking to cultivate political allies to place pressure on the government and serve as alternatives to the PPP and the PML-N. One figure that nicely fit the bill was the rising political star Imran Khan and his party, the Pakistan Tehreek-e-Insaf (PTI). Khan, a former cricket star-turned-politician, had a struggling political career for most of the past decade. However, according to Fair, 'with what Pakistanis suspect is support from the military and the ISI, Khan's. . . party has successfully wooed numerous turncoat politicians and their swollen vote banks'.[69] Khan was appealing to the military because he shares similar views on key issues. He advocates taking a tougher line with the US over Pakistan's continued military cooperation; he supports the Afghan Taliban; and he wants to make the military the last resort in dealing with Pakistan's domestic militants.

The sackings of prime ministers Gilani and Ashraf were accompanied by street protests organized by Khan's PTI. Khan demanded that Zardari resign and call for early elections. Also joining in street protests were Tahir ul-Qadri and his party, the Pakistan Awami Tehreek (PAT). Qadri, a Muslim scholar of Sufism, was born in Pakistan, but maintains Canadian citizenship. Late in 2012, Qadri returned from years in Canada to lead his followers in a series of protests against government corruption and in favour of electoral reform. According to one news report, 'Critics questioned how a little-known cleric, who had managed only a brief stint in Pakistani politics, could suddenly command vast crowds and pay for reams of television advertising, without secret and powerful backers'.[70] In answer to this query, 'Talat Masood, a retired general and analyst, said the Supreme Court appeared to be acting in concert with the military and Dr Qadri to influence the formation of a caretaker government'.[71]

While there were widespread expectations for Khan's PTI to do well in the May 2013 election, his party only captured 35 of the 342 seats. Benefiting from strong patronage networks in Punjab, the clear winner with 166 seats was Nawaz Sharif and the PML-N. Since assuming power, Sharif has cast caution aside and pursued policies aimed at asserting civilian control over national security affairs. The prime minister immediately took over the defence and foreign policy portfolios, which had been held by the military. He sought to improve relations with India and spoke of abandoning the age-old strategy of establishing a friendly regime in Afghanistan to obtain 'strategic depth' against India. On the domestic security front, Sharif promised to negotiate with the Pakistan Taliban. Perhaps of greatest concern for the military, Sharif sought to try Musharraf for treason for the 1999 coup and suspending the Constitution in 2007.[72]

Once again, it is widely believed that the military is using political mobilizations by supporters of Khan and Qadri to clip the wings of Sharif's fledgling government. From August to October 2014, the PTI and PAT launched massive, and sometimes violent, street protests around the Parliament and the prime minister's residence in Islamabad. Khan and Qadri claim they are protesting to pressure the government to investigate electoral fraud in the 2013 elections. Qadri and his followers are also protesting the killing of a dozen of their supports by police when they were congregating at a meeting in an upscale neighbourhood in Lahore in June 2014. As of this writing, Sharif has rejected calls to resign and appears to be standing firm. It remains to be seen whether he will finish out his term.

Conclusion

Attempts by the military since 2008 to manipulate politics do not bode well for the future of civil–military relation in Pakistan. They are a strong indication of the military's ongoing distrust and contempt for civilian rulers. While it is common for the armed force to maintain reserved domains of power in countries with histories of weak democratic governments and military rule, not all forms of military tutelage are the same. It is one thing for a military to limit civilian oversight over its budget and business interests. It is a much more serious matter when the military controls national security policy and plays king maker by manipulating electoral and party politics. So, what hope does Pakistan have for making progress in subordinating the military to civil rule? Short of the country suffering a devastating military defeat that gives civilian politicians the political capital and broad social consensus to undertake bold reforms, there is one approach that seems feasible. It would involve an agreement among Western powers, international financial institutions, and leaders of Pakistan's major political parties, to make financial assistance to Pakistan conditional upon the military implementing a series of reforms aimed at greater civilian oversight. These would need to be enacted incrementally, starting with less threatening reforms and gradually working towards more sensitive issues. Since this approach would likely require US backing, it would not be feasible until after NATO ends military operations in Afghanistan, which would put Washington in a position to apply greater pressure on Pakistan's military. This second scenario, while not guaranteed to succeed, would be much more preferable than the first.

Notes

1 This trend is noted by Samuel Huntington, 'Reforming Civil-Military Relations', *Journal of Democracy*, 1995, 6(4): 15; and David Pion-Berlin, 'Introduction', in David Pion-Berlin (ed), *Civil Military Relations in Latin America: New Analytical Perspectives*, Chapel Hill: University of North Carolina Press, 2001, p. 2.
2 Elaborated from data found in Peter H. Smith, *Democracy in Latin America: Political Change in Comparative Perspective*, New York: Oxford University Press, 2005, pp. 354–55.
3 Mariana Llanos and Leiv Marsteintredet (eds), *Presidential Breakdowns in Latin America: Causes and Outcomes of Executive Instability in Developing Democracies*, New York: Palgrave Macmillan, 2010.
4 Shuja Nawaz, *Crossed Swords: Pakistan, Its Army, and the Wars Within*, Karachi: Oxford University Press, 2008, pp. xxxv–xxxvi.
5 BBC News, 'Q & A: Turkey's Military and the Alleged Coup Plots', *BBC Mobile News*, 6 January 2012, http://www.bbc.co.uk/news/world-europe-16447625 (accessed on 20 January 2012).
6 Fabio Scarpello, 'Indonesia's Personalized Civil-Military Relations', *World Politics Review*, 8 July 2011, http://www.worldpoliticsreview.com/articles/9418/indonesias-personalized-civil-military-relations (accessed on 14 January 2012).
7 C. Christine Fair, 'Why the Pakistan Army is here to Stay: Prospects for Civilian Governance', *International Affairs* 2011, 87(3): 576; and Stephen P. Cohen et al., *The Future of Pakistan*, Washington, DC: Brookings Institution Press, 2011.
8 A more detailed analysis of the cases appears in Steven Barracca, 'Military Coups in the Post-cold War Era: Pakistan, Ecuador, and, Venezuela', *Third World Quarterly*, 2007, 28(1):137–54.

9 James L. Gibson, 'Mass Opposition to the Soviet Putsch of August 1991: Collective Action, Rational Choice, and Democratic Values in the former Soviet Union', *American Political Science Review*, 1997, 91(3): 677–84.
10 Daniel Sutter, 'Legitimacy and Military Intervention in a Democracy: Civilian Government as a Public Good', *American Journal of Economics and Sociology*, 1999, 58(1): 129–43.
11 Barracca, 'Military Coups', pp. 144–46.
12 William R. Thompson, 'Organizational Cohesion and Military Coup Outcomes', *Comparative Political Studies*, 1976, 34(8): 255–76.
13 Barracca, 'Military Coups', pp. 147–49.
14 Steven Levitsky and Lucan A. Way, 'International Linkage and Democratization', *Journal of Democracy*, 2005, 16(3): 21.
15 Dexter S. Boniface, 'Is there a Democratic Norm in the Americas? An Analysis of the Organization of American States', *Global Governance*, 2002, 8(3): 368–81.
16 Barracca, 'Military Coups', pp. 149–50.
17 Stephen Philip Cohen, *The Idea of Pakistan*, Washington, DC: Brookings Institution Press, 2004, pp. 42–48.
18 Ibid., p. 54.
19 Ibid., p. 47.
20 Husain Haqqani, *Pakistan: Between Mosque and Military*, Washington, DC: Carnegie Endowment for International Peace, 2005, p. 15.
21 Ibid., p. 42.
22 Ibid.
23 Ibid., p. 21.
24 Cohen, *Idea of Pakistan*, pp. 68–69.
25 Nawaz, *Crossed Swords*, p. 164.
26 Ibid., p. xxix.
27 Haqqani, *Pakistan*, p. 37.
28 Nawaz, *Crossed Swords*, p. 153.
29 Cohen, *Idea of Pakistan*, p. 56.
30 Haqqani, *Pakistan*, p. 41.
31 Ibid.
32 Ibid., p. 46.
33 Ibid., p. 47.
34 Ibid., p. 58
35 Ibid., p. 166.
36 Lawrence Ziring, *Pakistan: At the Crosscurrent of History*, Oxford: One World, 2003, p. 149.
37 Cohen, *Idea of Pakistan*, p. 79.
38 Ziring, *Pakistan*, p. 146.
39 Khalid B. Sayeed, *Politics in Pakistan: The Nature and Direction of Change*, New York: Praeger, 1980, pp. 91–96 and 157.
40 Haqqani, *Pakistan*, p. 124.
41 Ibid., p. 122.
42 Kanishkan Sathasivam, *Uneasy Neighbors: India, Pakistan, and U.S. Foreign Policy*, London: Ashgate, 2005, p. 130.
43 Haqqani, *Pakistan*, p. 131.
44 Cohen, *Idea of Pakistan*, p. 123

45 Jeffrey Goldberg and Marc Ambinder, 'The Ally from Hell', *The Atlantic*, 11 December 2011, http://www.theatlantic.com/magazine/archive/2011/10/the-ally-from-hell/8730/ (accessed on 25 January 2011).
46 Ahmed Rashid, 'Pakistan's Coup: Planting the Seeds of Democracy?' *Current History*, 1999, 98: 409–14; and Pamela Constable, 'Pakistan's Predicament', *Journal of Democracy*, 2001, 12(1): 15–29.
47 See BBC News, 'Pakistan awaits Military's Next Move', *BBC Online Network*, 13 October 1999, http://news.bbc.co.uk/2/hi/south_asia/473370.stm (accessed on 16 January 2012); and Jason Burke, 'Pakistan: Marching to the Brink', *India Today*, 25 October 1999, http://www.india-today.com/itoday/19991025/cover.html (accessed on 16 January 2012).
48 BBC News, 'Opposition Happy at Sharif's Dismissal', *BBC Online Network*, 13 October 13, 1999, http://news.bbc.co.uk/1/hi/world/south_asia/473124.stm (accessed on 16 January 2012).
49 Aqil Shah, "Pakistan's 'Armored' Democracy'," *Journal of Democracy*, 2003, 14(4): 37.
50 Rashid, 'Pakistan's Coup', p. 411.
51 Burke, 'Pakistan'.
52 BBC News. 'Pakistan's Coup: The 17-Hour Victory', *BBC Online Network*, 11 November 1999, http://news.bbc.co.uk/1/hi/world/south_asia/475195.stm (accessed on 16 January 2012).
53 BBC News, 'Clinton Urges Return to Civilian Rule', *BBC Online Service*, 14 October 1999, http://news.bbc.co.uk/1/hi/world/south_asia/473507.stm (accessed on 16 January 2012).
54 Constable, 'Pakistan's Predicament', p. 21.
55 Rashid, 'Pakistan's Coup', p. 409.
56 Shuja Nawaz, 'Army and Politics', in Maleeha Lodhi (ed), *Pakistan: Beyond the Crisis State*, New York: Columbia University Press, 2011, p. 583.
57 See Lodhi, *Pakistan: Beyond the Crisis State*, and Cohen, et al, *The Future of Pakistan*.
58 C. Christine Fair, 'Pakistan's Slow-Motion Coup', *Foreign Policy*, 5 January 2012, http://www.foreignpolicy.com/articles/2012/01/05/pakistan_s_slow_motion_coup (accessed on 1 October 2012).
59 Anatol Lieven, *Pakistan: A Hard Country*, New York: Public Affairs, 2011, p. 170.
60 Ayesha Siddiqa, *Military Inc.: Inside Pakistan's Military Economy*, London: Pluto Press, 2007.
61 C. Christine Fair and Shuja Nawaz, 'The Changing Pakistan Army Officer Corps', *Journal of Strategic Studies*, 2011, 34(1): 63–94.
62 C. Christine Fair, 'Pakistan's Own War on Terror: What the Pakistani Pubic Thinks', *Journal of International Affairs*, 2009, 63(1): 39–55.
63 Goldberg and Ambinder, 'The Ally from Hell'. Also see Dennis Kux, *The United States and Pakistan 1947–2000: Disenchanted Allies*: Washington, DC: Woodrow Wilson Center Press, 2001.
64 Ibid.
65 Fair, 'Pakistan's Slow-Motion Coup' and C. Christine Fair, 'Still Standing in Pakistan: The Protests, the Military, and What Comes Next', *Foreign Affairs*, 3 September 2014, http://www.foreignaffairs.com/articles/141954/c-christine-fair/still-standing-in-pakistan (accessed on 30 October 2014).

66 Fair, 'Pakistan's Slow-Motion Coup'.
67 Mira Sethi, 'A Hostage in Pakistan', *Wall Street Journal*, 21 January 2012, http://online.wsj.com/article/SB10001424052970204257504577154730006383176.html (accessed on 30 January 2012).
68 Ibid.
69 Fair, 'Pakistan's Slow-Motion Coup'.
70 Rob Crilly, 'Pakistan's supreme court orders arrest of Prime Minister Raja Pervez Ashraf, *Telegraph* (UK), 15 January 2013, http://www.telegraph.co.uk/news/worldnews/asia/pakistan/9802187/Pakistans-supreme-court-orders-arrest-of-Prime-Minister-Raja-Pervez-Ashraf.html (accessed on 30 October 2014).
71 Ibid.
72 Fair, 'Still Standing'.

8

WOMEN AT RISK
Militancy in Pakistan

Tahmina Rashid

Introduction

On 9 October 2012, Tehreek-e-Taliban Pakistan (TTP) accepted the responsibility of shooting 14-year-old Malala Yousafzai in Mingora, Swat, severely injuring her and three other young school girls sitting next to Malala in the school bus and declaring that 'anybody who speaks against us will be attacked in the same way'.[1] Malala was shot because she wanted restoration of law and order in the Swat Valley and demanded the right to go to school. Politicians have been careful to condemn the Malala shooting without censuring the TTP, while the Pakistan army chief has called for unity to 'fight the perpetrators of such barbaric mindset and their sympathizers'.[2] He also stated that 'We wish to bring home a simple message: We refuse to bow before terror. We will fight, regardless of the cost [;] we will prevail'. Ironically, after the military operation in Swat in 2009, the military had claimed that the valley is peaceful and people are able to resume life without fear. This incident highlights that the TTP would continue to terrorize women from public spaces, curtailing their basic rights to education or being in a public space. It also indicates that TTP is still active in the area and would continue its barbaric criminal acts against citizens, especially targeting women. However, it displays an apathetic attitude of the state that fails to criminalize TTP and similar outfits. Once again, the military can assert its role of a protector of the state and the citizens, especially women.

In several Pakistani forums and the media, there have been discussions about the impact of militancy on women. Still, the state ignores women voices and continues to display the hypocrisy in its policies (internal and external) that encourage, harbour, support, and protect TTP-like militant outfits as 'strategic assets'. The debates continue to revolve around national sovereignty, blaming US policies in the region as the prime reason for religious militancy and on the mainstreaming of religious discourse and politics of religion in Pakistan. Much of the existing research continues to focus on the role religious schools play in promoting and transmitting the militant ideologies, ignoring the broader civil society and public sector education system and curricula. It also needs to be recognized that the religious schools are not the sole cause threatening women; a greater threat to women stems from legitimacy given to religious arguments to define socio-economic and political crisis. Defining major structural and institutional issues in the language of Islam poses serious risk to the safety of women – and ultimately, to the state. In this broader context, it is paramount to appraise the status of women in Pakistan and to understand the context for their protection in various settings.

Women in Pakistan are not a monolithic group. The nature of barriers hindering their status and participation in the Pakistan polity varies from place to place, depending upon cultural practices of the region, geographical location, socio-economic status of women, and political settings. The socio-cultural formation of the society in Pakistan is deeply patriarchal and continues to be governed by tribal and feudal structures – a parallel governance structure that continues to determine and define roles and rights of women. These structures predate the formation of a modern state and continue to enjoy informal status, running parallel judicial systems and dispensing justice based on primitive notions of 'fairness', ignoring the principles of equality before the law, even passing judgements in violation of laws enacted by the state institutions. These patriarchal structures, assign women an inferior status, delegating men the role of a legal guardian (*wali*), thus reducing women's legal status to objects 'owned' by men (father, brother, husband, son) and depriving them of autonomy over their lives and protection by the state as equal citizens. Women are considered the symbols of men/family/tribe's honour; thus, their behaviour, especially towards men, is determined by these codes of honour, at times ending their lives through criminal cultural practices. Despite changes in the socio-economic and legal arenas, men continue to wield considerable control over women's lives as the 'providers' and 'protectors'.

Women's public roles and rights are determined by their tribal customs, cultural practices, and urban/rural location. Historically, the provincial politics of *Khyber Pukhtunkhwa* (KP) had been secular: however, since the 1980s, Afghanistan's entanglement with global/regional politics during the Cold War period, huge influx of Afghan refugees, mushrooming of madrasas (religious schools), and legitimacy crisis of the then military regime (of Zia-ul-Haq) have given rise to the politics of religion with serious consequences for the province, especially women. The Pakistani government and people continue to blame the US policies of the Cold War period that provided financial and logistical support to Afghan *mujahidin* fighting the Soviets, as well as accuse India for the politics of hegemony in South Asia. Similarly, Pakistan's support to various militant outfits continues to be justified in 'national interest' and remains aligned with the Pakistani establishment's policies on Kashmir.

Women and the polity in *Khyber Pukhtunkhwa* (KP)

The political situation in KP has been fragile since the 1980s due to the influx of refugees from Afghanistan and has deteriorated further as Pakistan has joined the US alliance in the War on Terrorism. During the Afghan crisis of the 1980s, locals suffered due to the sheer number of refugees (3 million) and the burden on resources and the resulting law and order situation. In the post-Geneva Accords between Afghanistan and Pakistan (1988), assistance from the international community dropped to an alarmingly low level, leaving millions of Afghan refugees and local Pakistanis to deal with the prevailing humanitarian crisis. In the current crisis, the presence of US troops, the International Security Assistance Force (ISAF), and NATO, and the increasing presence of militants have led to another wave of Afghan refugee influx into Pakistan. Global, regional, and local politics have intertwined with serious implications for the people in Federally Administered Tribal Areas (FATA) and *Khyber Pukhtunkhwa* province. On the one hand, there are US-directed drone attacks, and NATO/ISAF border attacks, promoting Taliban outfits to push out locals in Swat Valley as well as tribal areas of Pakistan and move to other locations for their own safety. On the other hand, various military operations by the Pakistan defence forces against the Taliban and foreigners supporting militancy are taking its toll on the locals in the Swat Valley. Retaliation to small-scale attacks by the military on the militants in FATA have resulted in attacks by the militants on state offices, increasingly targeting innocent civilians as well, which have heightened insecurity in the already troubled areas. The volatile situation resulting from Taliban's control in Swat led to the military operation in the Swat Valley, displacing thousands from the valley.

The Pakistani military operations in the Swat Valley against the militants in 2009 were followed by the flash floods of 2010, causing havoc to businesses and families. Through these troubled times, women continued to play an active role through civil society forums, calling for the protection of women from Taliban's onslaught on women. These organizations have lobbied for an increased role for women in the peace-making processes, as well as expressed women's concerns about the humanitarian crises caused by militancy in the region. It needs to be noted that the deteriorating law and order situation, target killings, terrorist attacks, ethnic and sectarian violence, and suicide attacks in public spaces have taken the lives of innocent children and women, even if most of the dead were men. Such huge loss of the male population has adversely impacted families where women lose the protection and financial support of male members.

Feeble governance by the government notwithstanding, the Zardari government during its tenure (2008–13) passed a series of laws focusing on crimes against women: Protection of Women (Criminal Laws Amendment) Act, 2006; Sexual Harassment at the Workplace Act, 2010; Anti-Women Practices Act, 2011, The Criminal Law Amendment Bill on Acid and Burn Violence, 2011 are some initiatives introduced by the administration. These laws specifically deal with the concerns of women and are applicable in all situations where women suffer because of cultural practices that dehumanize them.

In addition to being a signatory to various international protocols and humanitarian laws, Pakistan has a number of laws on the statue books that are relevant to the protection of women during civil conflicts. Pakistan has enacted as well as inherited from the British laws that deal with the protection of civilians. The Constitution of Pakistan provides the guiding principles for policy and guarantees fundamental human rights and special protection of women and children. However, Pakistan has a rich history of suspending the Constitution and seeking approval of unconstitutional acts in the name of 'law of necessity' or by invoking an emergency in a conflict zone. Even in 'emergencies', when the Constitution is suspended, laws remain relevant and applicable to crimes committed against citizens.

Succumbing to the pressure of militant groups such as TNSM (Tehreek-e-Nafaz-e-Shariat-e-Mohammadi – Movement for the Enforcement of Sharia), the Zardari government introduced the controversial *Nizam-e-Adl* Regulation, 2009 (based on Sharia law) in Malakand division, under clauses 3 & 4 of Article 247 of the Constitution of Pakistan.[3] Introduction of another legal structure (*Nizam-e-Adl*) has further complicated the judicial system, as already there are Shariah courts applying Islamic laws while the rest of the court system works under the Code of Criminal Procedure (CCP) and the Pakistan Penal Code (PPC), undermining the rights of women whose cases can be dragged from one system to the other. Legal ambiguities, societal attitudes towards women, and cultural constructions of masculinity have legitimized domestic violence in the garb of religion to regulate immoral 'behaviour', as well as condone militants' criminality against women.[4] Invoking moral, cultural, and religious arguments to inflict violence on women essentially absolves men from any responsibility, let alone acknowledging their criminal acts. As I have noted elsewhere:

> Women's experiences with law are different from men due to the inherent gender bias in the legal processes. The relationship between women and law is that of protection, which will continue to remain a problematic articulation of the principles of personal justice.[5]

The present conflict has extended the frontline of violence into villages and small towns that have become a challenge for the protection of civilians. Displacement, internal as well as across international borders, has ruptured social networks and community cohesiveness, making civilians, especially women, vulnerable. Two key points ought to be noted here: that such crises can potentially create more space and legitimacy for women's role in peace processes, and that not all women are victims. They are active agents involved both as perpetrators of various criminal acts (involvement in making and installing improvised explosive devices (IEDs), providing intelligence and support, and so on) as well as peacemakers in the post-conflict situation in the Swat Valley.

Displacement also has the potential to expand women's role in the refugee camps, as women have to perform or take over roles traditionally performed by men. Women lose the protection of their community and are vulnerable; these camps can also free them from an abusive relationship. Displacement exposes women to inadequate living conditions, lack of privacy, accidents, diseases, and food insecurity as distribution is mainly conducted by men and fails to reach single and elderly women. Women's access to income and education suffers badly; however, displacement also opens up opportunities for services unknown to them previously (reproductive health).

In women-headed households, accessing relief goods in camps or during movement/displacement has been identified as a serious concern,[6] which is exacerbated when women lose their homes, social and community support, as well as income and assets.

Many women cannot leave their homes because of the restrictions imposed by the local cultural and patriarchal practices on them, and in the absence of men of the family (who have been either killed during crisis or are away for work reasons), the women are not allowed to step out of the house alone. Leaving their home can pose potential harm, especially in the public space, which, in turn, has a consequential loss of access to employment and education. Since the focus remains on displaced people, those who are left behind are isolated from social and economic networks, especially food supply and health services, becoming far more vulnerable. They remain trapped and isolated from support mechanisms and their experiences are rarely documented in conflict management discussions.

It has also been recognized by international aid agencies that a number of women enter the sex trade or become beggars.[7] There is very little research available on the links between displacement and sexual exploitation and prostitution in Pakistan. In the absence of awareness about displaced women and lack of financial support for them, society takes a moral stand against vulnerable women, while the state has failed to provide support to women forced into street prostitution. Currently, neither is there sufficient acknowledgement of sexual exploitation nor is there any discussion around programmes to assist, re-train, or rehabilitate women into other forms of employment. Moral arguments around sex work/prostitution limit the possibility of valuing these women as being worthy of assistance. The media, both Pakistani and international, has widely reported the self-righteous militants publically flogging women for alleged immoral behaviour.[8]

During my fieldwork, many women made references to the sexual exploitation and abuse of women by the Taliban; a psychologist noted the sexual abuse of men by the militants during their control of the Swat Valley. However, I was unable to confirm these accounts as reports about such incidents are not publically available, and abused men are less likely to speak out for fear of shame. It, therefore, needs to be noted that sexual crimes against men during conflicts remain unacknowledged. NGOs have failed to document sexual abuse by defence personnel during the military operations in the Swat Valley; however, there have been anecdotal reports relating to the abuse of women by the Taliban during the Swat Valley conflict. Conflicts have the potential of increased sexual abuses, including trafficking, rape, abduction, forced and child marriages, and sexual servitude in exchange for food or services (identity documents),[9] exacerbating vulnerability to trafficking and domestic violence.[10] Older women are particularly vulnerable due to their limited mobility and reliance on family and community networks; they remain on the fringes of society, spurned in public and ignored by the state-supported development sector.[11] Similarly, women's involvement (forced or otherwise) or the family's association with militants puts them at the risk of isolation in their communities, making it harder for them to seek assistance from the civil society or the state.

Militancy in Swat – a local narrative

Locals in the Swat Valley argue that the Valley had schools and basic health facilities when ruled by *Wali-e-Swat* (princely state). Once the Valley became part of Pakistan in 1969, development stalled and it lagged far behind the rest of KP in infrastructure for the lack of investment. Tourism has been traditionally good in the summer and generated seasonal employment, although in the winter, the number of tourists would drop sharply. Lack of employment has resulted in internal migration, but also in overseas employment in the Kingdom of Saudi Arabia and the UAE. The authorities have ignored the social impact of employment-driven migrations on local communities. But clearly, in these communities, there is a higher proportion of female-headed households. Introduction to the Saudi or Middle Eastern Islam vis-à-vis Wahhabism is a notable influence among overseas employed men. The demand for the Sharia by local groups has been made since the 1990s and has been attributed to economic disparity and local tribal politics; there has been a steady rise in militancy in the Swat Valley from the early 2000s and continues unabated. The military operation in 2007 was a small-scale operation, which led to a dialogue and an accord reached in 2009, but it broke down and resulted in a major military operation in May 2009. Military sources claim that during the operation, 416 military servicemen lost their lives, while 3421 terrorists were killed and thousands detained. After the operation, the military introduced a 3D strategy 'Deter, Develop, and De-radicalize'. As part of the post-operation strategy to deter and de-radicalize, the following programs have been initiated:

- *Sabaoon* (The Dawn) – Juvenile facility for education and skills training of male youth between the ages of 12 and 17. This residential facility comprises a boys' school, dormitories, counselling and sports facilities.
- *Mishal* – Two Adult facilities for religious education, vocational training, financial assistance for self-employment or job-seeking assistance (in Pakistan or overseas).
- *Sparley* (spring)/*Roshni* (light) – Women's education and training programmes through vocational training centres established in different parts of the Swat Valley

I conducted field research in the Swat Valley in early 2011 and visited many areas in the upper and lower Swat Valley and some other parts of Malakand division.[12] The destruction caused by the militants who had blown up almost all girls schools in the upper Swat was visible from the ruined buildings across the area; whatever little was left intact was swept away by the floods in 2010 as the river on both sides had encroached the land where once there were 159 hotels. Alongside these ruined buildings, I could see the national flag of Pakistan painted everywhere – on doors, shop shutters, and walls all the way from Rashkai (Mardan) to the Peochar Valley (the stronghold of militants before the 2009 military operation). This puzzling exhibition made me wonder whether this was some sort of display of national identity or expression of a nationhood project or a symbol of the supremacy of the writ of the state. Many inquiries with locals revealed that militants had painted Taliban's flags to indicate their control of the area; and then, locals started painting these flags on the doors to indicate their support for the militant groups who controlled the area, to protect their businesses and homes from destruction by the militants. After the military operation, servicemen painted national flags where once militant flags were painted, to erase the visible presence and symbols of militant groups and assure locals that the army is in control. Each time I tried to count the number of flags, I lost count as they were in their thousands; it seems that removing Taliban flags was symbolic for the military to assure the people in the Swat Valley that the Taliban were gone (at least for now).

I was able to get insights into the role of women and the incorporation of radical and militant ideologies inside the households. Locals agree that women influenced by the jihad radio sermons of Tehreek-e-Nafaz-e-Shariat-e-Mohammadi (TNSM – Movement for the Enforcement of Islamic Law) have been a key influence on the youth, and that these sermons promote – and nurture – an environment conducive to the radicalization of the entire household. It needs to be noted that the area has higher proportion of female-headed households because invariably adult male members of the household would migrate internally (notably to Karachi/Quetta) or overseas (UAE/Gulf/Middle East) in search of employment as security guards and as semi/unskilled construction workers. These households have a population of young children, women, and the elderly and heavily rely on hard-earned overseas remittances.

In the three locations where I was able to meet local women, their narratives are contradictory on militancy, women's own roles in supporting/opposing militancy, and militancy's impact on their lives. I was informed that after the military operations, there was an influx of NGOs in the area; however, most of these organizations left within a few months because of security concerns, but also because of the lack of resources and the difficult terrain of the valley. There were hundreds of billboards, reminding locals of welfare and civil society organizations that mushroomed after the military operation in 2009 to 'develop' the area; however, after the initial few months, these NGOs left the area. There was consensus that the visible presence of the military in the area has legitimized women's presence in the public space and restored some confidence in going to schools and public places such as the market. Women in the upper Swat, a stronghold of militants during 2007–2009, suffered most; hardly was there any girls' school that was not blown up by the militants. Girls' education and female employment in the education sector was the first casualty of militancy in the area. It was evident that women's education irked the Taliban greatly, perhaps as a serious threat to the expansion of Taliban's militant agendas. The history of Islamization in Pakistan since the 1980s has shown that religious groups view women's presence in the public space as a threat, and policies of the decade are especially loaded with religious idioms.

One of the vocational training centres that I visited had a multipurpose facility for young girls, boys, and women. There is a computer room for boys and girls, sewing machines for women, and a salon for training future beauticians. Girls had access to the area from 9–12a.m., boys would come after school and work on computers from 2–5p.m. It was heart-breaking to see young children without any reading/writing skills and their attendance was recorded with a thumb imprint in the attendance log. The girls' primary school was destroyed by the Taliban, and the nearest high school was in a nearby village accessible only via transport, limiting the possibility of education: girls are either barred from travelling for safety reasons or cannot afford public or private transportation. Like millions of other Pakistani girls, these young girls will never have any access to education or employment, will be married at an early age, and continue to worry about feeding their young. For the only social worker at the centre, it is a hard task to visit nearby village communities and persuade families to send their girls and women to the vocational centre. There is still stout resistance to female education; there is dominance of patriarchal cultural control, and there is opposition by male family members to give permission to women to leave the house. Harsh winter weather and lack of public transportation are also cited as primary reasons for poor female education rates. It is dangerous to be a social worker in the Valley because it involves local travel.

> Although the presence of military has given me the confidence to work as a social mobilizer, still the community reminds me that if [the] Taliban comes back, they will slaughter me. I am not afraid of death. I want to do something for my country.. . . Since my husband is overseas, I am blamed [for being] a woman of 'loose

morals', one of the reasons that I keep both my daughters with me [to avoid such comments].[13]

The social realities around such women are a constant reminder that society holds primitive views about working women, and their independent presence in the public space continues to be controlled by men. She mentioned this a few times during the course of the interview, which indicates the stress it has caused her.

Another vocational centre was established in the newly constructed girls' school that was destroyed by the Taliban. It had 50 sewing machines for women to learn to stitch and embroider. However, the future of the vocational centre was uncertain because the winter was coming to an end and the building had to be given back to the school the next morning. Local women were hoping to get a sewing machine at the end of their training; however, there was uncertainty about whether or not the vocational centre will move to a new location. Women were worried as they could not come in the evening due to their domestic responsibilities, but also because leaving the house in the afternoon required permission from a male family member. One local schoolteacher stated:

> We received threats from the Taliban as warning letters were thrown on the school premises to close down the school; if the school continued they would destroy the entire building. We were thankful to the Pakistan Army for rebuilding the school. The school had 150 girls before the destruction; and now we are all looking forward to returning to the school.
> My husband was a teacher and not a Talib: he opposed them. After the Taliban took over there was chaos. He [my husband] died in the military operation even though he did not support the Taliban. I work two jobs to support my son's education; he is enrolled in a boarding school, and it is hard to make ends meet with my salary and my late husband's meager pension. Military has promised to take financial responsibility of my son's education that will reduce the financial burden. My in-laws are pushing me to re-marry but I do not want to marry an uneducated man. My son says from where can I find you an educated husband.[14]

She was of the view that the Taliban were outsiders who got the support of some locals, but she could not be sure which area they came from, as their accent was different. In her view, the Taliban were polite to women and did not harass them in public and were very civil to women. She said that some local supporters of the Taliban have disappeared along with their families and no one knows where they are, whether they have been detained by the army or have left the area. She stated that she was initially scared of the army, but now worries what will happen to her once the army leaves the valley.

Another teacher from the same school contradicted her views, stating:

> We were asked to wear burqas [at all time], although women traditionally cover themselves in public. We did receive threatening letters to close down the school; then a final letter came threatening us to stay away from the school or they (the Taliban) will bomb the school. The school lost its furniture and all belongings, including records, books, etc., and no one knows who took all the stuff.[15]

On the way to the Peochar Valley, I passed by the notorious 'Veenay' bridge (Blood bridge), a place used for executing and slaying the locals. The area is extremely remote, cut off from the rest of the Swat Valley during the entire winter due to heavy snowfall. The locals grow wheat, corn, and apricots, and the houses remain scattered in the mountainous valley. The army has rebuilt the bridge and people from the valley are able to move across the region again. The enormous number of national flags in the Peochar explains the fear of the Taliban; however, locals are quick to remind that there were no schools, hospitals, or employment opportunities in the area. Local women have indicated that local support for the Taliban was not merely a result of fear: many have willingly participated and benefitted from the militants, receiving weapons and money from the Taliban. They also expressed their fear that once the military goes back, these criminals will again gang up on women.

I was informed that none of the civil society organizations were willing to work in the Peochar Valley across the bridge. The only meaningful work women could engage in outside their homes was the makeshift vocational centre, run by a local teacher and comprising open space given by a local elder's family. I was told that the girls' school was one of the first casualties of militants' hatred for female education. Her frustration was obvious:

> There is no building now for my 150 students and I am the only staff in the school. There is no girls' high school in the area and they bombed girls' primary school. If I go to the Education Department at Saido Sharif the entire day is not enough and who will teach these girls if I am away? I have to close the school premises

to visit the office. I have rented a house (family had moved during the Taliban hold of the area) for Rs. 500, and pay the rent from my salary rather than wasting my time and money to travel to make any request. I am hoping that the military will rebuild the school as promised.

I was asked by the military to enroll 30 women in the vocational center but 70 came and more are coming to join but we do not have any extra sewing machines or fabric or raw material to train these women. What will happen to the center after the winter, we do not know yet. The schools will reopen after the winter break and I shall not be able to manage the vocational training center. I cannot be at two places during the day and women cannot come in the evening with their sewing machines; they have to look after their children and families and cook for them.[16]

Considering the lack of opportunities for girls' education in the area, it is going to be a huge task to de-radicalize women of the valley. Despite being active agents of radicalization and the Taliban, to my knowledge, there are no women detainees in military-run de-radicalization projects. They are encouraged to enrol in VTCs (Vocational Training Centres) and learn skills useful to earn a living. In keeping with the traditions of the area, cultural correctness requires not detaining any women, as they were not caught in combat. Does that mean that the ideology that they had subscribed to, has its verve diminished? Or, were they merely responding to the call to holy war from a firebrand *maulvi* who had come to the area to impose an 'Islamic way of life', paving the way to heaven for the sinful locals?

A ticket to paradise

Everyone has stories to tell: stories of brutality, inhuman acts, criminal behaviour, how the Taliban sexually molested the young and women with the promise that such servitude would earn them a place in paradise. Women were picked up randomly to engage in sexual relations or marriage; so were young boys (*bacha baazi*). Stories circulating about the youth joining the Taliban gangs only to marry girls of their choice are common. Locals shared gruesome details of how men were slaughtered publicly in the presence of young children. It is heart-breaking that, despite the large presence of locals, militants continued slaying to terrorize communities. It is also a testimony to local apathy towards such criminality. There were stories of sexual exploitation by the militants who manipulated abducted local young women of their choice into marriage during the reign of terror under the

Taliban. There were (unconfirmed) stories that many young women were married off in haste (after getting bride price), presumably trafficked overseas via Afghanistan or sold internally in the red light districts in Lahore and Karachi. Although trafficking is common during conflicts, the notion of shame and dishonour in Pakistan prohibits bringing such cases to light. In the absence of any such reporting or evidence collected by any organization, it is difficult to know the magnitude of the problem.[17]

The issue of women's role was raised a number of times during the field research. Women have not only been donating jewellery or cash, but they have also been forcing male members of the family to participate in the holy war against the 'infidel'. Hardly anyone articulated the rationale behind equating the US and Pakistan armies; yet, everyone blamed one or the other for the rise of militancy in the region. Locals indicated and confirmed that such support extended to providing intelligence, assisting in preparation and installing of IEDs, as well as supplying of food and weapons to the Taliban. Random discussions with women led to listing of a range of issues from detainees to the role of women and the need for de-radicalizing the entire community. In Malakand, another story about three young sisters (potential suicide bombers) was shared; it was stated that their brother joined the local Taliban and was killed during the military operation. Their drug-addicted father wanted to take revenge and was persuading his three daughters to undertake a suicide attack for revenge from the military by exploding themselves at an army checkpoint. A psychologist involved in providing counselling service to the alleged militant women was of the view that women's role was not that of active agents, though they have donated their jewellery. For that reason, women do not require de-radicalization training and *Sparley* (vocation centre) is already providing them vocational training. The divergent views of the role played by women, as explained by women and servicemen, raises some intriguing questions. If de-radicalization will occur through education, religious and vocational training, women also require a sustainable and tailored programme. Women's active agency and persuasion by male family members to participate in the holy war, donating jewellery or money, providing assistance in making and deploying IEDs, and giving logistical support in supplying food and information would require much more than vocational training. Perhaps the need for a universal education in the entire valley is a starting point that would have a curriculum different from what is being currently taught in the public school system or *madrasas* (religious schools).

Another urgent and compelling concern remains about women's deradicalization. Irrespective of the divergent viewpoints on the level of women's involvement with the militants, one can hear stories about women trained for suicide bombing, groomed to provide logistic support, and prepared to donate in cash and kind. The Pakistani authorities have detained no women, though there were some investigation and interrogation of potential suicide bombers. These women subscribed to the militant ideology; they were encouraged by male members to join jihad; and they rationalized their newly carved role as a service to God. Vocational training may provide an alternative peer group and give some earning capacity; yet, it cannot be expected to de-radicalize these women.

Subscribing to the jihadist ideology empowered these women in a way unknown or experienced by them previously. They have their first opportunity to serve God as well as their religion and country against the evil 'Other' – be it the West, America, Pakistan Army, or an imagined enemy of Islam. It guaranteed a 'ticket to heaven' for women who have always been told that women are sinful (*fitna*), and therefore, will go to hell in flocks. For these women who have endured a lower status within their household, community, and country, there was a new hope in the message of hatred and violence, a chance to earn a higher status in the afterlife. Will they ever forget those fiery religious messages that made them feel empowered? Will they content themselves with sewing and embroidering? The road back to the old life as if nothing at all had happened to them or their communities is difficult. Will they subscribe to a different ideology that believes in social harmony? In the absence of investment of resources in the local infrastructure, goods, and services, jihad remains their best hope of redemption.

One woman referred to the destruction caused by the 2010 floods that displaced over a million people and destroyed crops, houses, schools, hospitals, and buildings. It was suggested that these floods were the wrath of God because of the immorality and adultery in the area. As the conversation continued, references were made to the dead bodies of prostitutes who worked as dancers and comfort women in the tourism industry. It was alleged that these loose women died in the act of performing: 'Their bodies were recovered still wearing dancing costumes and ornaments' usually worn by women in local brothels. Further, it was stated that the immorality and prostitution is 'the cause' of all local problems, notwithstanding these women complaining about the lack of infrastructure and services and employment opportunities available to them. These are the core issues facing the people, while the state has remained wilfully indifferent to local concerns.

The social discourse moves in circles around issues of morality and ethics; it seems that morality is a prime concern, irrespective of who is defining morality. The local *maulvi* was able to convince women and men to lead a moral life, as defined in his view of Islam. Leading an ethical life based on principles of mutual respect, tolerance for diversity of political views, religious beliefs and practices, and being a law-abiding citizen remain absent from the prevailing discourse of moral police. Curbing the Taliban and restoring the writ of the state is one part of the problem; the other is dealing with morality that has become a part of the popular local discourse. It seems that anyone can declare another person an 'infidel', thus a target for killing in the name of Islam. There needs to be a frank discussion whether Pakistani society aims to be an ethical society or a moral society. While morality is subjective, the state can regulate a system that is based on ethical principles. If morality stays in the private realm and public matters are to be regulated based on ethical principles, Pakistan may achieve a moral society that is envisioned in local discourses.

There is no systematic collection of the stories of the locals. Accounts vary about who the Taliban is; who supports them locally and why; how the climate evolved from the emergence of the Taliban to the military operation in the Swat Valley? One can argue that not all of these accounts are verifiable; some accounts are, no doubt, exaggerated or even invented; still, they are a part of the Swat Valley folklore. These stories will be told to friends, relatives, and, more importantly, to the next generation. Collaborators may be transformed into heroes and heroes may become villains, depending on whose narrative one is listening to. These stories also reflect popular understanding of the Taliban phenomenon and its impact on the local understandings of the future. If one is able to record the stories of ordinary people, these may shed a new light on the causes and processes of the militancy, as well as provide a potential solution to end militancy. These stories offer early warnings of entrenched militancy.

One local story reveals many veiled realities: a *Maulvi* at the local mosque was given a local radio station as a gift, which he used for sermons all day long. He promised women that he would open a *madrassa* (religious school) for girls' education. He assured them that women can only go to heaven if they serve God and instructed women to play their Islamic role and encourage their husbands, sons, and brothers to join jihad. He declared that women are inferior to men and less pious in the eyes of God; the women therefore will go to Hell in large numbers for not serving God, unlike men have done. Women are convinced that they can play a role in ensuring their salvation in the afterlife; however, these women also allow their girls to go to school, which they believe is permitted by Islam. Women of the village were persuaded to contribute to the cause of Islam to ensure a place in paradise in their afterlife.

Many locals as well as servicemen confirmed that the Swat Valley women donated gold jewellery to the Taliban willingly in an effort to win a higher status. One local woman confessed that she did not contribute to the militants; those who did 'in the name of God' badgered her. Those who could contribute viewed their pious act with reverence. It is vital to note that Pakistani women receive jewellery (dowry) traditionally as a wedding gift from parents and in-laws; and dowry is considered as their personal assets. Donating jewellery is rare and parting with jewellery is complex and fraught with social taboos, such as widowhood or destituteness. Nevertheless, such donations have been given a new meaning as they are made in the service of Islam and for a greater cause in God's name. In the prevailing socio-religious discourse in Pakistan, women are viewed as half-citizens; they inherit half the share of their brother, are entitled to only one-tenth portion from their husband's wealth, are considered less rational, are viewed as the reason for all social evils in the society (*fitna*), even their witness status is half that of a man. By donating jewellery, they have acquired a newfound status in local religious discourse, a newfound meaning in life, an elevation of their religious status in the 'eyes of God', and a sense of empowerment.

The locals are of the view that the *Maulvi* got financial assistance from Waziristan (a militant hub) and recruited some unemployed youth. One such youth spent his time chasing young boys and girls before becoming the *Maulvi's* protégé. Access to money and weapons gave him the power to harass and terrorize the locals.

> He harassed women in the village and told them to stay indoors. He announced that it is forbidden in Islam to send girls to school. He also banned music and dancing at wedding ceremonies, even though we have always sung and danced on such occasions. Previously the entire village would celebrate weddings. But once the young man became agent of the *Maulvi*, from which time brides had to be given to the groom's family without any fanfare, as all local traditions were declared un-Islamic. Women even stopped visiting each other's house for fear of being harassed.
> Women could not be seen in public spaces and female education became a victim. Even the local police could not do anything. There were rumors that he slaughtered few men as well. All we could do was curse him and pray to God that something terrible happens to him.[18]

Local women were appalled at how women suffered, and provided horrible details of the time when the *Maulvi* and his protégé controlled the village. They told the story of the local thug firing and severely injuring a pregnant woman, who gave birth to a son prematurely, ultimately dying during childbirth. Another similar incident narrated was about a terrorized woman, who was hiding in an animal shed for fear of her life. She too gave birth to a premature child. Finally, after the military killed the local militant and allegedly dragged his dead body across the villages to assure the people that they were safe from the goon, the local community's reaction was puzzling. One can understand their repulsive response to the alleged inhuman treatment of the dead body. What was astounding was their praise for the goon and how bravely he fought with the military? It seemed as if, in death, he won applause for his bravery. His crimes against the people were forgiven, and ironically, the perpetrator had become a local hero. One comment by a woman captured the common sentiment: 'Sister, he fought with the army like a man and died as a brave man'.[19] It seems that such views are not isolated. Many in the community would share the stories of militants' criminality and its terrible impact on the community, especially on women; and then in the next breath, they would talk about their bravery and ill-treatment of these criminals by the military during the operation.

The reintegration programme involves the families of young children and adults and spans over a two-year period during which they are re-educated. However, unlike Rwanda, South Africa, Timore-Leste, and some Pacific islands, there are no truth commissions or reconciliation processes in place. These individuals and their families are receiving the support of the military, which is otherwise not available or even possible, considering the limitations of Pakistan. The trauma suffered by the communities is enormous and requires collective healing. Women also stated that those who supported the Taliban were receiving favourable treatment from the army: they are receiving training in specialized skills, have been offered preferential employment and health benefits, as well as assistance for marriages in their families.

As education remains an unfulfilled promise and gender mainstreaming is an unachievable goal of development planners, these young girls' existence seems to have lost relevance for the policymakers and development planners. These young girls will have little access to education and will be kept busy drawing flowers, huts, and mountains in their scrapbooks, and will learn embroidery skills. The Taliban has crushed their dreams for education, condemning them to marriage at a young age, which will leave them at the mercy of male members of the family; and local culture and traditions will force them to deal with the harsh realities of childbirth, caring for the family and the elderly. They will wait for years for their husband's visit and remain an easy prey of any mullah, who can convince them of their religious duty and promise of a ticket to paradise. Those who will dare to speak up for their right to education and public space will be attacked in an attempt to silence them. Pakistani society and the state need to deal with the demons within the country to defeat militancy. Otherwise, women would continue to pay the price by losing their right to life, which, in the end, does not bode well for Pakistan.

Notes

1 'Malala under treatment after being Shot', *The News*, 9 October 2012, http://www.thenews.com.pk/article-70817-Malala-Yousafzai-under-treatment-after-being-shot (accessed on 11 October 2012).
2 'General Kayani condemns Attack on Malala', *The Express Tribune*, 10 October 2012, http://tribune.com.pk/story/449540/malala-is-an-icon-of-courage-hope-kayani/ (accessed 11 October 2012).
3 Simi Kamal, 'Nizam-e-Adl Inside Out: A Study of Nizam-e-Adl in the Light of the Constitution, Women's Policies and the Perceptions of Pakistani Society', Islamabad: NCSW, 2010.
4 Tahmina Rashid, 'Radicalisation of civil society: A Case study of Pakistan', in Smruti S. Pattanaik (ed), *South Asia: Envisioning a Regional Future*, New Delhi: Pentagon Security International, 2011, p. 159.
5 Tahmina Rashid, 'Masculine Notions of Justice for Female Victims in Pakistan', *South Asia Journal*, 2008, (21): 65–81
6 Consultation notes, concern identified by Pakistani NGOs (Insan Foundation, 25 November 2011 Paiman – 24 November 2011) during consultation meetings in Islamabad.
7 Krishna Kumar, 'Women and Women's organizations in post-conflict societies: the role of international assistance', Washington DC, USAID, 2010. http://siteresources.worldbank.org/EXTGLDEVLEARN/Resources/KrishnaKumar.pdf (accessed on 20 September 2012); Wenona Giles, and Jennifer Hyndman, 'Introduction: Gender and Conflict in a Global Context' in Wenona Giles, and Jennifer Hyndman (eds) *Sites of Violence: Gender and Conflict Zones*, Berkeley: University of California Press, 2004; Sonja Wölte, 'Armed Conflict and Trafficking in Women', Eschborn: GTZ, 2004, http://www.gtz.de/traffickinginwomen (accessed on 15 September 2012).
8 Declan Walash, 'Video of girl's flogging as Taliban hand out justice', *The Guardian*, 3 April 2009, http://www.guardian.co.uk/world/2009/apr/02/taliban-pakistan-justice-women-flogging (accessed on 15 September 2012); 'Pakistani Woman Recalls Flogging by Taliban' CBS News, 6 December 6, 2010, http://www.cbsnews.com/2100-202_162-7122774.html (accessed on 15 September 2012); 'Teenage girl flogged by Taliban in Swat', The Dawn, 3 April, 2009, http://archives.dawn.com/archives/141743 (accessed on 15 September 2012).
9 USAID, '*Women and Conflict: An Introductory Guide for Programming*', Washington, D.C., USAID, 2007, http://www.popline.org/node/179756 (accessed on 15 September 2012).
10 'Impact of Crisis on Women and Girls in FATA', Peshawar: Khwendo Kor, 2011.
11 David Hutton, 'Older People In Emergencies: Considerations For Action And Policy Development', Geneva: World Health Organisation, 2008. http://

www.who.int/ageing/publications/Hutton_report_small.pdf (accessed on 15 September 2012).

12 I would like to acknowledge that this trip in early 2011 was facilitated by the Pakistan Army; staying in the area otherwise was not secure even though after the 2009 military operation, the security situation had improved.
13 Interview conducted with Participant A1, at Rahet kot, 17 February 2011.
14 Interview Conducted with Participant B1, at Fazel Bag 19 February 2011.
15 Interview Conducted with Participant B2, at Fazel Bag 19 February 2011.
16 Interview Conducted with Participant C1, at PeocharValley 19 February 2011.
17 One of the Peshawar based organizations promised to send me a documentary on human trafficking in Swat valley during the Taliban militancy; however, despite numerous requests, I was never able to get further details.
18 Interview conducted with Participant A1, at Rahet kot, 17 February 2011.
19 Interview conducted with Participant A1, at Rahet kot, 17 February 2011.

9

AT THE MARGINS OF PAKISTAN

Political relationships between Gilgit-Baltistan and Azad Jammu and Kashmir

Martin Sökefeld

Introduction[1]

Pakistan is a prime example of a state with significant political marginalization and unequal sovereignty among its political units. The country's territory is compartmentalized into sections with differential rights and diverse political processes. Pakistan's tribal areas, for instance, have for decades been almost stateless tracts. This chapter focuses on two other areas at the margins of Pakistan: Gilgit-Baltistan (GB) and Azad Jammu and Kashmir (AJK). Historically, both areas were part of Jammu and Kashmir state (J&K). With the beginning of the Kashmir dispute between India and Pakistan in 1947, they came under the control of the latter. The purpose of this essay is to explore relationships between these two uneven territories that, in spite of the shared framework of the Kashmir dispute, are subject to different political treatments. Although both are under Pakistani administration, they differ radically in the way in which Pakistan has exerted control over them. Pakistan has always been committed to maintaining an almost watertight division between both parts. One could almost say that Pakistan established a kind of second Line of Control (LoC) between AJK and GB, beside the LoC that separates Pakistani from Indian-administered parts of J&K. Recently, however, oppositional political groups from both AKJ and GB have questioned the Pakistani control over both tracts, and have attempted to overcome the division and to establish political cooperation between them.

AJK and GB in the framework of Pakistan

The state of Jammu and Kashmir was created as a result of the Treaty of Amritsar signed between the British and Gulab Singh in 1846, establishing

Gulab Singh as the ruler of the new state and ushering in rule of the Dogra dynasty. After 1947, Jammu and Kashmir state was divided into three parts. Two of them, AJK and GB, are controlled by Pakistan; the third one is under Indian control.[2] Before 1947, the southern part of present-day AJK belonged to Jammu province of J&K. The northern section was part of Kashmir province. GB formed, together with Ladakh, the frontier districts of J&K, which included the British Gilgit Agency. In 1947, there were independent uprisings against the Maharaja in what was to become AJK and in Gilgit. In the southwest of the state, the insurrection developed from early summer of 1947, mainly in Poonch. On 4 October, the insurgents formed the government of Azad Jammu and Kashmir and declared the Maharaja deposed.[3] Aided by 'tribesmen' from the Northwest Frontier Province and Pakistani paramilitary forces, the rebels advanced towards Srinagar, forcing the Maharaja to declare accession to India on 27 October for the sake of military support. When the accession became known in Gilgit, the paramilitary Gilgit Scouts imprisoned the Kashmiri governor and asked the government of Pakistan to take over administration of the agency.[4]

Although the territories of AJK and GB were never formed into a single administrative unit, the Government of AJK (GoAJK) claimed to represent GB, also vis-à-vis the United Nations.[5] But, in April 1949, the GoAJK signed the Karachi Agreement with the Government of Pakistan (GoP), which specified the political jurisdiction of the GoAJK. According to the agreement, the GoAJK was responsible for the internal administration of AJK while the GoP took responsibility for defence, foreign policy, the negotiations with the UN concerning J&K, and 'all affairs of Gilgit-Ladakh under the control of Political Agent'.[6] The Karachi Agreement formally separated the administration of AJK and GB, although they never had been united.

Both AJK and GB were controlled by Pakistan. Yet, while AJK enjoyed nominal autonomy and formally had its own government, in GB, the colonial agency system was continued. Like his British predecessor, the Pakistani political agent was the supreme power in the area, possessing executive, legislative, and juridical functions. GB's request for accession was never accepted by Pakistan. This caused considerable alienation. The GoP controlled both territories through its Ministry of Kashmir Affairs.

The limited democratization of Pakistani politics initiated by Zulfiqar Ali Bhutto at the beginning of the 1970s brought changes to both AJK and GB. In AJK, the local political monopoly of the Muslim Conference was broken by the establishment of a second party, the Pakistan People's Party AJK. The first elections of the Legislative Assembly in AJK took place in 1970 and the Azad Jammu and Kashmir Interim Constitution Act was brought into force in 1974. The interim constitution tightened Pakistan's grip on AJK by creating the Azad Jammu and Kashmir Council: the GoP held the majority of the Council's seats. Pakistan's control of AJK affairs was also ensured by the fact that the GoP appointed AJK's top-most officials – the Chief Secretary, the Inspector General of Police, and the Accountant General – who were not answerable to the GoAJK.[7] The strict orientation towards Pakistan is expressed by the oath of 'loyalty to the country and the cause of the accession of the State of Jammu and Kashmir to Pakistan' that members of government and the legislative assembly have to take.[8] The interim constitution further stipulates 'no person or political party in Azad Jammu and Kashmir shall be permitted to propagate against, or take part in activities prejudicial or detrimental to, the ideology of the State's accession to Pakistan'.[9] Thus, any person who favours the independence of J&K is excluded from official political processes and positions. AJK is not recognized as a state by any other country of the world. Its status in international law is that of a 'local authority' under the UN Resolutions.[10] For all practical and ideological purposes, AJK is Pakistan's placeholder for its claim on the whole of J&K.

Bhutto also brought changes to GB. From the local perspective, the Bhutto government's political reforms were in response to a local uprising, called the 'revolution of Gilgit'. Events escalated after a minor dispute with a Pakistani army officer in January 1970. Incidentally, a few weeks earlier, a political organization called *Tanzim-e Millat* (Association of the Nation) had been established under the leadership of a local political activist, Johar Ali Khan. The dispute was understood as a further example of abuse of locals by outsiders. When some local leaders were arrested, an angry mob attacked the jail and the police station. Finally, Frontier Scouts from the NWFP were called in to subdue the revolt.[11]

Bhutto's reforms incorporated some of the demands that had been voiced by the *Tanzim-e Millat*, and the *Tanzim* was turned into a local branch of Bhutto's PPP. The administration of GB was changed from the Agency system to a more regular administration that, to some extent, resembled the administration of a province. Bhutto renamed GB as 'Northern Areas of Pakistan', which can be understood as a symbolic incorporation of the region into Pakistan. In 1970, the first elections of a body called *Northern Areas Advisory Council* were held. Taxes were abolished and the semi-autonomous petty states such as Hunza were integrated into the Northern Areas. Many people in Gilgit demanded that the Northern Areas be declared a regular province of Pakistan and the steps undertaken by the Bhutto government pointed towards this direction. Reforms came to a halt when Zia-ul Haq seized power in 1977. Zia leveraged the martial law to further integrate the Northern Areas into Pakistan. The region was declared 'Martial Law Zone E' (the four provinces of Pakistan being zones A-D).[12] In 1982, Zia stated that the Northern Areas were part of Pakistan and not disputed territories.[13]

Legally, neither GB nor AJK is a part of Pakistan and the Constitution of Pakistan does not refer to these tracts as part of the state's territory.[14] However, the atlas of the Survey of Pakistan does not show GB ('Northern Areas') as a territory distinct from Pakistan, while AJK is identified as separate from Pakistan, as part of J&K.[15] Today, the official terminology identifies GB not a *de jure* but a *de facto* part of Pakistan.[16] This is also reflected in the citizenship status of the inhabitants of the GB. While the inhabitants of AJK are still considered state subjects of J&K and are issued *State Subject Certificates*, this status has been discontinued in GB. In May 1999, however, the Supreme Court of Pakistan gave the verdict that the people of GB should also be considered *de jure* citizens of Pakistan.[17]

In September 2009, the GoP introduced a new reform package, the *Gilgit-Baltistan Empowerment and Self-Governance Order*.[18] Like several previous reform packages, this one gave few new competencies to government institutions of GB. The region was officially renamed again as Gilgit-Baltistan. Besides, a Gilgit-Baltistan Legislative Assembly with very limited legislative powers was established. The designation of the administrative institutions now closely resembles the nomenclature of Pakistani provinces. But the GoP equally dominates the new GB Council, designed on similar lines as the AJK Council.

While AJK formally possesses most of the government institutions of a state, GB now formally has the institutions of a Pakistani province. However, AJK remains a quasi-state and GB a quasi-province because neither territory enjoys the full rights and powers connected with the respective political formations. In both areas, Pakistan retains ultimate control.

Politics opposing Pakistan

Yet, politics is not limited to official institutions and procedures. In both AJK and GB, there were a number of movements and oppositional initiatives originating from 'popular politics' that opposed Pakistani official politics. Noteworthy examples in AJK are the Sudhan revolt in Poonch in 1950 and the protest against the construction of the Mangla Dam in the 1960s. In Gilgit, the 'revolution' of 1970 was followed by political movements in the 1990s. Here, sectarian mobilization and violence that started in the 1970s partly intersected political movements.[19] Shias form the majority of GB's population, but there are strong Sunni pockets also.

Many people in Gilgit allege that violent sectarianism was endorsed by the Pakistan government by sending radically anti-Shia, "Wahabi" mullahs to the town, so as to drive a sectarian wedge into the region for a more effective control of the area. The most violent incident occurred in May 1988, when more than a hundred Shias were killed by intruding Sunni warriors in villages around Gilgit.

By the term 'oppositional politics', I do not refer to opposition within the current political setup in GB and AJK; rather, I refer to oppositional groups and activists that radically challenge existing arrangements, including control of their areas by Pakistan. Both in AJK and in GB, political activists who struggle for autonomy or independence of their respective areas call themselves *nationalists*. This self-designation reflects the conviction that the people of both territories form nations that deserve the right of self-determination. 'Nationalism' is contrasted with 'power politics' or 'loyalism', which means politics within the official setup, under the surveillance of Pakistan. A recent poll shows that around 44 per cent of the people in AJK are not content with the political status quo, but favour the independence of J&K instead.[20] Perhaps even more people in GB are dissatisfied with the present status of the area. Basically, there are three different positions in GB: a minority demands that GB becomes a part of AJK, a second position favours the full integration of the region as a fifth province into Pakistan, and a third position considers GB as entirely different from both Pakistan and Kashmir and demands actual autonomy or even independence. Most probably, the majority of people in GB would opt for provincial integration. Organizations that put forward the third option were established mostly after the end of Zia's military regime. They moved gradually from the demand for autonomy to the demand for independence.[21] All three positions affect the relationship between AJK and GB.

Relations between Gilgit-Baltistan and Azad Kashmir

From the perspective of the GoP, the Karachi Agreement of 1949 severed the relations between AJK and GB. According to the Agreement, the GoAJK has no say in the affairs of GB. Yet, from AJK's oppositional perspective, GB is considered a part of J&K, and should therefore be united with AJK. Perspectives in GB, however, are more varied and complex.

Even before 1947, Dogra rule was strongly resented in the Gilgit Agency due to taxation and other exploitative practices (Sökefeld 2005).[22] Johar Ali Khan, the leader of Gilgit's 1970 uprising, always asserted that GB could never become part of AJK. Referring to the proportions of both parts (29.814 sq. miles in the case of GB and 5.134 sq. miles in the case of AJK), he liked to compare GB with a bucket and AJK with a glass, emphasizing: 'You can only put a glass into a bucket but never bucket into a glass'![23]

The adverse attitude of the majority population of Gilgit towards AJK is mainly based on two factors: the history of Dogra domination of the region before 1947 and the fact that the population of AJK is largely Sunni. As a consequence, all Shias and Ismailis reject AJK. Shia political leaders regularly demanded the accession of GB to Pakistan as a fifth province. Yet, the GoP responded to this demand with nominal reforms only, thereby ducking the demand for the integration of the area with Pakistan. Consequently, demands by GB became radicalized and some activists raised the demand for independence. It was first put forward by the *Balawaristan National Front* (BNF), a small party established in 1988. This group coined a new name for GB: Balawaristan. The designation is derived from the Persian word *bala*, high, and translates as 'country of the heights', i.e. country of mountains.[24] Since that time, oppositional groups generally rejected the term Northern Areas because it designated the area in relationship to Pakistan only, as 'Northern Areas *of Pakistan*', and denied a separate identity. Besides the new Balawaristan, there was also a growing popularity of the old designation, Gilgit-Baltistan, in oppositional politics. The renaming of the erstwhile Northern Areas as Gilgit-Baltistan in the reform of 2009 is seen by many as a certain acknowledgment of identity by the GoP.

Nationalist groups define GB as a nation in its own right that is separate from both J&K and Pakistan, and that, therefore, is entitled to national self-determination. This position is supported by historical, cultural, and linguistic arguments.[25] According to this perspective, the Northern Areas are 'The Last Colony of the 21st Century'.[26] When, on 14 August 1997, Pakistan celebrated the Golden Jubilee on its 50th anniversary, nationalist groups in Gilgit mobilized for commemorating a 'Black Jubilee' instead. In Gilgit, November 1 is officially celebrated as *yom-e azadi* (freedom day). For years, on November 1, GB nationalists have been denouncing *'ghulami'* (slavery) under Pakistani rule.

It is difficult to assess the strength of the nationalist groups. They are not allowed to take part in council/assembly elections on a party ticket, although occasionally, individual nationalists have been elected as independent candidates. Yet, not all political activists in Gilgit share the perspective of the nationalists and reject Kashmir. In accordance with the sectarian rationale, some Sunnis demand instead the unification of the GB with AJK. In 1990, Malik Miskeen and Haji Amir Jan, two Sunni politicians from GB, together with an advocate from Muzaffarabad, filed a writ petition at the High Court of AJK that demanded the unification of the GB with AJK. In response to the petition, the GoP simply rejected the competence of the court because its jurisdiction was limited to AJK. Also, the GoAJK rejected the petition. In addition to the statements of the GoP and the GoAJK, statements of various political parties from AJK, both pro-Pakistan and pro-independence, were admitted to the case. All these statements affirmed that GB was part of J&K and that GB should be handed over to the GoAJK. In his verdict of 8 March 1993, Chief Justice Malik Majeed agreed with this position, admitted the petition and ordered:

I. (a) the Azad Government to immediately assume the administrative control of the Northern Areas and to annexe [sic] it with the administration of Azad Jammu and Kashmir;
 (b) the Government of Pakistan to provide an adequate assistance and facility to the Azad Government in [the] attainment of the said objective.
II. the residents (State Subjects) of the Northern Areas shall enjoy the benefit of the fundamental rights conferred by the Act [of]1974. They shall be provided representations in: (i) the Government, (ii) the Assembly, (iii) the Council, (iv) the Civil Services; and (v) other national institutions."[27]

The verdict had no practical consequences. The GoP and the GoAJK appealed to the Supreme Court of AJK, which rejected the High Court's verdict on 'technical grounds', the retired Chief Justice Malik Majeed told me in an interview.[28] On the GB side, the judgement was criticized and rejected by the nationalist groups. In an interview in August 2007, one leader objected that the High Court had not consulted anybody in GB, except the petitioners. While a number of parties from AJK were admitted to the case as respondents to the petition, no group from GB was included. This reaction to the verdict exemplifies the prevalent sentiment among most political activists in GB towards AJK: the impression that people from AJK – and this refers not only to the government, but also to oppositional Kashmiri groups – do not take the people of GB seriously, that they do not accept them as equal political actors. Until recently, few Azad Kashmiris have actually bothered to visit the area and to establish personal contacts. Generally, AJK is indifferent to the political and living conditions in GB. In Gilgit, the sentiment prevails that GB is considered a pawn in the power games of AJK.

In contrast, from the perspective of political activists in AJK, GB is considered, by default, as a part of J&K, and should therefore be united with AJK, as the High Court ruled. It seems that many members of the GoAJK share this perspective, albeit they never endorse it while in office. Until very recently, members of the GoAJK did not even visit GB. Although unification with AJK is still rejected by the nationalists in GB, there has been a certain rapprochement between oppositional political groups of AJK and GB. In a marked departure from earlier perspectives, some groups in Gilgit compared J&K favourably with Pakistan. This did not mean that they considered GB a part of J&K state. But they claimed that before 1947, under Dogra rule, GB had more political rights than subsequently under Pakistani administration.

In 2001, relationships between some nationalist and oppositional groups from GB and AJK led to the formation of the *All Parties National Alliance* (APNA). Wajahat Hassan and Nadir Hassan, the two sons of Gilgit's freedom fighter Col. Mirza Hassan Khan, are the principal activists of APNA from Gilgit. Wajahat Hassan had moved to Islamabad in the mid-1990s because, as he said, pressure on nationalists had become very strong in Gilgit. The brothers got involved with oppositional AJK activists. They organized demonstrations for the enforcement of State Subjects Status in Gilgit Baltistan. At a protest in February 2001 in Rawalpindi, they were arrested together with activists from AJK. Wajahat Hassan told me:

> We remained twenty or twenty-five days in Adiala Jail in Rawalpindi. There I realized that the others [i.e. activists from AJK] were really secular-minded and liberal nationalists. We wanted to establish a secular and liberal council with people from this Kashmir [AJK] and that Kashmir [Indian Administered Kashmir] and Gilgit Baltistan.[29]

The explicit purpose of APNA was to close the 'communication gap' between AJK and the GB. It is no accident that APNA was established in Islamabad, which is close to AJK and where many Kashmiri activists and groups are based. In Gilgit, not all people were happy about APNA and some criticized the Hassan brothers for having left the town for a more comfortable life in the capital. Still, there was a certain expectation that oppositional activists from GB and from AJK needed to join hands if they wanted to achieve anything. On several occasions, APNA delegations visiting Gilgit for seminars or to protest against conditions in their territories were forced to leave the town by the Pakistani authorities. For the nationalists in Gilgit, forming ties with groups from AJK is also an expression of their rejection of the *de facto* integration of GB with Pakistan. Thus, while in the past, they always underlined that GB was not a part of Kashmir, a new formula is used by nationalists, according to which GB is not a part of

J&K, but a part of the Kashmir dispute, and therefore, certainly not a part of Pakistan.

Still, the communication gap between AJK and GB has not yet been closed. In the summer 2007, the *Azad Jammu and Kashmir National Students Federation* (NSF), closely linked to oppositional politics and parties, organized a 'Long March' to Gilgit with the intention of establishing better relations between the two areas. On 13 August, a large group of students from AJK started to cross the high mountains into the Astore Valley of GB. The purpose of the march was the

> Remembrance of the reunification of our motherland and also solidarity with the most oppressed people of Gilgit Baltistan. People from northern province of Kashmir have been denied their basic human rights since last 60 years and kept under brutal Pakistani occupation. JK NSF ... will never forget their brothers and sisters living under worse conditions in occupied Gilgit Baltistan areas of Kashmir. JK NSF appealed to the youth from Indian occupied Kashmir (IOK) that they also can support and participate in this long march, starting from Srinagar towards Gilgit Baltistan. It will be an attempt to make LOC irrelevant for every Kashmiri living in three parts of forcibly divided Kashmir.[30]

Political activists in Gilgit had not been contacted before the march. They learnt about the upcoming event only through the press and regarded this as another indication that they did not really matter much for the Azad Kashmiris. Further, some fear was expressed that the students might move into Gilgit with the slogan that GB is a part of Kashmir and that this would certainly be detrimental to the intention of forging better understanding. Unfortunately, the march did not reach Gilgit. Being largely unaware of the topography of GB, the students lacked even the most basic equipment for a march over high mountain passes. Several students slipped down steep slopes. Two of them suffered fatal injuries. Only five students reached Gilgit and kept a low profile there, while the rest of the group returned to AJK. The tragedy of the long march demonstrated the difficulties of establishing communications across the GB-AJK divide.

Nationalists from AJK and from GB are united in their critique of the 2009 GB reform package, if for different reasons. Those from AJK allege that the reform cements the separation of GB from J&K while activists from Gilgit regard the reform as Pakistan's attempt to tighten its grip on GB.

Networking between activists from both territories is not limited to Pakistan or to the two areas themselves. Transnational relationships are especially significant for AJK because of the large Azad Kashmiri diaspora in Britain that mainly consists of people originating from Mirpur and Kotli.[31] Since the 1950s, transnational mobilization has played an important role in oppositional Kashmiri politics; for instance, activists in these diasporas opposed the construction of the Mangla Dam. Also, activists from AJK in Britain established the Jammu and Kashmir Liberation Front, which, in the late 1980s, initiated the insurgency on the Indian side of J&K.

More recently, Kashmiri activists from AJK in Britain have developed a strong interest in the political fate of GB. After the promulgation of the GB Self-Governance Order in September 2009 by the Pakistan government, both independence-oriented and pro-Pakistani Kashmiris in Britain voiced their protest against this Order. Yet, not all people of GB were happy with the sort of support given by Kashmiri diaspora groups. As AJK nationalists called a meeting in Brussels in December 2009 to discuss the GB reform package, and termed GB an 'integral part of Kashmir', an activist from GB issued a strong reaction on the email discussion group *Kashnet* to the effect that claiming GB to be an integral part of Kashmir was an insult to the people of Gilgit Baltistan. Further, he wrote that GB could be considered a party to the Kashmir issue, but not a part of Kashmir territory. He emphasized that Kashmir had occupied GB, but that the people of GB ended the occupation in November 1947. He stated that statements by any group that called GB a Kashmiri territory must be strongly condemned.

Still, there is also diasporic cooperation among activists from GB and AJK. Also, ideas that germinate in the diaspora feed back into the regions. For example the leftist Kashmiri Workers Association (KWA) in Britain introduced a new term for AJK into political discourse on the Pakistani side of the LoC: instead of speaking of Azad ('Free') Kashmir, the KWA started to refer to 'Pakistani Occupied Kashmir' (POK), similar to the expression 'Indian Occupied Kashmir' (IOK), or simply, 'Occupied Kashmir' (*Maqbuza Kashmir*), invariably used in Pakistan to refer to the territories controlled by India. The new designation filtered back into the discourse of the nationalists in AJK. This was taken up by nationalists in GB, who now refer to 'Pakistani Occupied Gilgit-Baltistan' (POGB). There are many political differences between nationalist activists in AJK and in GB, but on one point they agree: neither part is free.

AJK and GB: Ambiguity of status in the framework of Pakistan

Geographically, both GB and AJK are situated along the margins of Pakistan. Politically, however, this marginality needs to be qualified. These areas are marginal in that they have no say in Pakistani politics. Yet, both ideologically and economically, they are at the very centre of Pakistan. The national ideology of Pakistan is still based on the 'Two-Nations-Theory' that stipulates that Pakistan is the nation of South Asian Muslims. As a Muslim-majority territory, J&K is claimed as an essential part of Pakistan. As historical parts of J&K, AJK and GB represent Pakistan's claim. At the same time, while the two territories are claimed by Pakistan, they are not politically integrated territories: consequently, AJK and GB are kept in state of political limbo: the two territories are neither Pakistan nor *not* Pakistan. The status of GB is doubly equivocal: GB is neither a part of J&K nor *not* a part of J&K; it is neither a province nor *not* a province of Pakistan. The ambiguity of the territories enables Pakistan's unilateral control. While the government of Pakistan exerts power and control on AJK and GB, through the Ministry of Kashmir Affairs and the AJK and GB Councils, the people of the two areas, in their turn, have no right to participate in the formal political processes of Pakistan. The residents of GB and AJK are residents of their Pakistan controlled territories with limited citizenship rights.

Economically, AJK and GB are harbouring one of Pakistan's most needed resources: water. Most of the water that is required by Pakistan for irrigation and for generating electricity comes from these areas. The Mangla Dam on the river Jhelum in AJK and the Diamer-Bhasha Dam on the Indus that is currently under construction exemplify the marginal status of AJK and GB on the fringes of Pakistan in a literal sense: in both cases, the reservoir extends beyond Pakistani territory, into AJK or GB, yet the dams and powerhouses are situated just on the border. The resources generated through the dams are controlled by Pakistan, beyond the reach of the local population, which suffers displacement due to water inundation. Protest against the construction of the Diamer-Bhasha Dam frequently refers to another dam project on the river Indus: the Kalabagh Dam in Khyber-Pakhtunkhwa province. After thirty years of discussion and in consequence of the strong and politically articulated local protest, the Kalabagh Dam has still not been built. The disenfranchised people of AJK and GB, however, have no means to articulate their protest and resistance through Pakistani political institutions like a provincial or the national parliament.

Conclusion

Recent scholarship has described the state as a fragmented and unstable configuration with 'blurred boundaries'.[32] Introducing a volume on sovereignty and the postcolonial state, Hansen and Stepputat suggest 'that sovereignty of the state is an aspiration that seeks to create itself in the face of internally fragmented, unevenly distributed and unpredictable configurations of political authority that exercise more or less legitimate violence in a territory. Sovereign power . . . is always a tentative and unstable project whose efficacy and legitimacy depend on repeated performances of violence and a "will to rule"'.[33] In an echo of Radcliff-Brown's doubts about the 'reality' of the state,[34] Mitchell argues that the state is not a distinct powerful entity, but just an 'effect' created by multiple practices and processes.[35] From a different academic tradition, Jackson asserts that most postcolonial states are 'quasi-states' that are insubstantial and lack effective sovereignty.[36] All these concepts and analyses fit very well the case of Pakistan. Especially at present, Pakistan appears as an unstable project that is under heavy attack from many sides. Yet, this image remains incomplete as long as only instability and the fragmented character of the Pakistani state are emphasized. The idea of the state as an 'effect' has to be complemented by the recognition that this effect is extremely convincing and powerful. Indeed, the discourse of opposition groups in AJK and GB describe Pakistan as a pervasive and powerful entity. Not only the state itself but also its opponents produce a 'magic fiction'[37] of the powerful state. In spite of the apparent instability of the Pakistani state – and opposition and resistance to it from the areas notwithstanding – Pakistan's control over AJK and GB has been very stable. Fragmented sovereignty may not always simply indicate a state's weakness and fragility. In Pakistan, differential sovereignty is also a strategy of control. Pakistan creates a 'state of exception' in which AJK and GB enjoy neither constitutional rights nor actual autonomy.

Inequality does not only govern the relationship between Pakistan and the two tracts, but also between them as greater autonomy of AJK contrasts with more direct control of GB. The inequality between the two territories is embodied in the border that sets them apart. Being neither a provincial nor an international border, it is another irregularity. In contrast with the LoC that separates Pakistani and Indian-administered J&K, the line between GB and AJK is unnamed, unmarked, and unguarded in the high mountain territory that connects the two territories. The border does not need to be watched, as there is no road and traffic there. In fact, there is no direct road link between AJK and GB. The border is much more a symbolic construct that enables control than an actual line of demarcation. It enables control because the differentiated (and uneven) border regime extends into the centres of the separated territories, preventing officials from AJK to comment on the affairs of GB, and allowing Pakistani forces to banish unwelcome political activists and to prevent their free movement between the two territories. The border helps to impede joint political mobilization by GB and AJK. For AJK activists, the border is another 'line of division' – almost similar to the line that divides J&K into Pakistani and Indian-controlled parts

In July 2010, Prime Minister Raja Farooq Haider of AJK resigned in order to avoid a no-confidence motion in the legislative assembly. His was the third resignation or dismissal of an AJK Prime Minister within less than two years. As reasons for his resignation, Farooq Haider mentioned factionalism and opposition within his own party, the Muslim Conference, but he also held the GoP responsible for political crisis in AJK.[38] These resignations exemplify both the volatility of politics in AJK and the ultimate grip of the GoP. Robinson emphasizes that AJK (and GB, I might add) should not be considered a mere extension of Pakistan; it is a political entity in its own right and a quite dynamic one at that.[39] Yet, while the political situation within AJK is very fluid, the overall political arrangement with Pakistan is quite stable. The same applies to GB: Reforms notwithstanding, the ultimate control of Pakistan over GB has never been in question. In all likelihood, opposition political activism will not be able to change this as nationalist groups are no less divided than official Pakistani politics. The nationalists enjoy equivocal and probably limited popular support. On close inspection, beyond political rhetoric, anti-state politics is as fragmented and unstable as the Pakistan state itself.

Notes

1 Earlier versions of this paper were presented at the 22nd Pakistan Workshop, May 2008, Rook How, UK and at the International Symposium Jammu and Kashmir: Boundaries and Movements, June 2011, Frauenwörth, Germany. I am grateful to the participants of the workshops for their many useful comments. The paper is based on research which was generously funded by the Deutsche Forschungsgemeinschaft and the Wenner-Gren Foundation.
2 A fourth part of J&K, Aksai Chin, is under Chinese occupation.
3 This government was replaced by a 'Reconstituted Government of Azad Kashmir' on 24 October 1947, which, in official history, is regarded as the founding date of AJK.
4 Martin Sökefeld, 'Jang Azadi: A major theme in Northern Areas' History', in *The past in the present: Horizons of remembering in the Pakistan Himalaya*, ed. Irmtraud Stellrecht (Cologne: Köppe, 1997).
5 Nazir Anjam, *Shumali Kashmir ki siyasi tarikh* [Political History of Northern Kashmir, in Urdu] (Mirpur: Kashir Publishers, n.d.), 50.
6 For the text of the Karachi Agreement see Smruti S Pattanaik, 'How Azad is 'Azad Kashmir': An Analysis of Relations between Islamabad and Muzaffarabad', in *Pakistan Occupied Kashmir: The Untold Story*, ed. Virendra Gupta and Alok Bansal (New Delhi: Manas Publications, 2007), p. 179f.
7 This system started in the early 1950s and continues to the present, see Leo E. Rose, 'The Politics of Azad Kashmir', in *Perspectives on Kashmir: The Roots of Conflict in South Asia*, ed. Raju G. C. Thomas (Boulder: Westview Press, 1992).

AT THE MARGINS OF PAKISTAN

8 See AJK Government Act, 1970, in Syed Mazoor H Gilani, Constitutional Development in Azad Jammu and Kashmir (Lahore: National Book Depot, 1985), appendix VIII, 202f.
9 Azad Jammu and Kashmir Interim Constitution Act, 1974, section 7(2).
10 See UNCIP Resolution, 13 August 1948, Part II, A-3, in Gilani, Constitutional Development in Azad Jammu and Kashmir, p. 15.
11 Martin Sökefeld, Ein Labyrinth von Identitäten in Nordpakistan: Zwischen Landbesitz, Religion und Kaschmir-Konflikt (Cologne, Köppe 1997), 284ff.
12 Martial Law Order No 3, July 7, 1977, in Usman Ali, Gilgit ki rog kahani [The doleful story of Gilgit, in Urdu] (Lahore: Maqbul Acacemy, 1990), 233f.
13 Khalid Rahman and Ershad Mahmud, 'Northern Areas of Pakistan: Facts, Problems and Recommendations', Policy Perspectives 1(2004), 128.
14 Constitution of Pakistan, Part I, section 1.
15 Survey of Pakistan, Atlas of Pakistan (Rawalpindi, Survey of Pakistan, 2005).
16 In its reply to the Supreme Court of AJK in a case about the political status of the Northern Areas the Government of Pakistan stated that 'Pakistan exercises de facto sovereignty over "Northern Areas"'. See Samuel Baid, 'Suppression of Gilgit Baltistan', in Pakistan Occupied Kashmir: The Untold Story, ed. Virendra Gupta and Alok Bansal (New Delhi: Manas Publications, 2007), 150. Similarly, officials of the Chief Secretary of Azad Kashmir told me in summer 2007 that while AJK is a disputed territory, GB is not disputed.
17 This judgement was issued in response to the decision of the AJK High Court of 1993 to which I refer below.
18 Available online at http://www.gilgitbaltistan.gov.pk/images/stories/downloads/Governance-Order.pdf (accessed 6 July 2010).
19 Sökefeld, Ein Labyrinth von Identitäten in Nordpakistan, p. 203ff.
20 Robert W, Bradnock, Kashmir: Paths to Peace (London: Chatham House 2010), 15. Comparable data for GB are not available.
21 Sökefeld, Ein Labyrinth von Identitäten in Nordpakistan, p 296ff; Martin Sökefeld, 'Balawaristan and Other ImagiNations: A Nationalist Discourse in the Northern Areas of Pakistan', in Ladakh: Culture, History, and Development between Himalaya and Karakora, eds Martijn van Beek, Kristoffer Brix Bertelsen and Poul Pedersen.(Aarhus: Aarhus University Press, 1999), pp 350–368.
22 Martin Sökefeld, 'From Colonialism to Postcolonial Colonialism: Changing Modes of Domination in the Northern Areas of Pakistan', The Journal of Asian Studies 64 (2005).
23 Interview with Johar Ali Khan, Gilgit, 1992.
24 See also the first BNF-manifesto, Nawaz Khan Naji, Gilgit, Baltistan aur mulhaqa illaqajat par mushtammil Balawaristan [Balawaristan consisting of Gilgit, Baltistan and adjacent areas, in Urdu], Gilgit, 1988. Balawaristan resonates also with the historical regional name Boloristan.
25 See Sökefeld, Ein Labyrinth, 297ff.; Sökefeld, 'Balawaristan and Other Imagi-Nations'.
26 Abdul Hamid Khan, Balawaristan: The Last Colony of 21st Century (Gilgit: Balawaristan National Front, 2001).
27 Majeed Malik, High Court of Judicature Azad Jammu and Kashmir: Verdict on Gilgit and Baltistan (Northern Area) (Mirpur: Kashmir Human Rights Forum, n.d.). 173f.
28 Interview, 31 August 2007.

29 Interview, August 2, 2007.
30 Statement disseminated through the email-forum Kashnet, 4 July 2007.
31 On (Azad) Kashmiris in Britain, see Nasreen Ali, 'Diaspora and Nation: Displacement and the Politics of Kashmiri Identity in Britain', Contemporary South Asia 12 (2003); Nasreen Ali, Patricia Ellis and Zafar Khan, 'The 1990s: A Time to Separate British Punjabi and British Kashmiri Identity', in *Punjabi Identity: Continuity and Change*, ed. M Gurharpal Singh and Ian Talbot (New Delhi: Manohar, 1996); Patricia Ellis and Zafar Khan, 'Political Allegiances and Social Integration: The British Kashmiris', in *Roots and Routes: Ethnicity and migration in global perspective*, ed. Shalva Weil (Jerusalem: Magnes Press,1999); Martin Sökefeld, 'Diaspora und soziale Mobilisierung: Kaschmiris in Großbritannien', in *Praktiken der Differenz: Diasporakulturen in der Zeitgeschichte*, ed. Miriam Rürup (Göttingen: Wallstein Verlag, 2009); Martin Sökefeld and Marta Bolognani, 'Kashmiris in Britain: A Political Project or a Social Reality?' in *Pakistan and its Diaspora: Multidisciplinary Approaches*, ed. Marta Bolognani and Steven M. Lyon (New York: Palgrave, 2011).
32 Akhil Gupta, 'Blurred Boundaries: The Discourse of Corruption, the Culture of Politics, and the Imagined State', American Ethnologist 22 (1995); Michel-Rolph Trouillot, *Global Transformation* (New York: Palgrave Macmillan 2003).
33 Thomas Blom Hansen and Finn Stepputat, 'Introduction', in *Sovereign Bodies: Citizens, Migrants, and States in the Postcolonial World*, ed. Thomas Blom Hansen and Finn Stepputat (Princeton: Princeton University Press 2005), 3.
34 A.R. Radcliffe-Brown, 'Preface', in *African Political Systems*, ed. Meyer Fortes and E.E. Evans-Pritchard (London: Oxford University Press, 1940), xxiii.
35 Timothy Mitchell, 'Society, Economy, and the State Effect', in *The Anthropology of the State*, ed. Aradhana Sharma and Akhil Gupta (Oxford: Blackwell 2006).
36 Robert H. Jackson, *Quasi-States: Sovereignty, International Relations, and the Third World* (Cambridge, Cambridge University Press, 1990).
37 Das, Veena, 'The Signature of the State: The Paradox of Illegibility', in *Anthropology at the Margins of the State*, ed. Veena Das and Deborah Poole (New Delhi: Oxford University Press, 2004).
38 See *Dawn*, 27 August 2010 and *The News International*, 27August 2010.
39 Cabeiri Debergh Robinson, *Refugees, Political Subjectivity, and the Morality of Violence: From Hijrat to Jihad in Azad Kashmir* (Unpublished PhD thesis, Cornell University, 2005), 39f.

INDEX

Afghanistan, terrorism 28–32; CENTO and SEATO Alliances 31; extremist Islamic militancy 32; Haqqani network 29; HuJI 32; HuM 32; Iranian revolution, 1979 32; ISI support 31; JeM 32; Kerry-Lugar Bill 31; Khost and Gardez, captures of 29; LeJ 32; Quetta Shura 29; Shanghai Cooperation Organization 31; SSP 32; TTP 30
Afghan Taliban 12, 31, 35, 51, 140, 146, 149
Ahl-e-Hadith movement 87–8
AJK see Azad Jammu and Kashmir (AJK)
Akhand Bharat (undivided India) 6–7, 9
All India Muslim League, 1906 3
All Pakistan Mohajir Student Organization (APMSO) 111–12, 116
All Parties National Alliance (APNA) 181
al-Qaeda 28, 95–8; AQAP 97; AQIS 96–7; freedom fighters 89; global jihadist ideology 95; Indian Mujahideen network 98; Jund-ul-Fida (Army of Fidayeen) 97–8; Kashmiri Muslims 97; Punjabi Taliban 97; Taliban and Kashmiri militants, links between 30–1
al-Qaeda in the Arabian Peninsula (AQAP) 97
al-Qaeda in the Indian Subcontinent (AQIS) 96–8

'Aman ki Asha (hope of peace)' 50
Andrabi study 61, 73
ANP see Awami National Party (ANP)
anti-colonialism 16
anti-Soviet war, Afghanistan 139–40
Anti-Women Practices Act 158
APMSO see All Pakistan Mohajir Student Organization (APMSO)
APNA see All Parties National Alliance (APNA)
APP see Associated Press of Pakistan (APP)
Ashraf, Raja Pervez 148–9
Associated Press of Pakistan (APP) 42
Audit Bureau of Circulation (ABC) 43
Awami League 135–6
Awami National Party (ANP) 106, 108, 114, 116–17, 119–20
Ayub Khan: Chief of Army Staff (COAS) 133–4; economic and military development 133; guided-democracy 133; military rule 41–2; national identity 4–5; Pakistan–China relations 15
Azad Jammu and Kashmir (AJK) 174, 179–81; political activists 180–1; political crisis 186; Sunni population 179; see also Gilgit-Baltistan (GB) and AJK, political relationships
Azad Jammu and Kashmir Interim Constitution Act 175–6
Azad Jammu and Kashmir National Students Federation (NSF), 2007 182

INDEX

Balawaristan National Front (BNF) 179
Bandung Conference 15
Bangladesh, creation of 8–9, 12, 16, 27, 32, 97–8
Barelvi 23, 35, 87–8
Bengali movement (1971) 42
Bhutto, Benazir 35, 43, 136, 141, 148
blasphemy law 25, 52
blasts, Pakistani rationale 13
BNF *see* Balawaristan National Front (BNF)
British Raj, partition of 4, 7, 131
Business Plus TV 46
Business Recorder/Aaj TV 46

CENTO *see* Central Treaty Organization (CENTO)
Central Treaty Organization (CENTO) 14, 31, 132
Charlie Wilson's War 22
Chávez, Hugo 128
China 15, 36
Clinton, Bill 141
Code of Criminal Procedure (CCP) 158
Cold War security arrangements 14
colonial and pre-partition legacy 2–4; All India Muslim League 3; Indian Muslim elites and British rule 2; Indian National Congress 2; Muslim League, 1936 electoral defeat 3; partition of the British Raj 4; radicalization 2; refugee problem 4; South Asian Islamic culture 2
Committee to Protect Journalists 40
counter-terrorism laws 25
coup outcome, factors affecting 127–30; divisions within the military 128; OAS 129; popular support 128; putsch, Ecuador and Venezuela 128–9; threat of international retaliation 128; War on Terror 129
The Criminal Law Amendment Bill on Acid and Burn Violence 158

Dawn 45
Dawn News 46
defence policy 10–12; anti-Soviet Afghan jihad 11; defeat in 1971 war 11; fear of 'Hindu India' 11; 'martial races' concept 11; radical Islamist groups, support for 12
delegitimization 26
Deobandi–Barelvi violence 98
Diamer-Bhasha Dam and Mangla Dam 185
District Management Group 137
'Doctrine of Paramountcy' 7
Dogra rule 178–9, 181
Dunya TV 46

electronic media, rising power of 45–7; Business Plus TV 46; Business Recorder/Aaj TV 46; Dawn 45; *Dawn News* 46; Dunya TV 46; investment in audio-visual field 45; *Jang* (War) 45; Pakistan Broadcasting Corporation 47; Urdu channels 46; Waqt (Time) 45
English-language minority press 55
Erdogan, Tayyip 26
Ethan Bueno de Mesquita's model 77

FATA *see* Federally-Administered Tribal Areas (FATA)
fatwas 74, 136
fear of 'Hindu India' 11
fear of Indian hegemony 7–8
Federally-Administered Tribal Areas (FATA) 25, 62, 76, 86–7, 131, 157
Federal Security Force (FSF) 137
'flea market effect' 96
FSF *see* Federal Security Force (FSF)
FY2002 34

Gandhi, Indira 9
GB Self-Governance Order in September 2009 183
Gilani Research Foundation 2
Gilani, Yousaf Raza 148–9
Gilgit-Baltistan (GB) and AJK, political relationships 174, 178–83; APNA 181; BNF 179; communication gap 181; cooperation 183; Dogra rule 178–9; Economical resources 184; GB, defined by Nationalist groups 179; GoAJK and GoP 175; inequality

INDEX

185; IOK 183; Karachi Agreement 178; Kashmiri diaspora groups 183; 'Long March' to Gilgit 182; 'Martial Law Zone E' 177; Nationalism 178; networking between activists 182; *Northern Areas Advisory Council* 176; NSF, 2007 182; oppositional politics 178; POGB 183; POK 183; politics opposing Pakistan 177–8; revolution of Gilgit 176; revolution of 1970, Gilgit 177; *State Subject Certificates*, J&K 177; status of GB 184; *Tanzim-e Millat* (Association of the Nation) the *Tanzim* 176; transnational relationships 182–3; Treaty of Amritsar 174–5; unification, demand for 179–80; verdict, GB handed to the GoAJK 180; violent sectarianism, Gilgit 178; *yom-e azadi* (freedom day) 179
Gilgit-Baltistan Empowerment and Self-Governance Order 177
'guided democracy' 126

Haider, Raja Farooq 186
Haqqani, Hussain 12, 25, 28–31, 47, 53, 90, 131
Harkat-ul-Jihad-al-Islami (HuJI) 32, 87
Harkat-ul-Mujahideen (HuM) 32, 87
HuJI *see* Harkat-ul-Jihad-al-Islami (HuJI)
HuM *see* Harkat-ul-Mujahideen (HuM)
Human Rights Watch 54

identity 1–9; *Akhand Bharat* (undivided India) 6–7, 9; creation of a national identity 5; creation of Bangladesh 8; 'Doctrine of Paramountcy' 7; fear of Indian hegemony 7–8; General Zia's views 6; ideology 4; India–Pakistan trade agreement 9; Islamic Republic of Pakistan in 1956 5; Kashmir conflict of 1947–48 8; *lashkar* (irregular army) in Kashmir 7; Line of Control (LoC) 7; policies of Islamization 5–6; role of 1; territorial conflicts 8; 'two nation theory' 8; water dispute 8

IJT *see* Islami Jamiat-e-Tulaba (IJT)
India, self-identity and parity: colonial and pre-partition legacy 2–4; fear of Indian hegemony; identity 1–9; Jihadism 17; nuclear policy 12–13; Pan-Islamism 16; seeking military parity, Pakistan's defence policy 10–12; ties with Afghanistan 10; ties with China 15; ties with US 14
Indian National Congress 2–3
'Indian Occupied Kashmir' (IOK) 182–3
India–Pakistan trade agreement 9
India, terrorism 32–5; 11 September 2001 attacks 34; FY2002 34; Jamaat-ud Dawa (JuD) 33; Jammu–Kashmir Liberation Front 33; Line of Control (LoC), 1972 32; militant insurgency, tribal regions 34; Mumbai attack 33; Partition in 1947 32; 2006 Mumbai train bombings 33; 2008 Mumbai attack 33
Indonesia, progress in 126
Indo–Pakistan War 15, 135
Indus Water Treaty 8
Intelligence Bureau (IB) 53–4, 132
International Crisis Group (ICG) 61–2
International Security Assistance Force (ISAF) 29, 90, 157
'interrupted presidencies,' cases of 125
Inter-Services Intelligence (ISI) 22–3, 31, 132, 140
Inter Services Public Relations (ISPR) 53–4
Iranian revolution 16, 32
ISAF *see* International Security Assistance Force (ISAF)
Islamic Republic of Pakistan 5
Islami Jamiat-e-Tulaba (IJT) 110–12, 116
Islamist ideology 18, 135
Islamization 2, 5–6, 42, 87, 130, 132, 139, 163
ISPR *see* Inter Services Public Relations (ISPR)

Jaish-e-Mohammed (JeM) 32–4, 87–8, 90–1, 93–4
Jamaat-e-Islami (JI) 132, 137–9

INDEX

Jamaat-ud Dawa (JuD) 27, 33
Jamiat Ulema-e-Islam (JUI) 87–8
Jammu and Kashmir, conflict 131
Jammu–Kashmir Liberation Front 33
Jang (War) 45
JeM *see* Jaish-e-Mohammed (JeM)
Jihadism 17, 22, 35; anti-Soviet Afghan jihad 11, 16; domestic arena 17; foreign policy arena 17; global jihadist ideology 95; 'holy war' 22; interest in jihad 71; Islamist ideology, over-emphasis on 17; jihadists 35; military–intelligence establishment 17; over-emphasis on an Islamist 17; Pakistani jihadist community 92; revolutionary jihad 96; Salafist jihadists, profiles 64
journalism and power centres 47–9; Hussain Haqqani, 'Memogate' scandal 47; military establishment and the judiciary 48; Pakistan Telecommunication Authority, 49; political rewards to 'agreeable' journalists 48; programmes against parliamentarians without verification 48; proscribed outfits 48–9; public network, PTV 48; Syed, Mushahid Hussain (secretary general of the Pakistan Muslim League) 47
judiciary, manipulating 148
Jund-ul-Fida (Army of Fidayeen) 97–8

Karachi, battle for: ANP 106; democracy and militancy 113; domestic politics 113–14; 'the drug mafia' 120; episodic outbursts of violence 118–19; escalation of Lyari's gang wars 119; everyday political interactions 109–11; generalized violence 121; 'gray zone of politics' 114; gun battles 119; Karachi Agreement of 1949 178; KRC 120; law and order agency 120; *Mohajirs* 107; MQM 107–8; MQM and Jamaat-e-Islami 116; NATO forces in Afghanistan 119; naturalization of everyday violence 109; opportunistic violence 117; 'ordered disorder' 112–16, 121;
outbursts of violence (*hangamas*) 115–16; Pathan–Mohajir violence 107, 121; political entrepreneurs and violent specialists 114; political from criminal violence 112; politics of the MQM 112–13; protection rackets 117; Qasba Colony 107; rise in dacoities (robberies) 114–15; Saudi Arabia, political parties 117–18; Shia processions 120; state of violence 108; terrorist attacks 108; violence 109–11, 122; *see also* Muttahida Qaumi Movement (MQM)
Kargil War fiasco 141–2
Kashmir conflict, 1947–48 8
Kashmiri diaspora groups 183
Kashmiri Workers Association (KWA) 183
Kerry-Lugar Bill 31, 53
Khan, Liaquat Ali 4, 15
Khyber Pukhtunkhwa (KP), polity in 91, 156–60; Afghan refugees 156–7; civil conflicts, protection of women 158; cultural and patriarchal practices 159–60; displacement 159; domestic violence 158–9; international aid agencies 160; law of necessity 158; *mujahidin* 157; Pakistani military operations, Swat Valley 157–8; post-Geneva Accords 157; sexual crimes against men 160; sexual exploitation and abuse of women 160; TNSM 158; US troops 157; War on Terrorism 157; women in the peace-making processes 157–8; Zardari government 158
klashnis 110
KRC *see* Kutchi Rabita Committee (KRC)
Kutchi Rabita Committee (KRC) 120

Lahore Resolution 4
Lal Masjid operation 27
Lashkar-e-Jhangvi (LeJ) 32, 68–70, 87
Lashkar-e-Taiba (LeT) 68–70, 87–9, 140
lashkar (irregular army) in Kashmir 7
Leghari, Farooq 48

INDEX

LeJ see Lashkar-e-Jhangvi (LeJ)
LeT see Lashkar-e-Taiba (LeT)
'lifafa' (envelop) journalism 52
Line of Control (LoC) 7, 32, 68
'Long March' to Gilgit 182

madaris–militancy connections 67–73; Andrabi study 73; education, benefits 60; interest in jihad 71; LeJ militants 68–70; LeT's mission 69–70; militancy and human capital formation 70; militant field notebooks 68; militant recruitment; in militants production 59–60; open war with India, views on 71–2; operations of groups, comparison 68; pro-militancy families 73; public school curriculum 73; selection effects 70; support for terrorism 71
madrasah debates 61–4; Andrabi study 61; household-based surveys 61; informal 'mosque' schools 63; inventory of madaris 63; madaris and militancy, linkages 63–4; 9/11 Commission Report 61; penetration in educational market 61; school enrolment 63; socio-economic backgrounds 61–2
madrasas (religious schools) 167, 172
Mahuad, Jamil 128
'Martial Law Zone E' 177
'martial races' concept 11
media, evolution of 41–4; ABC 43; APP 42; appreciation of media 41; arbitrary action against newspaper 41; English-language minority press 55; General's Islamization project 42; ISPR 53; Kerry-Lugar Bill 53; 'lifafa' (envelop) journalism 52; military and media, communication 53; military rule under Ayub Khan 42; NTM 43; ordinances 43–4; Pakistan Naval Station Mehran 52; PEMRA 44; penalties on media broadcasting 44; politically motivated harassment 43; PPL 42; PPO 42–3; presence of Osama bin Laden in Abbotabad 53; security establishment 52–5;
state-controlled PTV 42; threat of a tax audit 41; Urdu Nawa-e-Waqt 41; Zarb-i-Azb operation 54; see also Religion and media
'Memogate' scandal 148–9
militant insurgency, tribal regions 34
militant recruitment: data collection, tanzeems and operations 75; intelligence collection and analysis, implications 74–6; madaris, in militants production 59–60; madaris–militancy connection 70–3; madrasah debates 61–4; madrasah education, benefits 60; madrasah–militancy connections 67–70; selection effect, impacts 74; 'supply-side' studies 64–6; tanzeems, efforts of 73–4; use of violence, edicts or rulings (fatwas) 74; US policy towards Pakistan 76–8
military aid 11, 15, 34
Military Intelligence (MI) 132, 135
military rule: Afghan Taliban, military to fight 146; cases of 'interrupted presidencies' 125; civilian-led 'guided democracy' 126; civil–military relations, developments in 127; consolidation of military regimes 146; coup outcome, factors affecting 127–30; dependence on the US 147; 18th Amendment to the Constitution, 2010 144; Indonesia, progress in 126; judiciary, manipulating 148; killing of Osama bin Laden 145; 'Memogate' scandal 148–9; military cohesion, support of military rule 145–6; military putsches, Ecuador and Venezuela 127; 1958 coup 133–5; 1977 coup 135–8; 1999 coup 141–3; party politics, manipulations 149; post-coup era 125; praetorianism 126; presidential breakdowns 126; revocation of the NRO 148; strategy of state-building 130–3; street protests, PTI and PAT 150; Turkey's Justice and Development Party 126; US, relation with 147; Zardari and military 148; Zia years 138–41

193

INDEX

Mirza, Iskander 133–4
Mohajirs 106–7, 112, 121, 130
Most Favoured Nation (MFN) 9
Movement for the Enforcement of Sharia *see* Tehreek-e-Nafaz-e-Shariat-e-Mohammadi (TNSM)
Movement of Pakistani Taliban *see* Tehreek-e-Taliban Pakistan (TTP)
MQM *see* Muttahida Qaumi Movement (MQM)
mujahidin, Afghan 157
Mumbai attack 33
Mumbai train bombings, 2006 33
Musharraf 142–3
Musharraf, Pervez 23, 89, 91, 119, 148
Muslim Conference 175, 186
Muslim League, 1936 electoral defeat 3
Muttahida Qaumi Movement (MQM) 51, 106; APMSO 111–12; ethnic and political violence 112–13; everyday political interactions 109; 'guided-democracy' regime 113

National Reconciliation Ordinance (NRO) 148
Nawa-e-Waqt, Urdu 41
Network Television Marketing (NTM) 43
9/11 Commission Report 61
9/11 September 2001 attacks 23, 34, 140–1
1958 coup 133–5; Ayub's decade in power 134–5; factors 133–4; foreign powers, Britain and United States 134; guided-democracy 133; Indo-Pakistan War, 1947 135; low-intensity warfare strategy 134–5; US agenda for country 134
1977 coup 135–8; Awami League 135–6; Bhutto years 136; District Management Group 137; fatwa 136; FSF 137; Islamist militias in Afghanistan 136–7; lack of retaliation by foreign powers 138; military–intelligence complex 135; nationalization of large businesses 137; nuclear weapons programme 136; opposition from JI 137–8; PPP 135; relations with countries 136; signs of factionalism in military 138
1999 coup 141–3; armed forces and prime minister 142; foreign powers, influence of 143; international debt 141; Kargil War fiasco 141–2; opposition to Musharraf 142–3; public support for the coup 142; United States and EU 143
Nixon, Richard 9
Nizam-e-Adl Regulation (Sharia law) 158
Northern Areas Advisory Council 176
Northwest Frontier Province (NWFP) 62, 79, 91
NRO *see* National Reconciliation Ordinance (NRO)
NTM *see* Network Television Marketing (NTM)
nuclear policy: blasts, Pakistani rationale 13; conventional military parity with India 12–13; nuclear technology, proliferation 28
nuclear weapons programme 13, 136, 139
NWFP *see* Northwest Frontier Province (NWFP)

Obama, Barack 31
Operation Zarb-e-Azb 86
opium trafficking 30
opposition from Jamaat-e-Islami (JI) 137–8
Organization of American States (OAS) 129
Osama bin Laden 26; in Abbotabad, presence of 53; US operation, killing of 76, 145

Pakistan Awami Tehreek (PAT) 149
Pakistan Broadcasting Corporation 47
Pakistan Electronic Media Regulatory Authority (PEMRA) 44, 46, 51–2
Pakistani counterterrorism efforts 98–9
Pakistani Occupied Gilgit-Baltistan (POGB) 183

INDEX

Pakistani Occupied Kashmir (POK) 183
Pakistan Naval Station Mehran 52
Pakistan Penal Code (PPC) 158
Pakistan People's Party (PPP) 45–8, 110, 113–14, 117, 120, 135–7, 142–3, 148–9, 176
Pakistan Resolution *see* Lahore Resolution
Pakistan Security Act, 1952 42
Pakistan Taliban *see* Tehreek-e-Taliban Pakistan (TTP)
Pakistan Tehreek-e-Insaf (PTI) 149
Pakistan Telecommunication Authority 49
Pakistan Television (PTV) 42, 48
Pan-Islamism 16
Pathan–Mohajir violence 107
PEMRA *see* Pakistan Electronic Media Regulatory Authority (PEMRA)
People's Student Federation (PSF) 110–11
'policy tripod' 131–2
post-coup era 125
PPL *see* Progressive Papers Limited (PPL)
PPO *see* Press and Publication Ordinance (PPO)
praetorianism 126
Press and Publication Ordinance (PPO) 42–3
Progressive Papers Limited (PPL) 42
pro-Pakistan regime 10
Protection of Women (Criminal Laws Amendment) Act 158
PTV *see* Pakistan Television (PTV)
public school system or *madrasas* (religious schools) 167, 172
Punjabi militant milieu: after 9/11 90–1; 'flea market effect' 96; al-Qaeda members 90–1; al-Qaeda, freedom fighters 89; al-Qaeda's global jihadist ideology 95; anti-state violence 93; clearing operation in 2014 95; contextualizing 87–90; crackdowns on LeJ 90; Deobandi Jamiat Ulema-e-Islam 87–8; FATA-based TTP 93; FATA-based TTP 93–4; ISAF 90; Lashkar-e-Taiba 87–9; militants migration 92; mosques and *madaris* 94; Musharraf regime 90–1; nuclear programme 89; Operation Zarb-e-Azb 86; Pakistan's FATA 86–7; Pakistani jihadist community 92; Punjabi *madaris*, Waziristan 92–3; religiously motivated violence 99; revolutionary jihad 96; 7/7 (2005 London) attacks 91; SSP and LeJ 95–6; SSP and LeJ members 88–9; state-allied militant organizations 94; Tehrik-e-Taliban Pakistan 86–7; threat to Pakistan 93–6

Quetta Shura 29

refugee crisis 4, 130, 156
religion and media 49–52; addressing religious issues 51–2; 'Aman ki Asha' 50; ban on telecasting 'immoral' programmes 49; blasphemy law 52; defensive mindset of Pakistan 51; denunciation of War on Terror 50–1; India–Israel–America axis 50; Muttahida Qaumi Movement 51; representation of India among Pakistanis 50; terrorism 49; two-nation theory 50; Urdu press 52; US–Pakistan relations, strained 50–1
'revolution of Gilgit' 176

Salafist and Wahhabi ideologies 35
Salafist jihadists, profiles 64
school enrolment 63
SEATO *see* South East Asia Treaty Organization (SEATO)
security tripod 26–8; al-Qaida 28; Jamaat-ud Dawa (JuD), branch of LeT 27; Lal Masjid operation 27; policy of strategic depth 28; proliferation of nuclear technology 28; unrest from Pashtun and Balochi separatist militants 27
'selection bias' 66
Sexual Harassment at the Workplace Act 158
Shanghai Cooperation Organization 31
Sharif, Nawaz 47, 89, 141, 149

INDEX

Sipah-e-Sahaba-e-Pakistan (SSP) 32, 68, 87–9, 95–6
South Asian Islamic culture 2
South Asia Terrorism Portal 23
South East Asia Treaty Organization (SEATO) 14, 31, 132
SSP *see* Sipah-e-Sahaba-e-Pakistan (SSP)
state-building, strategy 130–3; CENTO 132; civilian rule between 1947 and 1958 130–1; elite divisions 130; external threats 131; FATA 131; Intelligence Bureau 132; ISI 132; Jamaat-e-Islami 132; Jammu and Kashmir, conflict 131; lack of elite consensus 130; Military Intelligence 132; 'the mosque-military alliance' 132–3; partition 131; 'policy tripod' 131–2; SEATO 132; weak economy 130
State Subject Certificates, J&K 177
'strategic depth,' concept of 10
street protests, PTI and PAT 150
suicide operations 68–9
'supply-side' studies 64–6; high quality 65; Mesquita's theoretical models 65; Salafist jihadists, profiles 64; selection bias 66; *tanzeems* 65–6
Swat, militancy in 161–6; girls' education and female employment 163; militants hatred for female education 165–6; post-operation strategy, *Mishal* 161; *Sabaoon* (The Dawn) 161; *Sparley* (spring)/*Roshni* (light) 161; Saudi or Middle Eastern Islam 161; supporting/opposing militancy, women's roles 162–3; Taliban's flags 162; 3D strategy 'Deter, Develop, and De-radicalize' 161; TNSM 162; VTCs 163–5
Syed, Mushahid Hussain 47

Tableegi Jamaat 139
tanzeems 65–6; efforts of 73–4; and operations 75
Tanzim-e Millat (Association of the Nation) 176

Tehreek-e-Nafaz-e-Shariat-e-Mohammadi (TNSM) 158, 162
Tehreek-e-Taliban Pakistan (TTP) 30, 35, 51, 86–7, 140, 155
terrorism: Barelvi 35; China 36; costs of 23–6; counter-terrorism laws 25; delegitimization 26; extremist violence 24; jihadists 35; 9/11 24; Pakistan 35–6; public opinion 26; relations with neighbours 36; Salafist and Wahhabi ideologies 35; South Asia Terrorism Portal 23; Tariq-e Taliban Pakistan (TTP) 35; *see also* Afghanistan, terrorism; India, terrorism
3D strategy 'Deter, Develop, and De-radicalize' 161
Treaty of Amritsar 174–5
TTP *see* Tehreek-e-Taliban Pakistan (TTP)
Turkey's Justice and Development Party 126
'two nation theory' 8, 50

United Nations Development Programme (UNDP) 77
United Nations Educational, Scientific and Cultural Organization (UNESCO) 77
United States Agency for International Development (USAID) 78
US–Pakistan relations 50–1
US policy towards Pakistan, implications: colonial intentions 77; counter-insurgency in FATA 76; Ethan Bueno de Mesquita's model 77; law enforcement and counter-terrorism policy 76; preoccupation with *madaris* 76; school reform and employment generation efforts 77; third set of policy recommendations 78

Vocational training centres (VTCs) 163–5

Wahhabism 161
Waqt (Time) 45

INDEX

War on Terrorism 50–1, 129, 157
women at risk: Afghan *mujahidin* 157; deradicalization 167–8; donating jewellery 170; ethical society or moral society 169; holy war 167; immorality and prostitution 168; impact of militancy on women 155–6; jewellery (dowry) 170; jihadist ideology 168; marriage at a young age 171; *Maulvi's* protégé 169–70; polity in KP 156–60; public roles and rights 156–7; public school system or *madrasas* 167, 172; reintegration programme 170; religious schools 156; sexual exploitation 166–7; socio-economic status 156; suicide bombers 167; TTP 155 *see also* Swat, militancy in
World Trade Organization (WTO) 9

yom-e azadi (freedom day) 179
Yudhoyono, Susilo 127

Zarb-i-Azb operation 54
Zardari, Asif Ali 53, 143, 148–9
Zia ul Haq years 138–41; anti-Soviet war in Afghanistan 139–40; FATA 140; ISI 140; Islamic revival 139; JI and Tableegi Jamaat 139; LeT, terror attacks on Mumbai 140; 9/11, aftermath 140–1; nuclear weapons, acquiring 139; TTP 140